P9-CQM-432

States of Belonging

States of Belonging

German-American Intellectuals
and the First World War

PHYLLIS KELLER

Harvard University Press
Cambridge, Massachusetts
and London, England
1979

Library of Congress Cataloging in Publication Data

Keller, Phyllis, 1930–
    States of belonging.

    Bibliography: p.
    Includes index.
    1. Münsterberg, Hugo, 1863–1916.   2. Viereck,
George Sylvester, 1884–1962.   3. Hagedorn, Hermann,
1882–1964.   4. German Americans—Biography.
5. Intellectuals—United States—Biography.
6. German Americans—History.   7. European War,
1914–1918—German Americans.   I. Title.
E184.G3K39   973′.04′31 [B]   78-27544
ISBN 0-674-83595-6

For Mickey

ACKNOWLEDGMENTS

This book benefited from the support, cooperation, and criticism of others. Grants from the Radcliffe Institute, the Milton Fund of Harvard University, and the Rockefeller Foundation aided my research and writing. Dorothea Hagedorn Parfit, Mary Hagedorn DuVall, the late Ella Münsterberg, and Hugo Munsterberg II were unfailingly cooperative in responding to inquiries and lending me manuscript materials. Elzbieta Ettinger and Maria Chodakowska helped to decipher near-illegible documents and difficult German texts.

Rudolph Binion read a working draft of the manuscript with close attention to details of analysis and interpretation; the final text gained strength and clarity from his critical acumen. Richard Herrnstein, John Higham, and Arthur Mann also commented helpfully.

The photograph of Hugo Münsterberg is reproduced by courtesy of the Harvard Archives; that of George Sylvester Viereck, by courtesy of the Granger Collection; and that of Hermann Hagedorn, by courtesy of Dorothea Hagedorn Parfit. The material from Hermann Hagedorn's *The Hyphenated Family,* copyright 1960 by Hermann Hagedorn, is reprinted by permission of McIntosh and Otis, Inc.

I have several more personal debts to acknowledge. My parents, Sophie and Benjamin Daytz, gave me my first and fundamental understanding of the fact that one's loyalties *are* one's life. My children, Robin and Jonathan, reversed the usual direction of nurturing during long years of study and work. Finally, there is the greatest debt of all. My husband goaded and sustained me at a number of turning points. This book is rightfully dedicated to him: a small down payment on a life-long obligation.

CONTENTS

■ ■ ■

As historians we must be particularly concerned with the problem whether
major changes in the psychology of a society or culture can be traced,
even in part, to some severe trauma suffered in common—that is, with the
question whether whole communities, like individuals, can be profoundly
affected by some shattering experience . . . I hasten to say in advance
that I do not, of course, imagine the psychological impact of such crises to
be uniform for all members of the population, for if modern psychology
has demonstrated anything it is the proposition that in any given situation
individuals will react in widely diverse ways, depending on their
constitution, their family background, their early experiences, and other
factors . . . Over the long term . . . it seems likely that the group
would react in a manner most nearly corresponding to the underlying
requirements of the majority of its members—in other words, that despite
great variations as between individuals there would be a dominant
attitudinal pattern.

   William Langer

My writing was all about you; all I did there, after all, was to bemoan what
I could not bemoan upon your breast. It was an intentionally long-drawn-out
leave-taking from you, yet although it was enforced by you, it did take its
course in the direction determined by me.

   Franz Kafka to his father

INTRODUCTION

Before 1914, German-Americans were widely considered to be the "most assimilable and reputable of the immigrant groups" in America. They were a richly diverse ethnic group, differentiated by social and economic background, political and religious affiliation, stage of assimilation, and geographical location.[1]

Then came the First World War. Its effect was to draw German-Americans together: the threat that it posed to their status gave them an urgent need for self-defense—and ultimately for self-assertion. Those who were able to give meaning and direction to this group experience (which had no previous American analogues save the Tories in the Revolution and the pro-South Copperheads of the North in the Civil War) took on a special importance in German-American life. Intellectuals, editors, journalists, and college professors interpreted the "facts," developed the arguments, and manipulated the symbols that drew their audience to the cause of "justice for Germany" and the salvation of things German in America. They defined the range of options for their fellow German-Americans.

That range came to enclose a spectrum of sentiment reaching from extreme pro-Germanism to "one hundred percent" Americanism. Most German-Americans occupied a middle ground. They were indignant, ambivalent, vacillating, moving from issue to issue with responses keyed to the political conditions of the moment. They tried to balance their American interests with their sympathy for the beleaguered fatherland. They sought to refrain from actions that would set German-Americans apart. Most moderates tried to surmount their emotional involvement in the war, to negotiate their differences with critics, and to leave open the option of multiple allegiances.

Not so the pro-German militants. Their identification with the fatherland was rigid and unyielding, often going beyond the desires of the German government and occasionally subverting its interests. In many cases their militancy was as much an expression of negative attitudes toward America as of sympathy for Germany. Charles Hexamer, the American-born president of the National German-American Alliance, told his listeners:

We have before us a bitter struggle, and we can wage it successfully only if we are united . . . Whoever casts aside his Germanism from him like an old glove is not worthy to be spat upon. Such a rascal is a deserter . . . We have long suffered the preachment that "you Germans must allow yourselves to be assimilated, you must merge into the American people": but no one will ever find us prepared to descend to an inferior culture.[2]

Extremism was not limited to advocates of German victory. The range of German-American responses to the war included a party of American superpatriots, ready to identify with the Allied view of the conflict. Their Americanism took the form of rejecting rather than defending their ethnicity. They pioneered the path to total assimilation that in the end most German-Americans were to follow.

These three modes of activism do not exhaust the range of German-American responses to the issue of allegiance posed by the war. Many retreated into neutrality, apathy, privacy. Wealthy, assimilated German-Americans were conspicuously absent from leadership roles during the war years. Others were bound by religious conviction to adopt a neutral stance.

But it was among the activists that the several states of belonging evoked by the war found their sharpest and most poignant expression. And each of the subjects of this book came to symbolize one of these responses.

Hugo Münsterberg (1863–1916), Professor of Psychology at Harvard University, was the most powerful spokesman of the middle-of-the-roaders. George Sylvester Viereck (1884–1962), poet, novelist, and publicist, was the leading pro-German militant. Hermann Hagedorn (1882–1964), poet, playwright, and biographer, was foremost among the pro-Allied superpatriots.

To understand the choices these men made, it is necessary to explore their psychic and intellectual lives as well as their political activities. I have sought to do so through the traditional staples of biography: diaries, letters, printed sources. But I have also tried to comprehend, through these lives, the formation and dynamics of personality and the process by which personality interconnects with culture and history.

I begin with the assumption that adult political dispositions have their roots in childhood and adolescent family relationships. One's attitudes toward state and nation are significantly affected by perceptions of one's parents as love objects and authority figures. Post-Freudian theorists have argued persuasively that the raw experiences of childhood are reviewed and redefined throughout the life cycle. I seek to show how my subjects transformed the lessons of their early lives into character traits that shaped their adult attitudes and behavior.

The experience of these men had another crucial dimension: their social and intellectual careers. People generally act in a way calculated to reduce the dissonance between their inner and outer worlds. "Real" issues and events must be dealt with. Those who would be shapers of history must find a way to make their thoughts and actions, however subjective in character or unconscious in origin, intelligible to others. For Münsterberg, Viereck, and Hagedorn—men who lived by words and ideas—this was particularly true. In this fashion the history of their lives became part of the history of their time.

The studies that follow explore in depth this interaction between self and society. Each of these men sought (with varying degrees of success) to play an active role in American intellectual and cultural life. Their psychic and intellectual lives intertwined in revealing ways. With the coming of the First World War they were led to political commitments that merged with—and emerged from—these other modes of identity. The result was three very different states of belonging.

Part One

Hugo Münsterberg . . .

ON BEING GERMAN IN AMERICA

∎ ∎ ∎

In 1913, on Hugo Münsterberg's fiftieth birthday, George Sylvester Viereck
—then a young poet and journalist—saluted him as "Germany's greatest
single asset in the United States." He praised Münsterberg's vitality,
scholarly productivity, political insight, and interpretations of the German
and American national characters. "The intellectual leadership of the
German-Americans once held by Carl Schurz has fallen to him," Viereck
asserted.[1]

The final tribute was the more telling since Hugo Münsterberg retained
his German citizenship through twenty-four years of residence in America.
He believed himself to be "a man who sees both countries with the eyes of
love." He did not seek a new homeland in America, but came—and stayed
—as a scholar-ambassador whose mission was to promote ties of amity and
understanding between the two countries.[2]

Münsterberg had many homes, but none to which he fully belonged. Born
a Jew in Danzig, at a time in Germany history when the promise of social
equality beckoned Jews from their religion, he abandoned Judaism by his
early twenties. He converted to a secular religion compounded of German
nationalism and cultural romanticism. He was one of a number of bourgeois
intellectual Jews who aspired to an aristocratic lifestyle—the young Hungarian Theodor Herzl was another—and who fell prey to the common illusion
that assimilation was a simple matter of choice. He sensed that his two
allegiances could not be reconciled; that one must be denied. In renouncing
his Jewish identity, Münsterberg threw in his lot with the German nation.
It was a grave personal decision, the kind that few men later dare to
review. He took no notice of the shrill anti-Semitism that sounded in the
last decades of the nineteenth century in Germany, although it contributed
to the pressure on him to make his career elsewhere.

In America, Münsterberg became a renowned exponent of German
culture. In Germany, his good standing depended upon his American
associations. In each country he styled himself as a representative of the
other. German-Americans looked on him as an exemplar of their contribution
to America. Stressing the value of their heritage, he exhorted them to
resist assimilation, to retain their identity as Germans in America. If this
advice ran counter to his own behavior toward his Jewish heritage, it was
not because Münsterberg drew a distinction between religious and national
"faith." Rather, it was a matter of achieving the higher cultural status. In
Germany it was better to be a German than a Jew; in America it was
better to be a German-American than an undifferentiated citizen.

Like his national affiliations, Münsterberg's professional interests were
divided. He was a scientist and a philosopher, a scholar and a popularizer,
a teacher and an amateur politician. He was particularly prone to conflicting interests and incongruent ambitions. The new conditions created by
the World War transformed his personal experience into one widely representative of other German-Americans.

1 . . .
CHILDHOOD AND YOUTH

Hugo's father, Moritz Münsterberg (1825–1880), was born
into a middle-class Jewish family that had lived in Breslau for
two generations. One of Moritz's boyhood friends was the Jewish socialist intellectual Ferdinand Lassalle, with whom he
shared certain liberal, urban, and middle-class aspirations toward culture as a mark of status. At the age of nineteen Moritz
was apprenticed to a businessman in Berlin; subsequently he
moved to the prosperous city of Danzig to begin his own career. There in 1853 he married Rosalie Weinberg (1830–1857),
the daughter of a wealthy and prominent Jewish lumber merchant. He worked the family business in junior partnership
with his brother-in-law Hermann Weinberg until the latter
died in 1877 and Moritz assumed full control. The business
prospered and he realized a comfortable fortune. Although a
dedicated businessman, Moritz valued "the romantic side of
life," wrote poetry, and was "drawn to the world of books."
But these inclinations were distinctly subordinate to his drive
for control of the business and for financial security.[1]

Conveniently located on the Baltic Sea, the firm of S. Weinberg purchased lumber in Russia and shipped it to western
Europe, especially to England and Scotland. Moritz handled
direct relations with European buyers, and for this purpose he
travelled widely every winter for one to three months. A self-
educated man with a lively curiosity about the world beyond
Danzig, he brought home glowing tales of life in England
(where a married sister lived) and France. Much as he relished
culture and travel, Moritz's other ambitions were often frustrated by the demands of his business life. After the birth of
his first son, Otto, he transferred his own cultural aspirations

to the future prospects of his children. For Moritz was, above all, a family man, romantically adoring his wife and devoted to his children. In the diary that he kept on his business trips, he recorded the loneliness of his separation from them, his dedication to work on their behalf, and his thankfulness to God for familial as well as material good fortune.[2]

But Moritz's joy in life was severely tested. After four years of marriage and the birth of two sons, Otto (1853–1915) and Emil (1855–1910), Rosalie Münsterberg died at the end of a year-long illness (probably tuberculosis). Moritz's grief lasted for several years until, in 1860, he fell in love with his wife's first cousin, Minna Anna Bernhardi, who lived on the same street in Danzig and who had stepped in to help him care for his young boys. Their marriage was postponed until July 1, 1862, in an effort to temper opposition from the Weinberg family. This probably centered on the inheritance rights of Otto and Emil. In any event, documents securing those rights were registered at the Danzig City Hall on the same day as the new marriage. Anna's first and Moritz's third son, Hugo, was born on June 1, 1863. A last child, Oskar, was born in 1865.[3]

Moritz enjoyed thirteen years of marital and familial happiness before his second wife died in 1875. From that time onward, broken by grief, he lived only for and through his sons. His diary and letters show him to have been a fond and protective father, but one whose devotion did not impede a clear-eyed critical appraisal of his children. His ambitions and his standards of character and achievement were high. He rarely missed an opportunity to lecture the boys on the virtue of hard work and the benefits of delayed gratification. Each of them received *Konfirmation* at the synagogue as part of their moral and ethical training. They were expected to concentrate their youthful energies upon school work and music lessons, literary performance and rigorous physical exercise, and to seize the opportunities for intellectual and aesthetic cultivation that were available in Danzig.[4]

As a young child, Hugo did not enjoy robust health; doctors believed that he suffered from anemia. Various male members of the family from time to time had physical disorders as the result of nervous tension, and Hugo often was plagued by severe headaches and constipation, requiring treatment at a spa or daily medication. Family members observed an extraordinary politeness in him from the time he was four years old. As Anna's first-born son, he was the special pet of the Bernhardi family. He knew how to ingratiate himself with adults and they rewarded him with enthusiastic praise. Moritz, whose pride was injured by the academic ineptitude of his oldest son, warmed appreciatively to Hugo's early display of intellectual skills and literary interests. No doubt the child cultivated these skills in part because of his father's injured pride and his own eagerness to please. Moritz saw in the twelve-year-old boy a "deep mind," an exemplary manner, and a strong conscience. As his hope for the boy's future grew, his disciplinary control tightened.[5]

Whatever tensions were induced by Moritz's conception of character training and his ambitions for his sons, Hugo often nostalgically recalled his childhood as a happy and harmonious time. Moritz and Anna had many friends and extensive family ties on each side. When Hugo went to visit his father's family in Breslau he was lionized and pampered by adults responding to his respectful ways. Family members often gathered together during Jewish holidays, and in the summer months numerous young cousins visited the Münsterberg home in Langfuhr.[6]

Anna Münsterberg brought artistic and musical interests to the family. Hugo began to take music lessons at the age of six; he wrote his first poem at seven and began French lessons with his mother at eight. His childhood letters to Moritz exhibit a full measure of filial piety, but it is clear that he was more deeply attached to his "dearest" mother. The dutiful letters to his father told how hard he was working at his lessons, expressed pride in his achievement, and made excuses for his occasional lapses from exemplary performance. Later, in adolescence, he addressed his father "man to man" on general topics. But to Anna, when he had occasion to write, he poured out his heart and dwelt on every detail of his daily life. On one visit to Breslau he wrote to her of his loneliness and asked her not to show the letter to the rest of the family. Whenever she was away from home his headaches troubled him. His handwriting differs markedly between his casually sloppy letters to Anna, decorated with blots and drawings, and his carefully drawn, restrained, formal letters to Moritz.[7]

By his twelfth year, Hugo engaged in a wide variety of activities, centering on literature and science. He was an enthusiastic theatergoer, wrote poetry, read avidly, and published stories in a magazine (*Kinderlaube*) which he started with another boy. He also developed an extensive botanical collection: "In the first years of my school time [at the gymnasium] botany was all my desire. We lived in the summer in a country house with a large garden; and every minute I could spare belonged to the plants which I collected and pressed. It became a boyhood passion." After botany his scientific interest turned to physics, and he passed through a phase of fascination with electrical machines. But in his recollections of childhood, summers at Langfuhr always bulked large. They were rich in boyhood pleasures: rambling in the garden and woods, swimming and sailing at nearby Baltic beaches. In later years Hugo's imagination would often return to this "safe harbor" of his childhood.[8]

A few weeks before his twelfth birthday he was cast adrift by the death of his mother. The loss was stunning. To the extent that Hugo mastered his grief, he did so by turning to Moritz—whose bereavement overshadowed that of the four boys. In a moving letter written on his father's birthday in May 1875, Hugo promised to dedicate himself to Moritz's wishes in order to console him for the loss he had suffered. He began his task immediately by keeping an expense account to show his frugality. A year later, on the day of his *Konfirmation*, he expressed his resolve to put "lightmindedness" and "children's games" behind him and to demonstrate his love and gratitude to his parents by pursuing "noble ends."[9]

Hugo always had a strong identification with his father. One finds evidence of it in his boyhood religious piety, his literary interests, and his repeated expressions of male superiority over his aunts and female cousins. Their common loss enforced this identification, and made Hugo wholly dependent upon and doubly anxious for his father's approval and affection. He began to apply himself with diligence to the physical activities that

Moritz considered manly, to organize his time as if every moment had to be accounted for, to limit his pleasures—such as
the theater—when they interfered with school work, and to fill
his poetry with the fine and romantic sentiments that Moritz
recorded in his own diary. He struggled to produce an elegant
handwriting that would win his father's praise. He needled his
younger brother for nail-biting and "unfinished thoughts," and
even—jokingly but significantly—teased Moritz himself about
the latter's writing style. Emulating his father's pleasure in
travel, he seized every occasion to go on sightseeing trips and
to attend public lectures on unfamiliar parts of the world. In
the last letters to Moritz he expressed his deep satisfaction in
his work, his pleasure in the company of his brothers and the
frequent visits of relatives, and—like the twice-widowed, dis-
consolate Moritz—his sense of loneliness "deep inside."[10]

Returning from a business trip to Lisbon in November 1880,
Moritz Münsterberg died suddenly, at the age of fifty-five. His
last diary entry records the fact that since Anna's death "All
four [of my sons] think only how to please me." Shortly after
Moritz died, Otto took over the family business, married, and
provided a home for the younger boys. Hugo completed his
studies at the Danzig gymnasium with distinction by the end
of 1881. Free of the exacting obligations of filial piety and the
strict regimen of the gymnasium he was able, within certain
economic limits imposed by Otto's control over his inheritance,
to pursue his own pleasures, intellectual or other. In April 1882
he left Danzig to spend the summer semester studying French
at the University of Geneva. In his own mind this was to be a
condensed *Wanderjahr* in which he might see something of
the larger world, exercise his independence, and find the path
to his future.[11]

From the outset, Hugo's long letters "home"—to Otto and
Otto's wife Lotta—were filled with excited descriptions of new
sights, adventures, and experiences. But his excitement was
constantly tempered by anxiety over inadequate funds. Hardly
a letter failed to carry some reference to high prices, special
expenses, or persistent hunger—although he occasionally indulged himself in frivolous purchases or elaborate dinners.
Outbursts of irritation over his financial dependence and gra-

tuitous advice from Otto often were buried in lengthy passages revealing his keen interest in family affairs and his pride in the strong spiritual bond shared by the brothers. On his nineteenth birthday, in a euphoric mood, Hugo described how he had risen in the morning, cleaned his room, set out pictures of Moritz and Anna, and opened the thirty letters and packages received from family and relatives. Oskar had sent, at his request, "a game I used to play with Mother when I was four." "This is my weakness," he explained, "that I like to go back to my childhood, that in refreshing childhood memories I find the source of purest joy."[12]

Less pure, perhaps, but certainly more heady and stimulating, was the pleasure of mingling with wealthy and stylish Genevans:

having succeeded in becoming a member of the most elegant society in Europe, in one of the most elegant cities in Europe, I feel as if I am swept along by tempestuous waters which I find hard to handle . . . Unused to moving among glittering lights and shining mirrors, I must be watchful over each movement and each step . . . One must shrink in size to be able to sit on a small elegant soft chair, one must be able to quote the most fashionable writers and sayings . . . If you try to take part in social games you must know all the French painters, Italian poets, Russian commanders, Chinese mandarins . . . Still, I was never before so happy, I never enjoyed company so much, and I never made so much effort to sustain ties with society.

With his ingratiating manner, Hugo easily made the acquaintance of his professors, their wives and daughters, and others who crossed his path. He checked recurrent feelings of inadequacy with assertions to Otto about his "future laurels" or the fundamentally "meaningless" and "childish" character of social life. He rationalized—for his own as well as Otto's benefit—the time he spent in taking up invitations. It was, he argued, necessary for his future that he make his way into important circles and gather worldly experiences. In case Otto had "fears and reservations that I attend too small a number of lectures," Hugo assured his older brother that he was carrying more than the common workload, that he attended the theater and church services solely to improve his aural comprehension of French, and that he spent long and "systematic" days reading history and literature, writing poetry—and writing letters. "I am considered a fool by my peers," he reported, "on account of working so hard in the first semester."[13]

Hugo made a point of underscoring his dissimilarity from other students in Geneva. He was wary of joining the German student organization Teutonia because it was "nihilistic" and tended to attract students who preferred talk to work—although this evaluation may have been a protective response to its exclusion of Jews. During the first month of his stay in Geneva he was twice challenged to a duel by young students. In the first case, he told Otto, he was rudely accused of being a coward and called his challenger's bluff by insisting that "the only full satisfaction for me is to use a 5-caliber revolver and shoot from the distance of five steps." At this point his opponent apparently turned the challenge to a joke. Hugo was pleased with himself for having guessed in advance that it is "exactly . . . those who are marked with scars on their cheeks [who will] swallow every insult and take to their heels at the mention of firearms." On the other occasion, he received "a letter containing rude imputations from a young man I slightly knew." He threatened to turn the letter over to "more competent people to have their advice" and received a prompt apology.

Confident of his courage to go the limit in these affairs, he nevertheless proceeded on the assumption that his challengers were cowards. He assured Otto that his strength of will and common sense would prevent him from being trapped by "ancient humbug and senseless mores." When he felt the need to attend certain student meetings "where some general affairs are discussed," he reported that he was bored by the low level of intellectual activity and disgusted by the "outrageous effects" of "dreadful beer" on the other students.[14]

Still, Otto was alarmed by Hugo's endless accounts of what must have seemed a rather frivolous life in Geneva. In July he asserted his position as head of the family by rejecting Hugo's plan to spend the following year in Paris to prepare for the writing of a "major" history of culture. Hugo's disappointment was bitter. In his sixteen-page response he made the strongest possible case for further study at a French university, and tried to impress upon Otto how deeply his life was marked by self-denial. His funds were so short that he could not think of buying necessary clothing; his workday ran from 8:30 in the morning until 1:00 at night; much as he loved music, he felt he had to give it up:

Alas, I don't have time, like you, Otto, to go ahead in this direction. I would have to practice a lot and there is no time for this . . . [because] it is for my pleasure only, and for my personal pleasure I cannot waste two hours a day . . . In order to save time I do not practice fencing any more, I do not play cards, I do not take dancing lessons—which would be considered an outrage in any German university.

It was precisely the social rush of Geneva that made him want to move elsewhere, he argued. At the very least, he required a holiday in which to "live up to his dreams" by writing poetry, reading literature, finishing his novel, and designing an air-steered balloon.[15]

Otto relented somewhat in the face of this compelling account of intellectual ambition and self-privation. He was willing to entertain the suggestion that Hugo spend another year at Geneva. But Hugo was determined upon a contest of will with his brother. In his reply he renounced his holiday plan, arguing that after all his "real relaxation" was in working hard at his scholarly tasks. Then, as if to explain his sudden *volte-face*, he announced that he had fallen in love with a Russian girl: "I love with an elemental force, a force which is shattering my whole ego, which enslaves me, which is a preexistent sensation known only to some people, which hit me for the first time in my life." Mina Lapine was a medical student who lived in the same boardinghouse. She was "the most educated [girl] I've ever met . . . but without the ambitions of the bluestockings." Unlike the other girls at the university, she did not wield her feminine charms for the purpose of snaring a rich and handsome husband. They took long walks together and in the evenings talked in French about politics, science, and art. Mina spoke of her wish to alleviate human suffering and admired Hugo's determination "d'être utile à l'humanité par vos oeuvres littéraires et scientifiques." Then Hugo came abruptly to the point: "And now you know why I don't want to spend the winter in Geneva. A winter, day after day with her, I can't do it, I can't get along with it, it will upset my life or bring me to commit something stupid. Besides, people have started to talk already, and I feel guilty; I owe this girl a lot. She will be back in Geneva in the middle of September and I couldn't then abandon her." "I'm old enough to be able to govern my feelings and not to let myself be overcome by a temporary passion," he finally assured Otto—but, he added, surely it should be obvious that he must leave Geneva.[16]

The matter was left in abeyance until Emil came to spend his summer holiday with Hugo in Switzerland and Italy. In September, Hugo's new proposal—that he go to Leipzig—was accepted with alacrity by the family. Before beginning his "real studies" Hugo looked back with pleasure on the achievements of his *Wanderjahr:* "I did gain much that concerns my inner development, values which you can't measure." Whatever influence Otto and Emil were able to exert, Hugo's final decision was his own. He was sensitive about his position with respect to his oldest and younger brothers, taking frequent penswipes at Otto's provinciality and Oskar's childish enthusiasms. Complaining about his recurrent money shortage, he once told Otto that "we, all four brothers, are modest, undemanding and simple, but unfortunately each of us has three very elegant brothers, and mine, I believe, are the most elegant ones." It was a pattern of verbal humor, begun with his father, that sometimes masked his hostile impulses.[17]

On one matter Hugo ventured to give his older brothers stern advice. Otto wrote that he and Emil were concerned about the rising tide of anti-Semitism in Germany and especially the recent inflammatory speeches of Richard Wagner. "I have reason to believe," Hugo replied, "that in the place where you live you do not have right ideas about what's going on. Here, the news [about anti-Semitic meetings in Berlin] is received in quite a different way." It was all idle chatter, no different from the ignorant prejudices of some Frenchmen and Englishmen about the natives of Egypt. If Emil "suffered" over Wagner's speeches, Hugo would still "rather not see [him] defend his views publicly."[18]

Hugo's response was more complicated than a mere rebuke to his brother's provinciality. It was also a denial that anti-Semitism existed and an evasion of his Jewish identity. This evasion cannot simply be interpreted as—though it was in part —a rebellion against his father. Cultural conditions fostered it. Although Moritz Münsterberg was a leader of one of the Jewish congregations in Danzig, he came of age at the height of the period of Jewish emancipation in Germany, when upwardly mobile Jews expected to assimilate fully. In Danzig, the small Jewish community sustained steady losses through intermarriage and the emigration of young people to Western Germany.[19]

Thus Hugo's attitude toward his Jewish background reflected the drift of several decades of German liberalism and Jewish assimilationism. His social situation—that of a man belonging fully to neither German nor Jewish groups—was far from uncommon. His inability to call for or count upon psychological support from either Germans or Jews had at least one important consequence. Sensing that he must play a lone hand in life, he ventured everything in a quest for personal achievement and influence.

Some years after his father's death, Hugo became not a cosmopolitan German but an earnest nationalist and patriot. Significantly, he later defined the German national character in a way congruent with his Jewish upbringing. It, too, developed from a system of values that stressed rules, regulations, and injunctions to obey the law regardless of reason or pleasure. Thus Hugo retained the form while eschewing the content of his father's moral universe. His "rebellion" was, at the same time, an act of obeisance. Whatever signs of allegiance Hugo believed necessary for admission to the larger German world— renunciation, uncritical adulation—he freely gave. Nor did he subsequently allow himself any doubt as to the rightness of his choice. Several decades later he reportedly asked a graduate student in the Psychological Laboratory at Harvard "whether the 'Jewish Easter' was an important holiday."[20]

Despite his sense of destiny, Hugo's self-esteem evidently was insecure. He required constant reassurance and signs of approval from others. But his ingratiating politeness sometimes shaded into priggishness, for he was not always able to repress self-aggrandizing drives that gave offense. He learned to veil these impulses in a variety of ways. He was quick to assert his rights, but he never did so without justifying it as a defense against the hostility of others. This same need to establish his blamelessness (and worthiness of love) hearkened back to an earlier aim to please his father and forward to a later practice of attributing nobility to the German Kaiser and the German nation. He shared in the moral superiority of all his superego figures, thereby replenishing his self-esteem.

Under his father's tutelage he learned to value duty, self-control, and sacrifice. He was quintessentially German in holding that life was a struggle to serve ideal ends, though perhaps most human in tending to align those ends with his own wishes. Münsterberg was not consciously hypocritical. He simply transformed personal motives into abstract moral ideals, which he then served with a passion free of guilt or doubt. Likewise, his sentimentality—cloying in his letters and poetry—about his childhood, family, and loves was an affect attaching as much to his own feelings as to any external person or place.

This is not to say that he was without close personal attachments. On the contrary, his love for his parents figured prominently in his psychological development. Anna was a sublime and loving woman whom he trusted as he did no one else. She appeared constantly in his poetry—in association with other childhood memories, especially in her rose garden at Langfuhr and at her painting easel—as the poet's primary source of pleasure, the object of his physical desires and spiritual yearnings. When Oskar Münsterberg married a young American girl in 1913 and prepared to take her to live in Germany, Hugo feelingly assured his sister-in-law that "the land in which the love of your mother is with you in every hour will never appear far away to you." To Anna Münsterberg belonged the "glowing eyes which give my soul a feeling of freedom"; hers were the "sweet words" that made his heart beat. When Hugo describes a young poet's struggle to renounce temptation, he personifies allurement as a regal woman moving in a summer landscape.[21]

There is reason to believe that Anna's premature death left the youthful Hugo with a sense of deprivation and injury. Before he fully outgrew his childish love—the passive narcissistic pleasure he took in Anna's love—she was suddenly taken away from him. Later this frustration manifested itself as a sense of entitlement, a belief that he was *owed* gratification which was unjustly withheld. It was one of the factors contributing to his excessive concern for the perquisites of his rank, and it provided a source for his reflex-like rage over the "unfair" treatment Americans allegedly accorded to foreigners and over the lack of "Fair Play for Germany" in the controversy over World War I. He also clung to a fantasy of eternal life in which he expected to recapture his early bliss. So deep was this injury, however, that it created a permanent split in his feeling toward his mother. On the one hand, she was a sublime goddess; on the other hand she was a temptress who wantonly excited his low impulses to pleasure. Residues of the latter attitude would later appear in his outspoken contempt for "frivolous" women.

After Anna's death, Hugo's grief took the form of identification with his father through their common loss. To be sure, there was earlier evidence of identification in the young boy's range of interests, his entrepreneurship, his diligence and pride in achievement, his efforts to appear manly. Several of his later poems deal in an autobiographical tone with Oedipal conflict and its resolution. In "Dust," the poet describes a childish fantasy of power: bored with his books, he falls into a reverie and is "overcome with wild yearning." He grows as "wild and big as nature itself"—becomes superhuman (*übermenschlich*). In this fantasy state he feels omnipotent, capable of "tearing the sun out of the sky." He boasts to God that he is the stronger and bigger of the two, but as he speaks he begins to doubt his power and is struck by guilt: "I am strangled in my own words." At this point he bends his knee to God and is forgiven. Suddenly, he wakes from his reverie and picks up his interrupted studies with fresh courage and new hope.

Among other things, this poem graphically reveals Hugo's ambivalence toward work—which is both dry as dust and his sweet hope for the future. The alternative to losing himself in work, however, is losing himself in himself. The latter course leads to wild and confusing fluctuations between omnipotence and collapse. He plays with the fancy of self-exaggeration, conceiving power as an aggressive weapon to be used against God. But he is frightened by his destructive potential, doubts himself, and returns to reality, paying homage to God's greater power and taking up the tasks which are more properly his.

If Anna Münsterberg was the source of all of the poet's childhood pleasures, illusions and temptations, it was Moritz who, in the guise of conscience, duty and work, summoned him out of his uncertain dreamlike reveries and back to reality. The poet's early ambivalence toward work (and father) is apparently settled by an increasingly pragmatic emphasis upon Moritz's values. In the allegorical ballad "The Pearls," there is a marriage of id and superego principles as the poet undertakes a difficult life mission in the service of the Queen of the Forest. Here is a formula which combines the seeming irreconcilables: personal achievement for the sake of high ideals, charged with all the affect of those blissful childhood scenes and those days with the woman in the rose garden. For Hugo, personal achievement was a means to win social prestige and to replicate Moritz's idealized "conscious power, nobility and goodness." It was not the difficulty of the mission that sparked the poet's imagination, but the noble status derived from service to the Queen. "The Pearls" has significance in representing the inner springs of Münsterberg's ambition. His chief goal was neither Moritz's self-development nor external mastery, but the achievement of a status sufficient to confer authority and elicit respect and admiration.[22]

Defeat was built into this goal. He could never win enough social approval to sate his need for it. The transformation of his parental images into high ideals failed to account for contrary feelings of hostility and resentment that constantly needed to be restrained. When he was unable to repress forbidden impulses, or to project them, he was compelled to mask them as duty or the expression of conscience. Duty, or loyalty to ideals, became his preeminent conscious principle. With it were associated all the valued persons and places in his life: the beloved Anna, the noble and powerful Moritz, the family circle, and the German fatherland.[23]

The nineteen-year-old who set out for Leipzig carried within him certain character traits that would seriously hamper his ambitions. A loner by inclination, he was reluctant to trust others. The early injury of his mother's death impeded realistic self-perception. His failure to recognize and integrate contradictory feelings hindered his development of self-esteem and autonomy, leaving him inordinately dependent upon external signs of status. On the other hand, he had many strengths in his struggle for success: an abundance of energy productively focused on intellectual development and work from an early age; a lively and pleasing manner; a deep reservoir of ambition; a single-tracked self-interest. With intelligence, energy, ambition, and will, he manage: to surmount his weaknesses and make a distinctive mark on the intellectual and social history of his time.

2 . . .
CHOOSING A VOCATION

Hugo Münsterberg grew up with a wide range of literary and scientific interests. During his teenage years these focused on philology and archeology: at the age of fifteen he compiled a "Lexicon of Foreign Words used in German and their Etymology." He submitted a thesis for his gymnasium diploma on "West Prussia in Prehistoric Times." In Geneva he spoke of expanding his competence in philology by developing "foundations in other spheres of science" such as the history of culture, ethnology, and anthropology. He described a piece of fiction that he was writing as "a psychological study rather than a novel," as an extended essay in social psychology that might provide a basis for "solving social problems." But after the quarrel with Otto about continuing his "preparation" by living and studying in France, he pulled in his wings. He would never be his own man until he got on with the serious business of training for a profession.

In the fall of 1882 he began to study medicine at Leipzig, attending lectures and laboratories in anatomy and physiology for most of his first year. At this time, only about five percent of the students at Leipzig came from the same economic class as Münsterberg (that is, were the children of entrepreneurs and merchants). Most German university students were scions of the highly educated elite—government officials, professors, school teachers, jurists, clergymen, and doctors. Jewish families were represented in far greater proportion to their number than Protestant and Catholic families. But anti-Semitism kept Jewish students from pursuing government-related careers. Instead they tended to cluster disproportionately in the independent professions of medicine, law, journalism, and the arts.

Thus social conditions combined with Münsterberg's personal interests and needs to channel his energies into medicine. Not that he abandoned other interests. He entered into the lively student life at Leipzig, read philosophy, wrote poetry, played the cello in a quartet, and attended the theater and concerts as often as possible. His seriousness deepened, however, when in the summer of 1883 he attended a lecture course offered by Professor Wilhelm Wundt.[1]

Wundt had opened a laboratory at Leipzig in 1879 that quickly became the mecca of the new experimental movement in psychology. Trained in physiology, Wundt fruitlessly waited seventeen years for a professorship in that prestigious and over-crowded field. Finally, he accepted chairs in philosophy in-stead—at Zurich in 1874, then at Leipzig a year later. Wundt's appointments reflected the new deference that philosophy paid to science in German intellectual life; it was his scientific train-ing that made him an attractive acquisition. For his own part, in order "to preserve his scientific status, he was forced not only to carry out a revolution in philosophy by replacing logical speculation with empirical research, but also to widely adver-tise the fact that he was in a different kind of enterprise than the traditional philosophers." Wundt became the central figure in the founding of the new discipline of experimental psychol-ogy. Hugo Münsterberg, captured by the excitement of this venture, became a pupil of the master four years after Wundt's psychological laboratory opened.[2]

Wundt redefined psychology as the study of human reac-tions—the components of subjective experience—and assigned a key methodological role to the direct, controlled measure-ment of these reactions. The sciences of physics and chemistry provided his analytic models. But after resolving experience into its component parts, Wundt insisted that "the apparent separateness of the parts is only a necessary illusion of method." Wundt's overview of mental life involved metaphysical assump-tions about the fundamental activity of the will and its "cre-ative synthesis" of disparate elements. But it was not through his systematic psychology that Wundt fathered a new profes-sion; rather it was by training a whole generation of students in his empirical outlook and laboratory methods.[3]

Attracted by the academic profession in general and the new psychology in particular, Münsterberg took his medical qualifying examination in 1884 and remained at Leipzig to secure a D.Phil. under Wundt in 1885. According to one historian of psychology, Münsterberg fell into disagreement with Wundt over the interpretation of some experiments: whether the sense of effort in a physical action is produced by a discharge from the central nervous system toward the muscles or by sensations developed in the muscles themselves. This disagreement provided the kernel of a later public dispute between the two men —a dispute which established Münsterberg's reputation as a promising experimentalist in his own right. At the time, Wundt shifted his student away from experimental psychology for the subject of his doctoral dissertation: a historical and critical examination of "The Doctrine of Natural Adaptation."[4]

Moving on to Heidelberg, Münsterberg secured his M.D. degree in 1887 with a thesis based on an experimental study of eye estimation. That summer he won a position as *Privatdocent* at the University of Freiburg and married Selma Oppler, the daughter of a military surgeon who was Moritz Münsterberg's first cousin. Hugo had known Selma as a childhood friend and playmate in Danzig, where the Opplers briefly resided. He met her again in the fall of 1885 and became engaged after a whirlwind courtship of a few weeks. Neither bluestocking nor intellectual, Selma was a gentle and affectionate young woman with artistic interests after the fashion of Anna Münsterberg. Her father had long since converted to Christianity and achieved the position of chief physician in the Prussian army. The young couple settled down in Freiburg on Hugo's inherited income. While Selma produced two daughters (Anna Adelheid Margaret, b. February 14, 1889, and Ella, b. January 4, 1891), Hugo began to publish the works that would bring him international repute.[5]

The first of these was the product of his initial studies with Wundt, a treatise entitled *Willenshandlung* [Activity of the Will], which argued the central importance of motor processes in experience. William James called it "a little masterpiece," and in his own pioneering *Principles of Psychology* announced that "I shall repeatedly have to refer to it, and cordially recommend to the reader its most thorough refutation of [Wundt's] *Innervationsgefühl* theory" (that is, the direct experience of the will). Münsterberg's emphasis on motor processes placed him in open opposition to the Wundtians, who believed that feelings are central and fundamental responses of the organism to incoming sensations. Earlier critics of this position, principally Carl George Lange and William James, had argued that emotion was a peripheral phenomenon, that it followed upon organic changes taking place and qualified experience rather than defined it. *Willenshandlung* was an early example of Münsterberg's extreme physiological bias in psychology, and of the effectiveness of his firm separation of laboratory research from a more speculative approach to psychology.[6]

In 1889 Münsterberg began publishing a series of pamphlets later printed together as *Beiträge zur experimentallen Psychologie* [Contributions to Experimental Psychology]. These pamphlets described his work on eye estimation, kinaesthesis, the sense of time, fluctuations of attention, and auditory space-perception: research conducted in the laboratory fitted out in his Freiburg home. One of five experimental laboratories operating in Germany at the time, it was beginning to attract students from as far away as the United States. In 1891 Münsterberg published *Aufgaben und Methoden der Psychologie* [Aims and Methods of Psychology], emphasizing the scientific character of the new psychology and pleading the cause of rigorous laboratory research. While he was conducting research and training students in laboratory techniques, Münsterberg lectured and published in the more traditional domains of philosophy and, in his leisure, prepared an adaptation of Goethe's *Faust* for the leading playhouse in Frankfurt am Main. He was greatly interested in the work of Charcot and Janet in Paris, and Bernheim at Nancy, on hypnosis. In 1889 he lectured on hypnosis at Freiburg, and in the following year he published a paper on "Thought Transference."[7]

At the first international congress of psychologists in Paris (1889), Münsterberg met William James. James praised the young man's extraordinary "fertility in ideas," and later told him that "you seem to me to be doing more to open out new vistas in psychology than anyone today." When Münsterberg's

Willenshandlung came under attack by Professors Wundt and
G. E. Müller, James hastened to commiserate with the author:

Professor Müller's review [is] in many respects so brutal that I am im-
pelled to send you a word of "consolation" if such a thing is possible.
German polemics in general are not distinguished by mansuetude; but
there is something peculiarly hideous in the business when an established
authority like Mueller, instead of administering a fatherly and kindly
admonition to a youngster like yourself, shows a malign pleasure in
knocking him down and jumping up and down on his body. All your
merits he passes by parenthetically and *selberverständlich,* your sins he
enlarges upon with unction. Don't mind it! Don't be angry! Turn the
other cheek.

James was not in full agreement with Münsterberg's theories,
nor did he find his "general mechanical *Weltanschauung*" congenial. But he admired the young man's freshness of perspective and "sense for the . . . proportion of things." According
to James, Münsterberg's work was distinguished by a "flexible"
attitude toward existing theory and an "ingenious" approach in
subjecting new ideas to experimental tests. This intellectual attraction was reinforced by a certain fraternity of arms. James
and his friend Carl Stumpf, the chief rival of Wundt in German psychology, were held in some contempt by the Leipzig
group, in part because they dared to criticize the methods of
the Master. Münsterberg was considered heterodox from the
outset by his Leipzig colleagues. But in 1893 James reported
hearing disparaging remarks about him from Wundt and one
of Wundt's major disciples. "How can you arouse such malevo-
lence?" James asked Münsterberg with a mixture of sympathy
and perverse admiration.[8]

James himself had been doing amateur experimental work at
Harvard since 1875. But as the new movement took hold in
American universities with the establishment of major laboratories under German-trained psychologists, he realized that
neither his talents nor his interests were sufficient to meet the
needs of the time. Looking forward to a sabbatical leave in
1892–1893, he wrote to sound out Münsterberg ("the ablest
experimental psychologist in Germany") about a three-year
appointment as Director of the Psychological Laboratory at
Harvard: "The situation is this: we are the best university in

America, and we must lead in psychology. I, at the age of fifty
. . . am certainly not the kind of stuff to make a first-rate director thereof. We could get men here who would be *safe*
enough, but we need something more than a safe man, we need
a man of genius if possible." Flattered and excited by the prospect of a foreign sojourn, Münsterberg accepted the offer with
delight. He immediately secured a three-year leave of absence
from Freiburg (where he was then an Associate Professor).
James arranged for the appointment to commence in September 1892 and went out of his way to spend a few days with
Münsterberg in Freiburg late that spring. He reported to his
colleague Josiah Royce from Luzern on June 22, 1892:

He is an extraordinarily engaging fellow, not of the heroic type, but of
the sensitive and refined type, inclined to softness and fatness, poor
voice, vain, loquacious, personally rather formal and fastidious I think,
desiring to please and to shine, liberal of money, quick to forgive . . .
fond of travelling and of all kinds of experience, interested in many intellectual directions, and talking anything rather than "shop" when he
gets out of harness. I imagine him to be a man of the truest moral re-
finement and idealism, with probably a certain superficiality in his clever-
ness, and lack of the deeper metaphysical humor (such as the Harvard
philosophical department possesses in such unwonted measure). But he is
gentlemanly through and through . . . and is a man to whom I should
suppose one might easily become deeply attached. It is in the laboratory
that he appears at his best, and that best is *very* good. His indefatigable
love of experimental labor has led him to an extraordinarily wide range
of experience, he has invented a lot of elegant and simple apparatus, his
students all seem delighted with him, and so far as I can make out,
everyone recognizes him to be, as a *teacher,* far ahead of everyone else
in the field, whatever you may think of his published results. His brain
never tires; he is essentially a man of big ideas in all directions, a real
genius; and I feel more than ever, since I have been here, how great an
addition he will be to our strength.

James made particular note of the young man's formidable appearance—"round head, bristling moustache, stern eyes"—and
his eloquent German. He rightly predicted that Harvard and
Cambridge would "teem with anecdotes about him before he
has been there a month."[9]

Hugo Münsterberg was barely twenty-nine when he set sail
for New York in the fall of 1892 with his wife, two daughters,
and the children's nurse. He was in lengthy correspondence

through the summer with the chairman of the Department of Philosophy, Josiah Royce, who took great care to settle the visitors in domestic comfort. They met at North Station in Boston, where Münsterberg easily identified the genial Royce by a photograph the latter had sent of "my outer, or phenomenal self." Despite anxiety over his ability to express himself in English, Münsterberg was able to converse in the language within three months and to offer a full course of lectures (at Radcliffe) in eighteen months. Early in 1894, William James commented with evident delight, "He is a wonderful organizer, methodical to the last degree, our laboratory being a picture to look upon since he has taken hold; and he is, moreover, a most high-minded and lovable human being, so that I am thankful for the inspiration that led me to tempt him from Freiburg."[10]

Münsterberg's three-year sojourn was a brilliant success from every point of view. His colleagues in the philosophy department, especially Royce, James, Palmer, and Santayana, were unfailingly attentive and friendly. Neighbors in the Harvard community were solicitous of the visiting dignitary and his family; James's sister-in-law offered helpful counsel; and, when they found a house of their own on Quincy Street, their next-door neighbor Mrs. Louis Agassiz quickly became "like a mother" to Selma Münsterberg. Among the couple's intimate German friends were Dr. and Mrs. Max Poll (natives of Danzig) and Professor and Mrs. Kuno Francke. Münsterberg scored particular success with students working in the laboratory; Mary Calkins and Gertrude Stein were among his favorites. He also seized the opportunity to travel whenever he could—to Niagara Falls, to California, to Kansas and Nebraska, to the Chicago Exposition of 1893, to the psychological congress that met in Philadelphia the same year. Later in life he wrote of these initial American years in an idyllic and nostalgic vein.[11]

In the spring of 1895, Münsterberg returned to Freiburg with a proposal in hand from Harvard that he take two years to make up his mind about a permanent appointment in America. Harvard wanted him to remain, but he was unable to secure an extension of his leave of absence from Freiburg and was unwilling to relinquish his appointment there. He felt that he was obliged to return to Germany and wanted at least two years before deciding "whether I will become with my family Americans for a lifetime or whether I remain German."[12]

After the heady excitement of those days in America, Freiburg did not look the same. Münsterberg was haunted by happy memories and irritated by the lack of understanding about America among his German colleagues. Harvard's prestige, the high morale and intellectual distinction of its philosophy department, his senior rank at such a young age (the urbane and brilliant Santayana, born in the same year, held a junior, nontenured rank; in Germany, the average full professor was over fifty), and the possibilities of social contact and aristocratic lifestyle were values scarcely lost upon Münsterberg, despite the general disdain for America in German academic circles. He had long since convinced himself that the laboratory he had developed at Harvard was the "best" in America—the biggest and the hardest working—although G. Stanley Hall of Clark University took at least one occasion to admonish him that no comparative figures existed to support his claim. Back in Germany, Münsterberg's decision began to form at once: as Selma Münsterberg recalled, "in Freiburg we were naturally 'die Amerikaner.'" Numbers of American students, including Edwin Holt and Ethel Puffer, followed him to Freiburg to study in his private laboratory, and the Münsterbergs found themselves regularly playing host—on one occasion preparing a large Thanksgiving dinner—for visiting Americans. As if to close out past accounts he began to write the thinly veiled autobiographical poems (*Verses*) that were published together in July 1897, under the equally transparent pseudonym Hugo Terberg.[13]

But as the time for final action drew near, Münsterberg temporized by offering to return to Harvard, without his family, for the first semester of 1897–98. President Charles W. Eliot, however, on the advice of Palmer and Royce, insisted that "the University will not be content to have you return hither without 'burning your ships' . . . [and] making a visible transfer to this country of your household gods." Meanwhile, the government of Baden refused to fund a special laboratory at the University, leaving Münsterberg with the prospect of continuing to support his experimental work out of his own pocket.[14]

The possibility of a full professorship at Zurich fell through for shadowy reasons, possibly involving pressure applied by Wundt or Mueller. Heinrich Rickert, Münsterberg's close friend and intellectual companion, had already acceded to the prestigious chair in philosophy at Freiburg in 1894. Harvard was offering a handsome salary ($3500—probably equivalent to three times his salary at Freiburg) and a well-equipped laboratory. There was the remembrance of warm social ties and the homage paid to foreign scholars. For Selma Münsterberg, there was also the lure of educational advantages for the two girls which could not be matched in Germany.[15]

In March, Münsterberg wrote to William James, "Now I am yours forever and all my ships are burned . . . The University here did its utmost to keep me; they offered me a better position, but as it was nevertheless not just as I wished it . . . I declined here everything." Yet he did not fully turn his back on Germany. His psychological and intellectual ties to the fatherland were untouched by the move to America; in a sense they were fixed by it. From Münsterberg's perspective, his emigration was in large part an act of service to Germany. Henceforth he would be a unique ambassador, using his personal influence in the cause of international amity, uniting the best of both countries in and through his life.[16]

To the delight of his colleagues in Cambridge, Hugo Münsterberg at the comparatively youthful age of thirty-four became Professor of Experimental Psychology at Harvard. Within a year he was elected President of the American Psychological Association. Within two years he became chairman of the Philosophy Department and published his first book in English. The years from 1900 until his death in 1916 were filled with publications (books at the rate of more than one a year and scores of popular articles on a wide range of subjects), with academic honors, with biennial trips to Europe, and with an everwidening circle of acquaintances among prominent and influential American scholars, businessmen, and politicians. According to his colleague George Palmer, he was "confessed by all to be one of the most brilliant Harvard professors of his time":

Yet he had quite as many foes as friends, and these two groups were about equally ardent. They agreed, however, in calling him puzzling . . . His was ever a twofold nature, both sides of him genuine, both followed eagerly, but in themselves somewhat conflicting. He was a profound and capacious scholar, but none the less a popularizer, a producer of books and talks for the million. He loved seclusion and quiet almost as much as he loved the limelight and the front page. His intellect was exceptional in range and penetration, but often one had to think of him as a big boy who had never grown up.[17]

3 . . .

AN AMERICAN CAREER

At the beginning of his American career, the basis of Münsterberg's national reputation was his position as the leading experimental psychologist at Harvard. His gifts as a laboratory director were an orderly, analytic mind and a rich imagination with respect to experimental subjects and investigative techniques. "The roving, observant blue eyes, the springy step, the slight bend in the body in a kind of forward lunge, all suggested an alertness which characterized him throughout. He was all alive, perpetually creative."

In the late 1880s and early 1890s, laboratories had sprung up in several parts of the country, and Wundt's students became the patriarchs of American psychology. First among them was Edward B. Titchener of Cornell, whose devotion to methodology won him a reputation as the purest scientist of them all. Münsterberg was his chief rival for professional leadership. His claim to preeminence was enhanced by Titchener's reluctance to participate in professional organizations. Knight Dunlap, when he came to Harvard to work with Münsterberg in 1900, joined a group of gifted graduate students (Roswell P. Angier, Edwin Holt, Robert Yerkes) who, according to his recollection,

were all drawn to Harvard by the same force—it was the center for psychology at the time, and, in spite of the informality and laxness of instruction, we were confirmed in the scientific path . . . [Münsterberg] radiated scientific impulses . . . There was at least one giant in those days, although his publications do not show it. [He] made no converts to his philosophy. He was not a man to have disciples. But I think the modern trends in American psychology, and especially its experimental interests, are easily traceable to Münsterberg as their father.[1]

Following in Wundt's footsteps, both Münsterberg and Titchener imposed their own interests on students. But Münsterberg's were broader, and his personal supervision of laboratory work was so loose that talented students were relatively free to chart their own courses. As he grew increasingly absorbed in other affairs, he became a remote presence at the laboratory. He made regular rounds and was technically available for conferences,

but students were too awed by his extra-curricular activities to bother him . . . Not that he discouraged his students. On the contrary, he was genial and friendly, even if he would often indulge in mild sarcasm, the banter of the superior; and he always seemed to be conscious of his station in the cultural world—but such stereotyped expressions as "Well (ooell) now Mr. _____ you are on the (zee) right track and I expect a fine piece of work from you" could hardly be of any value to one who is groping.[2]

Some students took exception to his Germanic manner. Even the kindly disposed Gordon Allport described him as "looking like Wotan" on the lecture podium. And others were offended by his pedagogical dogmatism. But reminiscences abound of the kindness and hospitality shown by Münsterberg, who often "made his house a resort for homeless students, looked up the penniless, and furnished continual charity to stray fellow-countrymen." The cascading intellectual energy that led him to explore new areas of psychology impressed observers. Even Edwin G. Boring, who believed that Münsterberg's contributions to the experimental movement were negligible, attributed his failures to the fact that he was "too original; his energetic mind went on at once from experimental to still newer psychologies."[3]

Münsterberg's theoretical formulations are less important in the history of psychology than the fact that he was a forerunner of the functionalist school, which shifted emphasis from the structure to the operations of the mind. He resolutely set himself against the ascription of behavior to "some spiritual principle in the mind," and in his Action Theory proposed an exclusively physiological explanation of the phenomena of vividness and inhibition. He inverted the basic scheme of the associationist school by insisting on the primary importance of motor activities. The strength of a sensation, he argued, came not from the intensity of an external stimulus, but from action in the motor sphere: from the transformation of excitation into discharge. This transformation depended upon whether proximate pathways were open or closed to motor expression. The more open the pathways, the more conscious and vivid the sensation. Sensation thus hinged on a receptivity to sense data, and its quality was related to the spatial position of the pathways of discharge and the strength of the discharge itself. The basic unit of conscious life, Münsterberg argued, is neither the sense datum nor the nexus of sensations, feelings, volitions: it is a unified sensory-motor process. The study of this physiological unit, its multiplications and combinations, is the province of a truly scientific psychology.[4]

Münsterberg's theoretical contribution derived from and supported his physiological bias, his belief that psychology is a natural science wholly objective in character. He did not deny the personality or "self" as an original power, but excluded it from the domain of what he called "causal" psychology. If this left important questions unanswered, it was because the laboratory was not the proper place to develop a full picture of man. That task belonged to philosophy, and Münsterberg no less than James and Wundt was drawn to philosophy for a larger understanding of human experience.

Münsterberg and James held very different views of the domain of philosophy, and a comparison of their perspectives is instructive. Both men were trained in medicine, and shared a special interest in physiology. Both directed experimental laboratories and gravitated toward speculative philosophy. But for James the shift from psychology to philosophy was nominal: "He was so far indifferent to formal distinctions as to be scarcely aware whether he was treating psychology philosophically or philosophy psychologically." James believed that all experience was susceptible to scientific inquiry. Münsterberg, on the other hand, inclined to make a fetish of distinctions, and the philosophic system that he ultimately developed placed severe limits on objective knowledge.[5]

Beginning with *Psychology and Life* (1899), Münsterberg elaborated a philosophy that posited science and idealism, facts and values, as complementary orders. Scientific or *causal psychology* deals with phenomena, which are essentially mental constructs. In contrast, *purposive psychology*—historical and philosophic studies—treats the "real world of ideals and values." Man's inner self is a subject with wills and purposes linked by a hierarchy of values to overarching metaphysical principles. That subject is inaccessible to the scientist, who pursues truth limited to causal explanations. Science and idealism are compatible nevertheless, for "the labors of objectivist psychology" are required by "the subjective purposes of real life." This conception of science in the service of idealism provided the background of Münsterberg's later pioneering work in applied psychology.[6]

The style of Münsterberg's intellectual arguments is revealing. Defining subjects by the method of exclusion, he asserted that "only this" is psychology, "only that" is philosophy, and "only that philosophy" is true. Where William James avoided systematizing the variety of experience, Münsterberg imposed a rigid order. He reduced dissonance at the intellectual level in the same way that he coped with his affective ambivalence toward authority and love objects: by keeping the elements of thought and feeling strictly separate and compartmentalized.

It was in the area of applied psychology that Münsterberg made his most lasting professional contributions. His earliest work dated back to a set of lectures on hypnotism at Freiberg in 1889. He followed the publications of European scientists interested in various practical applications of psychology, and through his own investigations stimulated the thinking of younger American researchers in that direction. Beginning in 1907, his popular writings aroused widespread interest in psychology and its application to law, medicine, industry, education, and vocational selection. While some of these works were popular in the worst sense, they often flashed with insight and helped focus professional as well as lay interest on applied psychology. Richard M. Elliott, a student in the laboratory during the heyday of Münsterberg's work on applied psychology, suggests that while he seems "statistically naive" to later generations of psychologists, he was "a supremely ingenious pioneer and the only one at the time whose prognostication matched up to the accomplishments of applied psychology in the quarter century following his death."[7]

One episode, growing out of Münsterberg's research on the mental functioning of individuals in a group setting, reveals his originality, his methodological naïveté, and his injudicious haste to trade upon his professional position. Elliott tells the story:

I was a member of his seminar where student-subjects were asked to estimate in writing the relative number of dots which occupied the four quadrants into which a large piece of cardboard was divided by black lines, the whole card briefly exposed to observation. A week later the experiment was repeated with a longer period of observation, and the subjects were given an opportunity to influence one another's judgment in discussion. We individually changed our minds and improved our judgments over the earlier ones so much more flexibly than did the students of his Radcliffe seminar under identical conditions that Münsterberg announced himself opposed to the service of women on juries!

However freewheeling Münsterberg's conclusion, his experiment did effectively display the workings of group pressure upon individual judgment. His students were intrigued by his often ingenious application of measurement techniques to a host of human behaviors. His work led to his "classic text," *Psychology and Industrial Efficiency* (1912).[8]

One of Münsterberg's special contributions as a scholar reflected his early ambition to write a history of culture. In a number of essays exploring the national character of Americans, he brought together his interests in cultural history and social psychology. He began to write about American culture as early as 1894, when he published three essays on "The Americans" in a German newspaper. In "A Letter from the Journey" he offered an extended description, in verse, of American shortcomings in the context of an overriding admiration for the "energy, verve, scope" of the society.[9]

American Traits: From the German Point of View (1902) brought together a number of essays previously published in American periodicals. They take a close, systematic look at aspects of American life: the educational system, scholarship, the role of women, and democracy in its social and political forms. In each sphere, Münsterberg probes for the values un-

derlying specific practices. His psychological theme is that social norms affect individual "mental-functioning" or choice-
making. Comparisons with Germany enable him to show how
the same "facts" have entirely different meanings in different
value contexts. In both countries, for example, he notes marked
tendencies toward the emancipation of women. In the fluid
social organization of America, this emancipation leads to a
downgrading of family life and a feminizing of high culture
(that is, the introduction of "hysterical sentimentality, illogical
impulses, and the lack of consistent obedience to abstract
law"). In the fixed and hierarchical social order of Germany,
the primary place of family life and the masculinity of high
culture is determined by tradition, so that the "liberation" of
women merely introduces a controlled degree of individual
freedom. Similarly, the accumulation of wealth in industrial-
izing America creates the conditions for the emergence of a
largely "pseudo-aristocratic" class. In Germany, the same economic development tends to democratize an already established aristocracy.[10]

Despite its insights, there are built-in biases and distortions
of emphasis throughout the book, the effect of which is to play
to Germany's strengths and America's weaknesses. The relative lack of individual freedom in Germany is seen as the
product of a voluntary self-subordination to the welfare of the
whole society. German reverence for authority is taken to represent a high degree of civilization. The book's preface asserts
that Münsterberg's emphasis on American weaknesses is tacti-
cal. These essays, he writes, are intended for American eyes
only. They are meant to dispel American prejudices about Germany and to help correct American shortcomings. Drawing in-
vidious comparisons between American behavior (based on
pleasure-seeking) and German behavior (based on moral obligation), Münsterberg celebrates his own Germanness: duty
alone compels him to dwell on unpleasant circumstances in
America.

If *American Traits* exhibits Münsterberg in the role of moral-
ist, *Die Amerikaner* (1903) displays his more scholarly gifts.
The intended audience for this book was the cultivated German public. And if there is an element of distortion in con-

sistently putting America's best foot forward, this effect is minimized by the range and depth of Münsterberg's analysis. The book is divided into four main sections which describe the characteristic forms and institutions of American political, economic, intellectual, and social life. Drawing on a wide range of materials and using cross-cultural comparisons, Münsterberg interprets the practical life of Americans in terms of their commitment to the democratic ideals of self-direction, self-initiative, self-perception, and self-assertion. These ideals, he argues, make up the philosophy of Americanism and show "the true ethical meaning of American culture." He suggests to his German audience that the accumulation of wealth in America is not a function of greed but rather a consequence of the moral value assigned to work, productivity, economic progress, initiative, venturesomeness. "The real attraction which the American feels for money-making does not lie in the having but only in the getting . . . The American chases after money with all his might, exactly as on the tennis court he tries to hit the ball, and it is the game he likes and not the prize."[11]

In the preface to the English edition of this book, Münsterberg expresses his fear of feeding American self-satisfaction with an "optimistic" and positive interpretation of "the American man and his inner tendencies." Remarking upon the differences between *American Traits* and *Die Amerikaner*, he describes them as "two pictures of a stereoscope," one offering a critical and the other a roseate view of the same material. The first book was designed to show Americans how they measure up in comparison with Germans; the second to inform Germans about America. Yet there is no serious analysis of German biases in either work. The subject is America and the perspective is German in each. Taken together, the books display the negative and positive poles of Münsterberg's ambivalent attitude toward America.[12]

These books may also be seen as an expression of Münsterberg's status preoccupation. *American Traits* provided him with an opportunity to enhance his position in America by testifying to the superiority of his native German culture. *Die Amerikaner*, on the other hand, offered him a chance to exalt his position in Germany by praising his American associations.

Brilliant as were his insights, serious and "idealistic" as were his ends, Münsterberg was not a disinterested observer.

By the turn of the century Münsterberg set himself an extraordinary pace of activity: writing, teaching, and administering the affairs of the Philosophy Department at Harvard; lecturing to academic and other groups throughout the country; attending congresses in Europe and America; and leading a lively social life in Boston. Despite incidents in 1891, 1895, and 1901 that aroused fears of serious heart trouble, he barely slackened his pace, was careless in his eating habits, and was prone to mild depression. He contracted diphtheria in February 1893. In the spring of 1902 he succumbed to a second bout while visiting in New York. Immediately after recovering, he threw himself into the writing of *Die Amerikaner,* but suffered a nervous breakdown in the course of the ensuing summer that effectively curtailed his activities for the rest of that year.[13]

Nevertheless, in the fall of 1902 he began work on a project of great personal interest: a detailed plan for the Congress of Arts and Sciences to be held at the St. Louis Exposition in 1904. Members of the planning committee agreed that the Congress should be international in character, that it should bring European and American scholars together on American soil. But Münsterberg pressed for something more than a demonstration of the unity of scholars in a common endeavor. He wanted to make the Congress a testimonial to nothing less than the unity of knowledge itself, to the interrelationship of all categories of expression and inquiry. His detailed plan for the meetings, "so arranged that they formed one connected presentation of the whole universe of knowledge . . . logically organized," was accepted by his committee colleagues, and Münsterberg was given charge of securing the participation of German scholars. Afterward, one disgruntled critic of the elaborately structured Congress called it a "Münsterbergian Circus . . . a case of the pure love of schematization running wild." To William James the plan of the Congress was a revelation of Münsterberg's tendency "toward artificial bureaucratization and authoritarianism." But for Münsterberg it embodied a harmony to which he himself aspired. Significantly, a description of the plan was

Münsterberg's major contribution to the eight-volume edition of Congress papers.[14]

In the spring of 1905, the University of Königsberg offered Münsterberg its chair in philosophy once held by Immanuel Kant. According to his daughter Margaret, he always planned "to end his career and his life in the land of his birth." But his involvement in American life and—at this particular moment—in his professional career at Harvard, where he was on the verge of completing a long campaign for a new philosophy building, was so deep that once again he hesitated to make a major change. He accepted the offer, at first, on condition that he be permitted another full year to wind up his affairs in America. But shortly thereafter (as Münsterberg remembered it in 1916),

> Josiah Royce sat with me a long Sunday morning and insisted that it was my highest duty to stand by my Harvard post. Others might fill that German chair . . . but I was needed for more than the mere professional work. The Philosopher must not be a patriot only, but at the same time a citizen of the spiritual world in all lands, and I should be among true friends here all my life long. That night I sent a second telegram declining the call.

Others recalled the gist of this meeting with Royce somewhat differently. Mrs. William James reported that her husband hoped Münsterberg would leave Harvard, but that Royce urged him to stay on the condition that he give up his nonacademic activities and devote his energies to psychology. Perhaps neither version records the meeting exactly. In any case, the chair was not one of the juicier academic plums in Germany. And Münsterberg was not prepared to give up his vision of himself as an international ambassador, which depended on his remaining in America (where he also enjoyed considerable success as a popularizer of psychology).[15]

It is interesting to note that Münsterberg's chief criticism of the American academic community was that it failed to place scholarship at the center of its concerns. American universities, he argued, shared the same purpose (though not the same practices) as German gymnasia: the distribution of basic information through general courses. Thus the American professor, encouraged "to follow the leadings of his surroundings, becomes merely a good teacher, writes text-books and magazine essays and popular lectures"—becomes, in short, an academic businessman. The system does not foster specialization or productive scholarship. Instead, it "forces upon a serious scholar such self-destructive activity" as the pursuit of money. In praising the ideal of German mandarin scholarship and in deploring the coercive effects of the American system, Münsterberg avoided recognizing that his own inclination was toward the life of the academic entrepreneur.[16]

Münsterberg claimed that he also declined two other professorships in Germany—at Göttingen (1907) and Berlin (1909). There is no evidence as to the firmness of either offer. Berlin might have tempted him if the overture had involved a professorship in psychology or philosophy. Instead, what was under discussion was the directorship of the Amerika Institut, a position that at best might have been extended to a marginal status in the University (where not a single Jew had yet received a professorship). In any event, neither overture developed into an offer sufficiently attractive to warrant Münsterberg's serious consideration. Nevertheless he used them in an attempt to secure a salary increase, arguing that his refusals evidenced his full commitment to Harvard, to America, and to "the scholarly plans which I have set for myself in the coming years."[17]

By 1905 Münsterberg was a nationaly known figure in America. Between 1904 and 1914 he published, by his own count, over sixty articles, forty of them in large-circulation magazines. His professional interests moved from laboratory research to applied psychology and speculative philosophy. One of the consequences was a certain resentment of Münsterberg at Harvard which began with William James's "defeated . . . hope of acquiring . . . a great leader and exponent of experimental research."[18]

James's growing estrangement was based on more than disappointment over Münsterberg's professional course. Although each inclined to make allowances for the other, differences in their philosophic views and personal styles inevitably abraded their relationship. To these James added a mounting personal distaste. After the dedication of Emerson Hall, Harvard's new philosophy building, on December 27, 1905, he publicly complained that Münsterberg, presiding over the ceremonies, "made five speeches in the course of an hour." From the beginning James was unable to comprehend Münsterberg's consuming passion for the new monument to philosophy, arguing that "philosophy, of all subjects, can dispense with material wealth, and we seem to be getting along very well as it is." But Münsterberg saw the coming building as "a mother calling all her scattered children home to rest in her bosom." Informed of James's complaint against him at the dedication, Münsterberg immediately resigned as department chairman. Only after James was forced to apologize for his remarks, and President Eliot gave assurances that "I do not at all sympathize with Professor James's feeling that a Yankee would have been better than a German to guide the very simple ceremony," did Münsterberg withdraw his resignation.[19]

James generally kept his differences with Münsterberg on an intellectual level. In 1900 he was mildly discomfited when Münsterberg's *Grundzüge der Psychologie* appeared with a dedication to "my dear colleague at Harvard University, William James, in sincere admiration and cordial friendship." In a letter to Münsterberg he spoke of his "imperfect" sympathy with its theoretical conclusions and the "unaccountable hardening of my heart towards many of your beliefs." But the tone of the letter was friendly, jocular and affectionate. James remained friendly as late as June 1904, but by the end of that year his acutely observant brother Henry, on a visit to Cambridge, sensed a certain coldness. On December 11, 1904, Henry made a special entry in his novelist's notebook to remind himself to write something about Harvard as an American institution with incalculable resources and undetermined future, and to "glance at the 'sinister,' the ominous 'Münsterberg' possibility—the sort of class of future phenomena represented by the foreigner coming in and taking possession."[20]

Münsterberg's own response to the Emerson Hall incident in 1905 mixed anger and self-pity. When he offered his resignation to President Eliot, he wrote that "after all I am merely 'a

German' . . . a born American ought to take my place at once." Characteristically, he exaggerated his injured innocence as part of his bargaining for vindication. He was unable to take any sign of disapproval as other than a reflection of the mean spirit of his critic. His deliberately accented role as a German in America was so much a replay of his father's role as a Jew in Germany that he lived in constant expectation of antiforeign (the equivalent of anti-Semitic) prejudice. Despite James's apology, he later informed Eliot that the Emerson Hall imbroglio "changed totally my feelings toward this community."[21]

Yet relations between James and Münsterberg were restored to seeming friendship. When in February 1909 Professor Lightner Witmer published an article attacking James's "unscientific" indulgence in psychical research, Münsterberg, although in fundamental agreement with Witmer's position, rose to the defense of his colleague. He refused to allow the American Psychological Association to hold its scheduled meeting at the Harvard Laboratory as long as Witmer was a member. James persuaded Münsterberg to back down on his ultimatum, arguing that "temperamental antipathies"—as he termed the differences between Witmer and himself—should be allowed to express themselves. James evidenced surprise at finding Münsterberg so quick to champion his "greatness" as a psychologist. But Münsterberg would not be toyed with; he had disregarded his own self-interest, he advised James, out of a sense of personal loyalty.[22]

It was in response to the charge of "shallow dogmatism" leveled against him by James that Münsterberg agreed to observe the renowned medium, Eusapia Palladino, in 1909. James had argued on behalf of the serious investigation of psychic phenomena. He was a prominent supporter of the Society for Psychical Research in England, which printed a report about Mme. Palladino in its November 1909 *Proceedings*. In February 1910, Münsterberg published an essay on "My Friends, The Spiritualists" (in the *Metropolitan* magazine) that included his observations at a series of Mme. Palladino's seances in New York. He characterized those scientists who took psychical research seriously as men of "negative suggestibility," disposed by prejudice to assert the opposite of prevailing beliefs. But what made the essay a sensation was his account of how one participant had caught Mme. Palladino in a piece of trickery. Münsterberg implied that the participant acted as his agent: "I had told him that I expected wires stretched out from her body and he looked out for them. What a surprise when he saw that she . . . was reaching out and fishing with her toes for the guitar and the table in the cabinet" in order to make them sound and move respectively.[23]

His essay had mixed consequences for Münsterberg. It momentarily added to his fame, but it also aroused "hostility in many quarters." The negative reaction developed as it became known that the man who exposed Mme. Palladino was not Münsterberg's accomplice; he had acted on his own initiative. When the original article was reprinted in *American Problems* (1910), Münsterberg did not correct the misleading implication. Among those who believed he had been party to the exposure, some thought that he had planned the incident simply to make headlines. Five years later, Professor Joseph Jastrow claimed that the entire episode left such a bad impression of publicity-seeking that he was unable to secure approval for Münsterberg to give a series of lectures at the University of Wisconsin.[24]

Münsterberg probably did exploit the incident for self-advertisement. But he was more interested in using it to attack "My Friends, The Spiritualists," among whom he included William James. He undertook his observations, he argued, strictly in response to James's challenge, and he published them as a "public duty." Several years later, Münsterberg would allege that he spent "twenty years [in fighting a losing battle] against the cheap mysticism of the New England public." He had other personal stakes in the controversy over psychical research. There was, first of all, his instinctive aversion to disorder and uncertainty, which would surface as a pitched battle with the "pragmatists." There was also his habitual status anxiety, shared to a lesser extent by a number of contemporary medical psychologists. They felt threatened by the new movements in mind exploration and the vogue of faith healing that flourished after 1890, and feared the incursion of quackery into the domain of science. To Münsterberg, popular support for spiritualism was essentially antiintellectual and antiscientific; recognition of the occult by fellow academicians was "personally humiliating."[25]

Münsterberg's taste for fame led him to make numerous forays into the popular press. In 1906 he publicly declared his belief in the innocence of the defendant in a notorious Chicago murder case. Convinced that the man's confession was the product of an agitated mental state, Münsterberg felt vindicated when, before the death sentence was administered, the condemned man denied his confession. Münsterberg in 1907 attracted considerable attention in connection with the celebrated trial of William (Big Bill) Haywood and other officials of the Western Federation of Miners in Boise, Idaho. Harry Orchard, a confessed killer, testified that eighteen murders were committed by him at the behest of the union's officials. The charges against them hinged on the veracity of Orchard's testimony. Münsterberg went to Boise and spent seven hours observing Orchard, submitting him to word association tests, which he claimed were "more scientific and objective and convincing than the whole process of legal inquiry." Münsterberg's ostensible purpose in studying Orchard was to test his methods of determining veracity rather than to provide evidence in the trial.[26]

Before undertaking his investigations, Münsterberg inclined to doubt Orchard's character (a point he later cited as proof of his own objectivity). But the results of his word association and time reaction tests convinced him that Orchard was telling the truth. On the way back to Boston, Münsterberg "inadvertently" told a reporter of his conclusions. After his statement appeared in papers throughout the country, Münsterberg felt obliged to elaborate. In the ensuing tumult he was accused of being influenced by friends of Orchard, of taking money to support him, and of being "used" by the magazine publisher S. S. McClure, who had agreed in advance to publish "an article on his experiments." There was such a storm of controversy over his actions and motives that Münsterberg withdrew the article from publication. But he discussed his methods and theories about legal psychology in several popular articles later gathered, along with a review of the Orchard case, in his widely popular *On The Witness Stand.*[27]

Münsterberg's interest in the veracity of testimony takes on added significance in the light of a later quarrel that developed between him and his once devoted student Edwin B. Holt. Holt confided to William James in 1909 that "for him the profession of psychologist meant to be able to work with Münsterberg. If he couldn't do that, he would become a business man, and give up psychology." In 1915 Holt published a book called *The Freudian Wish,* in which he contended that a number of critics were skeptical of Freud's theories because they wished them to be untrue. One was a "fairly well-educated business man" who "passionately rejected" Freud's theories about the psychopathology of everyday life and was himself "one of the most unconscionable liars who ever lived." According to Holt's account, this unnamed businessman distorted everything to his own liking and made of his life "one long unconscious self-exposure." It was his frequent habit to introduce a lie in the form of a reluctant admission: to say, for example, that he could no longer resist the conclusion that Mr. X (a successful rival) was a failure. He repeatedly asserted that "the word lie is not in my lexicon," but was so devoted to lying that later in life he evidenced "emotional recoil at any mention of deceit or untruth."[28]

Münsterberg read this passage as a vicious personal attack on himself, for many of the attitudes and statements attributed to the businessman were recognizably his own. Holt almost certainly intended to refer to Münsterberg in this passage and in his statement that Freud's work made "established professors" look "hopelessly incompetent." What is most interesting about Münsterberg's response is that he took scant notice of the more obvious derogations of his person and position as a leading critic of Freud, but fastened instead on the almost buried anecdote about the lying businessman.[29]

His sensitivity to a charge of mendacity is understandable.

Münsterberg's deceptions ran the gamut from false candor to distortion; they were part of a system of necessary defense mechanisms. Most often they involved an unconscious self-falsification designed to make contradictory actions and beliefs appear congruent. He repeatedly cloaked his wishes as duties and justified aggressive behavior as self-sacrificial and self-defensive. Both action and belief strengthened self-esteem, but each followed a different principle: self-inflation and aggrandizement on the one hand, submissive conformity to external authority on the other. In Geneva, his declaration to Otto of a "shattering" passion for Mina Lapine was both a piece of self-exaggeration and a manipulation of his older brother's credulity. In childhood his extraordinary politeness demonstrated an overrespectful obedience to the demands of a stern and imposing father.

The source of Münsterberg's aggressive-submissive behavior pattern lay primarily in his ambivalent feelings toward his father. In part he directed his affection toward a purified and idealized parental image. This prepared the way for a strong identification with Moritz. Like his father, he was ambitious, industrious, strong-willed and compulsive; he wrote poetry, developed wide interests, enjoyed travel, pursued money, maintained strong family bonds. Despite a limited evasion of Moritz's authority in disavowing his Jewishness, Münsterberg replayed his father's role as a Jew in Germany by insisting upon his own marginal position as a German in America. He denied that anti-Semitism existed in Germany, but he dwelt upon the xenophobia of Americans. After 1914, when anti-Germanism in America began to correspond to his imaginings, he enjoyed a perverse sense of vindication.

But Münsterberg's hostility to and resentment of the punitive side of Moritz remained a source of aggressive impulse. He habitually displaced and projected these negative feelings onto others. His essential need to conform to an idealized parental image required constant self-falsification, for the price of failure was a disastrously lowered self-esteem. It is under these conditions that one must view his sensitivity to charges of deception and his near obsession with the issue of veracity. He chose to protect himself from anxiety over his own untruthfulness by adopting the role of an expert detector of the trickery of others.

Münsterberg was engaged for almost a decade in the task of informing the lay public about the principles and prospects of scientific psychology. In 1909 he published a popular work, *Psychotherapy*, which attempted to review systematically the applications of psychology to the practice of medicine. Part of his purpose was to "counteract misunderstandings which over-flood the whole field" of psychotherapy—chiefly the notion that man's will or inner purposes are accessible to science—by giving a lucid presentation of the physiological basis of be-havior. But his main concern was to point out the ways in which scientific psychology might be used as a technological resource by the therapist, whose task is "treating the sick by influencing the mental life."[30]

Following Pierre Janet's dissociation theory, Münsterberg interprets psychical disturbances as expressions of the dis-equilibrium of normal mental functioning. It is the job of the psychotherapist to repair disequilibrium. Through suggestion, he argues, the therapist can help "the weak mind" to overcome or inhibit abnormal impulses and reinforce "sound desires." Drawing upon a conception of the brain as the switchboard of an arc from sense to muscle, he perceives that suggestion (of an idea, belief, or action) "has a power in our mind to suppress the opposite idea." It can influence the balance of motor im-pulse in a predetermined direction. The suggestible person is one whose psychophysical apparatus is such that "new propo-sitions for action easily close channels for the opposite." The key elements in therapy are that the patient must struggle to overcome obstacles to normal functioning and that the thera-pist initiates the process by forceful suggestion. Thus Münster-berg defines psychotherapy as falling between causal and pur-posive psychology. The psychotherapist manipulates material reality (the sick patient) in the direction of ideal reality ("normal" functioning). Mental illness is essentially a sign of constitutional weakness which can be overcome by the willed repression of "bad" impulses and the reinforcement of "sound" ones.[31]

Needling Freudian and other theorists of dynamic psychia-
try, Münsterberg asserts that "There is no passing mood, and
floating half-thought in our mind, no dream and no intuition,
no slight change of attention, no instinct and desire which cannot be analyzed . . . into its sensation elements." "The story
of the [Freudian] subconscious mind," he claims, "can be told
in three words: there is none." There are no purely mental
mechanisms. Whatever is "unconscious" in the mind is merely
dissociated from the main contents of consciousness; normal
mental life is characterized by the *connectedness* of all contents at any one moment. The therapist works to restore connection both with physical (pharmacological) and psychical
(suggestive) means. In his own practice, Münsterberg reports,
he uses explanation, persuasion, assurance, and placebos, in
order to secure the patient's belief in the possibility of a cure.
He offers suggestions of a specific or general nature (work,
contact with beauty, pleasant company) and often prescribes
autosuggestion. By means of hypnosis, he claims, he can induce
a heightened state of suggestibility in his patients. He allows
that he sometimes works toward a catharsis through the "loose
dreamy play of ideas"—as he characterizes Freud's "talk" cure.
In direct suggestion, he prefers to reinforce ideas opposite to
the troublesome one; in autosuggestion, he advises patients
to cultivate discipline, repression, inhibition.[32]

Münsterberg's book on psychotherapy appeared a few
months before Freud lectured at Clark University. He had
read Freud and listened to Ernest Jones expound psychoanalysis at Morton Prince's house in 1908. But he was so convinced of its fatuousness that during the period of Freud's
lectures he preferred to accept an invitation to tour Canada
with the British Association for the Advancement of Science.
Writing at the end of a decade which teemed with popular
psychotherapies and mental health movements, Münsterberg
declared in his preface to *Psychotherapy:*

The aim of the book is not to fight the Emmanuel Church Movement, or
even Christian Science or any other psychotherapeutic tendency outside
of the field of scientific medicine. I see the element of truth in all of
them, but they ought to be symptoms of transition. Scientific medicine
should take hold of psychotherapeutics now or a most deplorable dis-

organization will set in, the symptoms of which no one ought to over-look to-day.

After Freud's visit, debate among the practitioners of medical psychology intensified. Münsterberg threw in his lot with the older generation of neurologists (including Wundt) who questioned the scientific status of psychoanalysis, and shuddered at its potential impact on "civilized" morality.[33]

Hypnotic suggestion, after Freud gave up its use, became the rallying ground for many who opposed psychoanalysis. It particularly appealed to Münsterberg as an application of the mental power of the practitioner. Despite claims to the contrary, he was uninterested in the scientific investigation of hypnosis or in its possible diagnostic uses. It was simply a preferred therapeutic device. He often terminated treatment quickly when he encountered a resistant patient.[34]

In Münsterberg's hands, the process of psychotherapy was one of imposing a strong will upon a weak one. The definitions of good and bad, of "proper" behavior goals and normal functioning, were ultimately supplied by the therapist. Evading the ethical implications of this method, he insisted that hypnosis does not eliminate the moral will of the patient but removes obstacles to its exercise. Furthermore, it is the physician's *duty* to serve the ideal of mental health—which Münsterberg defined in terms of self-discipline, energy, ambition, and initiative in the service of moral virtue.[35]

The year 1909 was a remarkably productive one for Münsterberg. In the six months from January to June he wrote the texts of *Psychotherapy, The Eternal Values* (an English version of *Philosophie der Werte*), *Psychology and the Teacher*, and numerous popular articles. For this brief period he rivaled the extraordinary output of his early mentor, Wilhelm Wundt, whose lifetime record of publication averaged "nearly one word every two minutes, day and night." Münsterberg's conception of applied psychology as an instrumental science proved to be exceedingly fertile, for he could address himself to an unlimited number of human aims and endeavors. With his "wonderful knack for perceiving and defining issues"—his passion for abstract order and exclusive categories—he divided the new field into applied psychology proper (the use of psychological principles to explain and interpret a wide range of human behaviors) and "psychotechnics" (the use of psychological principles to predict and control human behavior with respect to specific and narrowly defined activities).[36]

When Münsterberg turned his attention to the uses of psychology in commercial and industrial life, he embarked upon his most significant venture in practical psychology. While visiting at the University of Berlin in 1910, he offered a new lecture course which provided the outline of *Psychologie und Wirtschaftsleben* (1912). The work of Frederick W. Taylor set the stage for Münsterberg's new enterprise, but he shifted his emphasis away from the rationalization of the production process to broad problems of personnel selection, labeling Taylor's earlier efforts in this area "dilettantism." Specifically, Münsterberg devised ways to measure the "mental traits" or abilities required for the successful performance of certain jobs. In a famous study of the requirements for effective motormen (for the Boston Elevated Company) he developed laboratory test situations that identified the most effective job performers in actual service. These tests were then turned over to the company to be used in hiring replacements.[37]

In 1911 he cultivated contacts with businessmen and large factory managers for the purpose of studying work and management operations. Letters were sent to a thousand companies, requesting information about the essential mental traits for various jobs. At first he concerned himself exclusively with the problem of selecting the best human instruments to achieve the goals laid down by business enterprises. After he developed an experimental means for locating "the best possible man," he moved on to the problem of eliciting "the best possible work" from employees. Finally, shifting from industrial to commercial concerns, he investigated "the best possible effect" that various techniques of business promotion might have on the human mind. Salting the text of *Psychology and Industrial Efficiency* with vivid illustrations and case studies, Münsterberg set down "the principles and methods of [an] experimental economic psychology," which caught the attention of the business world and, according to one historian, effectively "sparked a movement." Despite his insistence that psychotechnics concerned itself with means alone, Münsterberg characteristically invoked the "general social welfare" as its ultimate justification. In effect, he argued that the work ethic and industrial efficiency were ideal values; thus whatever served economic interests served society at large.[38]

Significantly, it was a German critic who first questioned the ambiguous role of the psychotechnician and Münsterberg's "amerikanistische Tendenz" to assume that only good can flow from the fount of economic prosperity. Nor was this Münsterberg's only American deviation. In *Psychologie und Wirtschaftsleben* (1912) and the far more comprehensive *Grundzüge der Psychotechnik* (1914), he moved away from the German traditions of systematic and experimental psychology to focus on individual differences and practical interests. In German academic circles, the conventional wisdom argued against the pursuit of knowledge that was "merely" useful—against the practical and technical specialists who threatened to dislodge academic mandarins from their cultural hegemony. Even the experimental work of Wundt, Stumpf, and Müller fell into disfavor after the turn of the century for its "mechanistic analysis" and "naturalistic errors."[39]

Münsterberg was always concerned about his professional standing in Germany. He published his most ambitious scholarly works in German first. His English writings and translations were merely part of a noble mission to infuse America with German enlightenment. Through them he hoped to provide an antidote to the primitive "naturalism, and positivism, and scepticism" of American intellectual life. In aligning himself with the values of the German mandarins, he resolutely refused to see how much his own work was affected by the suspect traditions.[40]

One of the ingenious ideas spun off from Münsterberg's work on psychotechnics was a career guidebook, *Vocation and Learning* (1912), written for the general public. It was his "too long neglected duty," Münsterberg declared, to provide "right guidance of the youth to the special life occupations . . . What seems necessary is not a superficial outside view, but an understanding of the deeper inner demands of our occupations and professions." There followed an elaborate schematization in which he classified the motives, abilities, and knowledge requisite to eleven selected vocations. The book was far more informed by a priori judgments than by experimental data. It suffered from the subordination of Münsterberg's scientific perspective to his role as a guidance counselor, and it finally devolved into a long sermon on moral idealism.[41]

Emphasizing the "particular duty of the psychologist from time to time to leave his laboratory . . . to serve the outside interests of the community," Münsterberg addressed himself, in *Psychology and Social Sanity* (1914), to a selected set of social problems that he said could be "cleared up with the methods of modern psychology." Once again his stance is prescriptive. His essays are a characteristic compound of acute observations and moralistic dicta on subjects ranging from sex education, socialism, and commercial advertising to popular psychology and the current "dancing craze." His lengthy discussion of sex education begins with a declaration of his duty both to defend an unpopular point of view and to overcome his reticence and "feeling of disgust" about public discussion of sexual problems. He bases his argument on the "fact" that free discussion stimulates young minds and leads to immorality. The general social welfare demands *individual* repression of sexual impulses and *social* suppression both of vice and information about sex. Having examined the issues from the point of view of "objective science," and having exposed the uninformed opinions of the "thoughtless public," he asserts that "from now on I shall stick to the one policy in which I firmly believe, the policy of silence."[42]

In all, Münsterberg published four volumes of collected essays on American social and cultural life. *American Traits* (1902) examined selected topics "from a German point of view." But *American Problems* (1910), *American Patriotism* (1913), and *Psychology and Social Sanity* (1914) were written from the perspective of a professional psychologist. "While I have remained a German citizen," Münsterberg wrote in the preface to *American Problems*, "I naturally have . . .[come to accept] the American point of view more and more . . . the angle from which I see [American problems] has become a new one. It is no longer the national differences but more my professional lifework which has influenced my attitude toward the public questions. Not as a German but as a psychologist I have begun to take sides as to the problems which stir the nation."

Yet there is very little change in his critique of American life. Instead of measuring America against the yardstick of Germany, he claims to measure it against objective psychological laws. But the results are the same. *American Problems*, for example, teems with Münsterberg's by now familiar indictments of the shortcomings of Americans: their lack of self-discipline, their disrespect for experts and scholars, their narrow utilitarian philosophy, their conformism, and their inferior education. American women are described as passive, superficial, and given to an intemperate craving for frivolity.[43]

One essay in this volume, "Prohibition and Temperance," vividly illustrates the way in which Münsterberg's manner—regardless of the degree of reason in his argument—inevitably provoked controversy. It is a reprint, with an epilogue, of an article he wrote for *McClure's Magazine* in 1908. His position is that Prohibition will have little effect on alcoholism. A harsh, restrictive law will only breed violations. He claims that he is a recognized temperance leader in Germany and that his opposition to Prohibition is in fact designed to aid the temperance cause, not saloon keepers. But his initial focus and significant emphasis are ad hominem. The supporters of Prohibition are categorized as "hysterical": "only cowards who have no trust in their own will prefer to be removed from every temptation." The intelligent opponents of Prohibition are too intimidated to speak out. The whole public discussion reveals "the fundamental evil of American public opinion": that the fashion of the moment dominates all and "no one dares to be on the unpopular side."[44]

Prohibitionists (at least) were incensed by the article when it originally appeared, and some charged that Harvard accepted a gift of $50,000 from brewer Adolphus Busch for the Germanic Museum as a payoff to Münsterberg. Detailing his relations with the Busch family to President A. Lawrence

Lowell, Münsterberg reported that Busch once asked him to "do something" with a congressional commission working on prohibition legislation. But he refused and carefully avoided discussing the matter with his good friend Hugo Reisinger, Busch's son-in-law. "There is no money in the world which could induce me to write anything in the interest of any business," he told one advertising agent. "I write my articles exclusively in the interest of truth and moral reform, never asking whether any commercial interests gain or suffer from it."[45]

The essays collected in *American Problems* deal primarily with current domestic concerns. The most interesting essays in *American Patriotism* (1913), in contrast, deal with aspects of German life—as Münsterberg observed it during his exchange year in Berlin—and with American attitudes toward Europe. Once again he tries to dispel popular American misconceptions of Germany, which he alleges to be the product of a biased press, and to assert the fundamental kinship of the two countries. He praises German nationalism, which he defines as a "loyal belief in the mission of the German spirit in the world," denies any trace of chauvinism (that is, any lack of respect for the values of other countries), and breathes a sigh of relief that the "colorless and characterless cosmopolitanism" of humanist intellectuals "has been swept away by the enthusiasms for the German Empire." He believes that pride in the German army is an integral part of the new nationalism and "ultimately in deepest harmony with . . . peace-loving internationalism." According to Münsterberg, "weak cosmopolitanism" is the true enemy of peace, for it erodes the unique moral character of the individual nations and dangerously saps the healthy thrust toward national self-realization. The peace and disarmament movements in America, he charges, derive from a moral superiority complex, which encourages Americans to view themselves as world preceptors and supreme judges.[46]

In contrast to worldly-wise German nationalism, exuberant American patrotism draws "a disproportionate part of . . . its strength from a glaring ignorance of the rest of the world." "An aristocratic minority" of Anglo-Saxons nurtures this ignorance in order to preserve the dominant influence of England in America. Nevertheless, he looks to the forging of a "new patriotism" in America, spearheaded by "the non-Anglo-Saxon majority," which will reassert the paternity of continental Europe and pay it due respect. America, he argues, must define itself by the national task of all its people, and not by their national origins.[47]

In *American Patriotism* Münsterberg developed many of the themes that were to inform his wartime writings. His praise of "the Germany of to-day" is unstinted, and with it goes a marked decline in the quality and organization of his material from the level of *American Traits*. He begins to see a resolute idealism everywhere in Germany. In contrast, American society is impulse-ridden, wasteful, extravagant, pleasure-seeking, and self-divided. Germany stood for all the qualities Münsterberg wanted to possess; America, for the tendencies he feared in himself. His fundamental insight into the difference between Germany and America was that the former was given to "social idealism" and the latter to selfish individual pursuits. His idealization of Germany was not merely a grounding for his sense of "racial" superiority. He projected onto Germany his ideal conception of himself. His oft-repeated mission to bring Germany and America together derived its imperative force from his own psychic needs.[48]

The diversity of Münsterberg's interests and activities encountered few limits save those of time and energy. But some of his ambitions ran counter to the interests of Harvard University, and President Eliot reluctantly rebuked him.

Eliot's relationship with Münsterberg had a long and difficult history before their differences erupted into mutual censure. The president had dealt with Münsterberg on cordial terms with respect to his appointment at Harvard in 1892 and again in 1897. In the spring of 1904 Eliot told him that "your coming to the University, and your service to it, have been among the very interesting features of my work during the last twelve years." But already minor irritations had been sustained by each party. On several occasions, Eliot firmly rejected Münsterberg's suggestions for revising Harvard's administration and curriculum along the lines of German universities. A number of incidents between 1899 and 1902 aroused Münsterberg's suspicion of anti-German prejudice on Eliot's part. In fact, Eliot made a considerable effort to deal even-handedly with Münsterberg. After the unfortunate Emerson Hall affair in 1905, he wrote to William James:

The fact is that Münsterberg, like most men who think rather too much about themselves and their doings, is oversensitive . . . Of course Münsterberg has a German way of doing things, which is different from our Yankee way. For instance, his introduction of me on that occasion would have been absolutely impossible for any born Yankee, and it grated on the ears of all Yankees. But when you recommended Münsterberg for an appointment here you must have expected that he would be different from us and doubtless reckoned on those very differences as part of the profit to the University. We cannot expect to profit by his merits without ever having to wince at his defects.[49]

But statesmanship in the handling of strictly intrauniversity affairs stiffened into partisanship when larger interests were involved. In the spring of 1908, Eliot and Münsterberg began to tangle seriously. Münsterberg involved himself in raising money for an international exchange of students with German universities. Eliot cautioned him that this project was not of particular interest to the university, which was quite satisfied "with its present modest contribution towards larger intellectual intercourse between Germany and the United States." More pointed was his admonition to cease soliciting money from regular contributors to Harvard.[50]

By the fall of 1908 the two men were exchanging heated letters over Münsterberg's alleged interference with the professorial exchange program between Harvard and German universities. For several years Münsterberg had criticized the mechanics of the program. He objected to inviting German professors for a full year because American students, who might beneficially attend a short series of lectures in German, were not able to handle a full course in a foreign language. In his own department, he argued, the program was a complete failure for this reason, and in addition key men such as George Santayana and Francis Peabody were lost for a year as part of the exchange. When Münsterberg learned that persons in high places disapproved of his "interference" with the program, he defensively wrote to Eliot asserting that he acted only in its best interests.[51]

Eliot took a different view of the matter. He charged Münsterberg with opposing the exchange program in principle from its beginning, behaving coolly toward a number of the visiting German scholars, and exerting an influence in Germany "adverse to the continuance of the present arrangements." Eliot barely stopped short of alleging jealousy of rivals as Münsterberg's motive. Münsterberg denied Eliot's charges, including the unwritten one. His only grievance against other German scholars was toward the "haughty" professors at the University of Berlin, many of whom had agreed among themselves not to come to an American university—provincial by definition. Wounded by Eliot's tone, he recited a defensive litany of personal sacrifices he had made to stay at Harvard, of personal achievements that redounded to Harvard's honor, and of numerous services he had rendered to the university—including the unsolicited use of personal influence with German and American officials on Harvard's behalf. As for his role as a mediator between the intellectual communities of the two countries, he advised Eliot to "ask any educated man in all Germany who has done the most in the last ten years . . . and my name would be given."[52]

Avoiding the other points of controversy, Eliot tried to focus the issue on Münsterberg's conception of his unique mission as an international ambassador:

What I wish, and what the Corporation wish, is that you should give over your efforts as a special agent or adviser of German authorities about American affairs, or of American authorities about German affairs; that you should limit your activities to your professional and literary work . . . [and] cease to communicate on your own initiative with German officials . . . concerning the affairs of Harvard University . . . We should be glad to have you alter your conception of the "one great task for which I stayed in this country."[53]

Münsterberg was infuriated by this lack of appreciation for the work he had done to secure "that sympathy and interest which the European continent today has for Harvard." Under Münsterberg's needling, Eliot's tone hardened. He did not mince words in telling him that his "influence" was as much a hindrance to Harvard as a help and that his claim to have secured a world position for the American university "would not be taken seriously by well-informed persons." Unable to deal with this insult, Münsterberg convinced himself that the crux of the matter was anti-German prejudice: "It is the curse of the world that the foreigner is always wrong . . . he has no chance for an unprejudiced jury." He believed that the Harvard Corporation conducted a "secret trial" against him, admitting malicious slander and rumor as evidence.[54]

Moving decisively to head off a further exchange of pointless insults, Eliot advised his correspondent that the Corporation would certainly be pleased to have him remain at Harvard in the role of teacher, scholar, and public figure as long as he did "not become a political or industrial agent." But he added that "they are also willing that you should accept a suitable appointment elsewhere, and should on that occasion give such publicity as you thought best to your reasons for feeling dissatisfaction with the service of Harvard University." Münsterberg, although he previously made a vague threat to take his talents elsewhere, had no intention of leaving Harvard and therefore managed diplomatically to find himself "in far-reaching harmony with . . . your last letter." In the course of the whole affair and under the strain of conflicting obligations to the various roles he played, he gave way to outbursts of pettiness and self-exaggeration. His long letters to Eliot, written in the heat of passion, were blunt without being entirely honest, logical without being quite rational, and sprinkled with idle threats. When his passion subsided at last, it was chiefly because he convinced himself that his various roles could be reconciled, without diminution, to the demands of the university.[55]

Less than two months later Münsterberg was again self-confidently acting on behalf of his conception of German and American interests. Visiting French journalist and statesman André Tardieu, whom Münsterberg believed to be a "mere politician," one of "a little band of [anti-German] demagogues," was delivering a series of lectures at Harvard. Münsterberg complained to Eliot that the Frenchman came in the hope of stirring up American opinion against Germany and that his presence on the campus would result in the "unwillingness of German professors [here] to continue the professorial exchange." He asked Eliot to restrain the visitor.[56]

Eliot became concerned over the amount of passion Münsterberg invested in his various activities. A little over a year later, he took occasion to express this concern when told of a threat to Münsterberg's life by a deranged woman whom Münsterberg had treated under hypnosis:

You seem to me to work with too much intensity and too constantly, and to work on topics which are peculiarly stirring and exciting. I hope that you will moderate your rate of work and of publication, and will take up some systematic course of interesting out-of-door exercise, with frequent absences from Cambridge between Friday night and Monday morning for change of scene and change of thoughts. I also advise you not to have anything to do hereafter with the hypnotic treatment of women.

Relatively tolerant and patient with Münsterberg on matters pertaining strictly to his position at Harvard, Eliot flared up only when this position was made subservient to Münsterberg's other concerns. Later, after the outbreak of war in Europe, relations between the two men turned to open and bitter hostility.[57]

In 1910, Münsterberg secured an exchange professorship at Berlin as a reward for his willingness to organize the new Amerika Institut founded there under the auspices of the Prussian Ministry of Education. He was instrumental in raising funds for the new Institut, securing a $25,000 grant from his friend Jacob Schiff (and additional money from James Speyer) to add to the capital fund raised in Berlin. Some potential contributors raised questions about the venture because of the prior establishment of an American Institute at Berlin under the aegis of Columbia University. But Münsterberg argued that the new agency would perform different work by virtue of its German management. "The Amerika Institut," he modestly wrote, "is an administrative, governmental institute for the systematic furthering of the official cultural relations between Germany and the United States. It advises universities and governmental bureaus of Germany and the United States, it regulates the cultural relations, it transmits the official printed documents between the two nations."[58]

A few years later he would proclaim that "in the whole history of civilization probably no such enterprise has ever been recorded, and what it aims at may truly be the model for future developments. It works for the necessary modernization of international intercourse, a kind of efficiency management in the world of ideals." But it was also a project touching Münsterberg's less exalted ambitions. The existence at Berlin of several operations controlled by Columbia University (the American Institute, the Roosevelt Room, and the Roosevelt Professorship), was a thorn in his side. He feared that Columbia might become the "central agency working in international affairs," that Harvard would be locked out of the picture, and that Columbia president Nicholas Murray Butler would be the dean of American university presidents through his control over foreign professorships. The only thing that kept Butler from sweeping all before him, Münsterberg told Harvard president A. Lawrence Lowell, was the Prussian government's request for a Harvard man to head the Amerika Institut.[59]

Once settled in Berlin, Münsterberg divided his time between the Institut, his university lectures, and more popular addresses on American culture. In retrospect, he was to call this "the crowning year of my life." But in fact his sojourn in Berlin was far from serene or triumphant. Shortly after his arrival, he became enmeshed in a series of ludicrous contretemps stemming, in part, from his obsessively competitive attitude toward the Columbia University exchange program in Berlin.[60]

Earlier entanglements with Nicholas Murray Butler had set the stage for these developments. In 1904 Münsterberg provoked Butler into making an impolitic statement about the vanity, egotism, and unmannerliness of German university professors—and in particular about the financial greediness of a certain German scholar who refused to lecture at Columbia on his way home from the St. Louis Congress because the fee was not high enough. The mutual dislike of the two men hardened in 1907 when they shared a Carnegie Hall platform at a public meeting held under the auspices of the National Arbitration and Peace Congress. Münsterberg presented a case for the healthy influence of military conscription in Germany; Butler laced into him for defending "German militarism." By 1911, the two episodes fused in Münsterberg's mind. He looked back upon the "silent warfare [between us] in which I have never been the aggressive party. On the contrary, I have always avoided every fight, even though I had the weapons in hand."[61]

Münsterberg thought Butler resented the fact that the Amerika Institut was in the hands of a Harvard man. He came to believe that the entire purpose of the Columbia operations at Berlin was to humiliate Harvard (and, by extension, himself). He advised Lowell that Columbia scored great social successes at Berlin by selecting professors for their "brilliant parlor qualities," while Harvard in its innocence merely counted upon superior scholarship. He was certain that Harvard's best interests were seriously endangered: "I beg you not to underestimate the influence which this international relation of the various American universities has on the tendency of the German-American families to send their sons to one or another place. Columbia's pro-German policy, however hypocritical, probably involves a gain of several hundred German-American students a year, besides the large gifts from German-American bankers."[62]

The whole Berlin year started off badly, despite Münsterberg's initial boast that "my work here surpasses my best anticipation." It was bad enough to have competition from Columbia for the spotlight, but in addition he believed that he was undercut by the press corps that supplied American newspapers with news from Germany. This corps, he charged, was made up of English and American correspondents attached to anti-German papers in London. When a frivolous item appeared in American papers reporting that the emperor, at a reception in the fall of 1909, spoke for fifteen minutes with the Columbia representative, C. Alphonso Smith, and for only five minutes with Münsterberg, he lost all sense of proportion in his frantic effort to correct the story. In the heat of indignation he wrote self-pitying letters of denial to a number of prominent Americans. Lowell, attempting to calm Münsterberg down, did not refrain from inflicting further humiliation. Untoward concern, he cautioned, over "the question of the length of time the emperor talks to different professors, the invitations to court balls, and the precedence among professors has the effect here of lowering the dignity of Harvard's representative; it raises a smile that does not heighten the respect for professors." When Münsterberg did subside he attributed the "wholly fabricated" news item to the malice of anti-German reporters determined to avenge themselves for his disclosure of their biases. "The invention was so absurd," he pretended, "that when the reports [of it] came back from America to Berlin, it occasioned great amusement and not least among those most intimately concerned."[63]

The most serious contretemps of the year involved both of Münsterberg's *bêtes noires:* the Columbia representative and the American press. He was completely unaware of the hostility he bore toward the incumbent of the Roosevelt professorship, C. Alphonso Smith. At the beginning of the Berlin year he sent a patronizing letter offering his personal services to Smith. Münsterberg later claimed that he went out of his way to be helpful despite "all of the gossip which was brought to me about his jealousy." To Lowell he reported that Smith was full of "little intrigues," that he had orders to deliver "pro-Columbia speeches" whenever the name of Harvard was mentioned in public. Yet Münsterberg argued that he did everything possible to cover for the man's "tactlessness" and the "failure" of his allegedly inept and second-rate German lectures.[64]

Antagonism between Smith and Münsterberg finally flashed over the pettiest of affairs, involving a special invitation issued to Smith and his wife to attend a formal reception at Schleppencour given by the emperor. No foreigners previously presented to the emperor were supposed to be invited, but an exception was made in Smith's case because he had erroneously been promised an invitation and his wife had ordered a gown by the time the mistake was discovered. Münsterberg raised a storm of protest over the exception (which was arranged by Ambassador David Jayne Hill); he wanted either an invitation for himself or the cancellation of Smith's. According to

Smith, Hill told Münsterberg that "he could . . . [only act on behalf of] Americans and as German citizens [the Münsterbergs] did not come under his jurisdiction." Münsterberg flew into a rage at this and threatened to cable President Taft to secure his rights as an American representative.[65]

Reporters, getting wind of the story, had a field day. Various garbled versions of the initial controversy and the confrontation between Münsterberg and Hill appeared in the American press, consistently casting Münsterberg in the worst possible light. An editorial in the *New York Times* on March 20, 1911, chastised him for childish behavior and noted that he was an unpopular figure at Harvard, widely disliked for his vanity. Several months later, Dr. Frank McLean of the Waltham Hospital, in a friendly letter to Smith, reported that in "certain Harvard circles" Münsterberg's conduct was deemed disgraceful and many "are heartily ashamed of him."[66]

But Münsterberg insisted on viewing the incident and the news coverage as vindictive attacks upon his person and his legitimacy as an American representative. In a letter to President Taft he accused the ambassador's wife of leaking the story to the press. She acted against him out of prejudice, Münsterberg explained, because he had never become an American citizen. He also charged the Germanophobic press corps with personal malice. For his part, Ambassador Hill reported that while Münsterberg "has not been kindly treated in the newspaper representations," he was responsible for raising the whole tempest in the first place. In reply to Münsterberg's letters, Harvard's president once again took occasion to speak caustically: "It is of very little consequence what people say of you unless it is true."[67]

In the end, Smith's invitation to the reception was withdrawn. He was so angered by Münsterberg's actions that he placed his version of the story before German officials in order "that those in authority might know Dr. Münsterberg's attitude toward the holder of the Roosevelt chair (of which this is only one evidence) and that the chair might thus be protected against him in the future." One consequence of the affair was that the Minister of Education, Friedrich Schmidt, declined to accept the German-born Professor Kuno Francke of Harvard as Exchange Professor in 1913. He preferred to receive the nomination of an American professor who would be "less inclined to sympathize with German affairs" after "taking into especial consideration the [experience of the] Münsterberg year."[68]

The episode revealed Münsterberg's extreme sensitivity to his position as a distinguished American representative in Germany and an international dignitary in America. He had set out to apply his conception of a spiritual dual citizenship. But his acute status anxiety and compulsive self-assertion defeated his purpose. During the year in Germany his excessive loyalty to what he believed to be Harvard's best interests was in fact antithetical to them and to cultural *rapprochement*. It was not so much the variety as the intensity of his commitments that brought about his humiliation. Insecure, he required constant approval from others; aggressive because insecure, he aroused hostility instead, thereby thwarting his needs and ambitions. Once again he ascribed his difficulties to the faults of others: to malicious anti-German prejudice and to resentment of "my unusual situation of being a German in an important American place." The hostility that he provoked gave a basis in reality to the hostility that he projected onto others. Thus he was able to protect his altruistic and innocent self-image.[69]

Despite the unpleasant incidents that marred his Berlin year and the variety of involvements in America to which he returned, Münsterberg's direct ties to Germany remained strong. Family bonds were reinforced by the sojourn. The four sons of Moritz Münsterberg had pledged themselves to mutual support through the mechanism of a family foundation created on their father's birthday on May 29, 1880. Over the years, they established the practice of holding yearly reunions, of collecting family memorabilia (for eventual deposit in the municipal library of Danzig), and of increasing the capital of the foundation through individual gifts marking important occasions in their lives. These arrangements formalized a sense of kinship and dynasty that permeated their relationships.[70]

Hugo was particularly close to his older brother Emil, a scholar and philanthropist who won considerable renown as the chief administrator of public charities in Berlin before his death in 1911. The oldest brother, Otto, remained head of the family in Danzig until his death in 1915. The youngest brother, Oskar, lived in Leipzig and became a wealthy businessman and a collector and scholar in the field of Chinese and Japanese art. Each of the brothers visited Hugo in the United States at various times.[71]

Hugo was a highly successful fund raiser for German causes. In addition to support for the Amerika Institut, he helped secure funds for a Helmholtz memorial in 1895, a Schiller *Stiftung* in 1905, and a tuberculosis institute in Berlin in 1909. In the spring of 1910 he raised money for a gift to the University of Berlin in honor of its hundredth anniversary, and in 1912 he secured backing for a special effort to preserve "the old and interesting buildings of Danzig." His technique for obtaining money was to approach "a small number of the best known men" to head a subscription list; to these men he argued not for a gesture of international friendship but for the repayment of a debt to German culture.[72]

At the same time Münsterberg played a prominent role in the cultural life of Boston's German-Americans, serving from 1908 to 1910 as president of the Boston German Association, whose membership numbered six hundred and included a few prominent figures in the Boston community. Münsterberg was, in fact, recognized as a leader of the German-American community. He traveled widely to address German-American audiences. In a letter to President Taft he boasted of his influence upon their political behavior:

You know that the German-American vote will be of great importance this year [1912] both at the nominations and at the elections. You know on the other hand that those millions have no leader and on the whole no reliable political instincts. They are therefore more accessible to honest influences than other factions of the population, and words from those few Germans to whom they are accustomed to listen can be of consequence. I had the honor to do my little share in that direction in the last three presidential elections, always on the Republican side. Let me say that I am at your disposal in this spirit. I think I have succeeded in undermining the German-American indignation concerning the Anglo-French treaties. I was asked to speak at various indignation assemblies . . . and instead . . . I have succeeded in destroying the plans for those meetings altogether.

When Congressman Richard E. Bartholdt asked him to support Taft in 1912 and to work against a third term for Theodore Roosevelt, Münsterberg replied that "a number of opportunities are before me in which I shall work in that direction . . . I think that I shall be able to do quite a man's work in the coming months without publicly posing as an official campaign speaker." By the end of his first three years of residence in America, Münsterberg considered himself an expert on the political relations between Germany and America. After two decades of residence, he believed that he was a key mediator between the American government and the German-American community. On numerous occasions he offered advice and services in these matters to three presidents: Roosevelt, Taft, and Wilson.[73]

Münsterberg viewed his leadership of German-Americans as unique, for he was involved in their communal concerns and yet was apart from and above them. In 1911 he collaborated with a "small circle" of like-minded men to help George Sylvester Viereck launch "a high class" English-language monthly for German-Americans. In 1913 he helped plan for a weekly newspaper in German that would report on political and economic affairs in Germany. But these were minor activities on the part of a man who considered himself to be a German, an international cultural ambassador, a scholar, and a public figure in American intellectual and political affairs.[74]

When war came in 1914, German-Americans had no more prestigious and articulate spokesman for their cause than Hugo Münsterberg. A man of exceptional intelligence, versatility, forcefulness, and vitality, he had a deep personal stake in the issues raised by the war. He rose to the crisis with an unaccustomed singleness of purpose. There were many who thought that his considerable involvement in the pro-German cause represented a "wholesale devotion to German interests." In a sense this was true. But Münsterberg's "German interests" were not those of the German government. Unlike George Sylvester Viereck, he was never a German agent, and his wartime attitudes both reflected and helped to shape the experiences and responses of many German-Americans. Extremely sensitive to anti-German prejudice—sometimes flashing with indignation at imaginary slights—he was deeply engaged in the German-American predicament between 1914 and 1916. His "unusual situation of being a German in an important American place" challenged and restrained him at once. Events and circumstance were to place large numbers of German-Americans in a similar bind. Despite their differences, they soon were subject to a common fate.[75]

4 . . .
THE WAR

Hugo Münsterberg's romantic German nationalism remained untempered by his ever growing involvement in American life. In his estimation the American nation was inferior to Germany. But America was not merely a nation; it was also a symbol representing the fusion of the best elements of other nations. In this sense America went beyond nationality to denote to Münsterberg something akin to his own international mission. If his commitment to the symbolic meaning of America proved deeper and stronger than his special "German interests," it was only after a bitter struggle to keep both loyalties congruent in the face of gathering pressure to choose between them.

Münsterberg's initial response to the First World War crisis was so intense that he often failed to differentiate between himself and the German cause. His was not a unique reaction. For many German-Americans, group identity came to be defined by a common posture toward the war. Between 1914 and 1917 this self-definition increasingly conflicted with other allegiances and associations on the part of individuals, until at one point or another the conflict became unendurable. After months of heightened concern and activity, under growing social coercion and psychological strain, Münsterberg's focus too began to disintegrate.

The war came as a staggering blow to Münsterberg. His spontaneous sympathy for the German cause was augmented by pressure for several quarters. He had two brothers and innumerable friends and correspondents in Germany who urged the German view of the war upon him. His prewar eminence among German-Americans automatically placed him in a position of leadership. And his location in the heartland of Yankee culture made him an early target in the partisan strife that followed upon the outbreak of war. For decades before, New England Yankees had emphasized their English ancestry as a way of distinguishing themselves from the encroaching Irish. The political association of Irish- and German-Americans in 1914 only reinforced the disposition of influential New Englanders to censure the German cause and back the Allies. At Harvard, Münsterberg faced a growing personal suspicion and hostility: "the air . . . had suddenly grown chill and raw . . . From October [1914] on, [he] stayed away for a year from that small number of distractions that his constant work allowed him—from symphony concerts . . . from occasional club meetings, from dinner parties and receptions . . . In October . . . [he] appeared for the last time at a faculty meeting." Harvard's historian Samuel Eliot Morison recalls that "at the western university where I was teaching when the war broke out in Europe, it seemed to the average student as unreal as the Wars of the Roses; returning to Harvard early in 1915, one was on the outskirts of battle . . . sympathy for the Allied cause was unconcealed; not for a moment was Harvard neutral in thought or deed."[1]

In the meantime, pro-German elements in the country took their first steps toward organization. Beleaguered German-Americans, native Americans with pro-German sympathies, and the official German establishment cast about for effective spokesmen. Münsterberg quickly took a national role. From August 1914 until the spring of 1915 he devoted considerable time and energy to organizing pro-German forces, and set himself the task of influencing public opinion and policy in favor of American neutrality. His new role as pro-German propagandist afforded fresh opportunity for the gratification of private needs: for self-inflation in praising German nationalism, for acting out his aggressive impulses while vigorously denying "German" aggrandizement. So strong was his identification with the embattled German nation that in writing of its moral idealism, its entitlement to glory, its unjust injuries at the hands of sibling rivals (England, France, America), he poured out the passions of his inner life.

Münsterberg's first article on the war, entitled "Fair Play," appeared in the *Boston Herald* on August 5 and was reprinted in fifty large-circulation newspapers throughout the country. Two years later he wrote that this

was a week in which the whole Eastern press fell upon the good reputation of Germany, denounced the Emperor as a criminal, accepted blindly the English tale that Germany wanted the war and had started it, and in which no one had a word of defence for my fatherland. By chance I met on the street the editor of the Boston Herald and he suggested to me to write an . . . interpretation of the German side . . . The letter made a great stir . . . and, as the first reaction against the uniform pro-ally view, was harshly cried down.

But he did, in fact, find many eager readers. The article was subsequently incorporated into *The War and America,* which came out late in September 1914 and went through a first printing of 2500 copies in five days. By the end of the month a second printing of the same size had sold out.[2]

The book contains twelve essays that examine the issues of the war and their moral significance for America. Münsterberg called it a "diary . . . [which] views the events as they unfold themselves from week to week, from the angle of personal experience." But the character and tone of the book are polemical. The "true facts" about the war are derived from his a priori belief in German innocence. The German nation, dedicated to the peaceful development of its inner strengths, was forced to war as a last resort against Russian expansionist greed, English economic jealousy, and French desire for revenge. Pacific and industrious, Germany is surrounded by neighbors who "begrudge" her prosperity. With reluctance, the same German Kaiser who had been "almost forcing peace on Europe for twenty-seven years" prepared to attack before Allied mobilization placed Germany at a hopeless disadvantage. One has to be a German, Münsterberg argues, fully to understand why Germany was alert and ready for war. "Nature formed from its clay no creature with more peaceful instincts than myself," he explains, and yet he can remember "from his childhood days" the constant tension under which Germans lived, ever fearful of their vengeful and threatening neighbors. The passage makes explicit Münsterberg's self-identification with a

Germany forced into aggression by the jealous prodding of morally inferior rivals.[3]

The idea of Germany's defensive aggression was developed by intellectuals such as John L. Stoddard, Edmund von Mach, Kuno Francke, John Burgess, and Münsterberg. In Münsterberg's view, Germany had nothing to gain from the war while Russia stood to win control of the Balkans, France to recapture Alsace, and England to destroy the potential power of her chief imperial rival. He made a point of "understanding" each country's concern with national self-interest. For them, as for Germany, "the life needs of a healthy nation are decisive." Each country, in fact, had a moral obligation to perform "its national duty." He sees no contradiction between his beliefs that war is an inevitable instrument for adjusting "the power of countries to the changing stages of their inner development" and that Germany had nothing to gain from war. No one's motives are morally reprehensible in his view, though one might —and Münsterberg does—accuse the Allies of ganging up against Germany.[4]

The second major theme of his book is that the European conflict is essentially a war of ideals between Germany and Russia. German culture represents the "active and productive"; it "aims to raise even the lowest by better education and by the stimulation of his free energies to the level of the highest." Russian culture, on the other hand, is "passive and unproductive"; it "aims to bring high and low to the same level by lowering the high . . . The result is lack of education, complete submission to the church, a pathetic mixture of ignorance and superstition." A sensual people given to "orthodox belief" and "blind brutality," the Russians conspire to overrun Europe. Germany stands alone against this threat to enlightened European culture. It is the "great historical blunder" of England and France that they fail to perceive where their long-term interests lie. Morally, they are guilty of racial treason.[5]

The style and argument of Münsterberg's book won substantial approval from German-Americans. In the theme of Germany's encirclement by hostile forces they saw a foreshadowing of their own fate. Indeed, what gave a note of urgency to the book—for Münsterberg as for his readers—was as much the development of anti-German sentiment in America as the difficult position of the fatherland in Europe.[6]

The lengthiest essay deals with the two large camps developing in America in response to the war: "the one controlled by anti-German sentiment; the other by fair play sentiment." Biased news reports from English sources set up "a vivid impulse against Germany" in suggestible minds. Münsterberg claims that English money and influence dominate the American press and that blind Anglophiles act essentially as English agents. They are intent upon subverting America's neutrality and estranging her German-American citizenry. The argument forges another link between German-Americans and Germany, for it implies that each is victimized by the same English enemy.[7]

According to Münsterberg, the leader of those bent on establishing German guilt—"leader by age, by authority, by mastery of diction and by the importance which the press gives to his utterances—is Charles W. Eliot." Other publicists joined in making Eliot a scapegoat for their resentment of the Anglophilic leanings of the American intellectual establishment. "The advanced decay of the old New England stock in the East" was a theme that embattled German-Americans in the East and Midwest found eminently congenial. If Münsterberg's attack on Eliot echoed earlier rancor, he implicitly denied it. Taking what he believed to be the highest possible moral ground, he compared his own "understanding" of the mistaken judgments of England and France with "the denunciations which the anti-German party thunders against the one people which is suddenly attacked by the guns of all Europe."[8]

Münsterberg's personal involvement in the issues raised by the war colored his arguments and released a flood of barely controlled aggression. Yet it also exercised a restraint on conscious levels of expression. Despite his emotional commitment to the German cause, he had to protect his self-image as an intellectual above the plane of battle, a moral philosopher, an international ambassador of good will, and a political power in America. He sought, therefore, to dissociate himself from fierce partisans who claimed absolute truth for one side or the other.

Arguing that the position of each combatant rested ultimately on a system of national beliefs rather than on objective facts, he posed as a moral relativist. In particular, he attempted to place himself above the vulgar partisanship of the Anglo-phobes: "I have certainly not joined in the widespread anger and indignation against England which my fellow [German] countrymen have often expressed. On the contrary, I have always emphasized my admiration for England and have always stated that in my opinion England has taken wrong steps in its policy, but was morally perfectly within its rights." It was a stance calculated to win American respect and to neutralize the moral indignation aroused by Germany's invasion of Belgium. A few months later he wrote to a fanatical anti-English partisan, "my sympathies, of course, are on the German side, and if America were beginning war against Germany, it would be the saddest fate I can imagine. But this does not make me wish at all that America enter into war on Germany's side." By implying that partisans on both sides sought to thrust America into war, he made his own support of neutrality seem a non-partisan, exclusively American interest.[9]

Münsterberg's sympathetic explication of the German position outraged pro-Allied sensibilities. Reviewers found his book a "blend of dogmatism, innuendo, sophistry and gush." John Cowper Powys quickly published *The War and Culture: A Reply to Professor Münsterberg*, charging him with deliberate and deceitful omissions in describing German culture, and with dishonest catering to American opinion. For every letter Münsterberg received from those who professed disagreement but believed that he should "continue your residence among us . . . [and] write anything you please" came a sheaf of letters addressed to "Professor Hugo Monsterbug" or "Baron Monchausen." For himself, Münsterberg believed that his analysis was, if anything, overly generous to England. He took the critical reviews to represent a personal bias against him which was arbitrary and unjust.[10]

His pleas for a suspension of moral judgment brought irate responses from militant pro-German partisans who accused him of cowardice, as well as from pro-Allied stalwarts. His old antagonist, Charles W. Eliot, charged that American sentiment was "not always appreciated by persons of German birth who have lived long in the United States," and was dangerously misrepresented by Münsterberg to the German government.[11]

Despite public and private jabs from Eliot, Münsterberg stuck to his relativist position in the belief that it would provide a basis for reconciling extremists and thus keeping America neutral. In October he wrote to Eliot on behalf of the German magazine *Nord und Süd,* which planned to devote its December issue to the opinions on the war of scholars from neutral countries. Politely, he asked

whether you would be willing to use this opportunity to speak a serious word to the Germans. Needless to say, the whole character of the enterprise is one in which nobody expects agreement with the German views, and I will also try to secure other contributors who feel themselves in opposition to the German side. I may say even for your orientation that Mr. [Kuno] Francke and I have agreed both to write articles in a critical vein.

However, he could not resist a glancing reference to "the *officially* neutral countries" that raised Eliot's dander. Eliot's refusal was intemperate and his reasoning evasive. He used the query as a pretext for sounding off against the German invasion of Belgium. Münsterberg's rejoinder was characteristic of his earliest quarrels with Eliot: a mixture of self-justification and assertiveness. Calling Eliot an extremist bent on war, he charged him with representing a "thin upper layer" of American society whose "fashionable" views were not widely shared. "The American people stands partly where Wilson stands and partly where Roosevelt stands, and I am in full harmony with either." He laid claim to a "fuller knowledge than the public has" about the trumped-up character of the Belgian-English protest against the violation of Belgian neutrality, referring to an alleged Allied understanding that England or France might use Belgian territory to launch war against Germany. Eliot refused to discuss the matter further, but repeated his warning to Münsterberg that false reports of American sympathy for Germany would stiffen German resistance and thus prolong a war that could only end in harsher defeat.[12]

Münsterberg could not suffer Eliot's reproaches silently. Convinced of Eliot's wrongheadedness and humiliated by his curtness, Münsterberg lost his judgment. On November 18, 1914, he sent Eliot a sealed envelope with a covering letter explaining that the contents offered secret information supporting his contention that American opinion was kindly disposed toward Germany. Eliot returned the envelope unopened, refusing to be a party to "secret affairs." Münsterberg then relayed the "secret" information in a regular letter to Eliot dated November 20. The gist of the matter was an alleged conference between Münsterberg and William F. McCombs, chairman of the Democratic National Committee and a former "intimate" of Woodrow Wilson, held at McCombs's request in early November. According to Münsterberg, McCombs believed that the Democratic party had suffered in the previous election from the defection of German, Irish, Jewish, and Swedish voters. He thought he could use his influence to swing both the administration and the public to the German cause if Münsterberg would exercise his "connections" in raising a certain sum of money, "which he supposed correctly would be easily at my comand, if the goods to be delivered were desired by me." Münsterberg went on to declare his horror at McComb's corruption, but did not doubt his ability to make good his alleged promises. He was convinced that whatever pro-English sentiment existed in the United States had been "purchased" in this same way and was therefore unreliable and unrepresentative. He had been urged by other German-Americans, he added, to seize this opportunity, but had turned from temptation because he believed that truth rather than influence would prevail in America. Eliot's reply was quick and stinging: "I must frankly tell you what impression your letter of yesterday produced on my mind. It seems to me to be the composition of a man who has been overwrought, and who is laboring under grave hallucinations. I beg you to consult at once the physician in whose judgment you have the greatest confidence."[13]

There is no record of what McCombs actually said to Münsterberg, but an approach of some sort certainly was made. It is not clear how much Münsterberg's imagination added to the bare fact of the meeting between himself and McCombs. According to Ambassador Bernstorff (who heard of the approach to Münsterberg through Bernhard Dernburg in New York),

McCombs was a trustworthy man whose sympathetic attitude toward Germany derived partly from an interest in the German-American vote and partly from his friendship with Bernstorff. But whatever McCombs said or intimated, he could give no guarantees of successful influence-wielding. Nevertheless the meeting with McCombs enlarged Münsterberg's sense of self-importance and moral rectitude. He referred to it on subsequent occasions as evidence of his own incorruptibility. His poor judgment in telling the tale to Eliot may be attributed, in large part, to the stresses and strains he endured at Harvard during the fall months of 1914—pressures that placed him beyond the pale of the community in which he had labored for almost half his life.[14]

When the outbreak of war in Europe wrought deep cleavages of opinion in the Harvard community, President A. Lawrence Lowell took plains to treat Münsterberg respectfully and to make conciliatory gestures. "You are certainly right," he wrote in September 1914,

in the resolution not to bring the war into the university lecture room, and I think you are wise also in declining to speak in public on the subject. But I see no reason whatever for keeping away from faculty meetings, or even for any interruption of social life. We ought all of us to be broad-minded enough to realize that the war will provoke differences of opinion backed by strong feelings; and all ought to be generous enough not to permit those differences to engender bitterness among colleagues, or to imperil friendship.

But within weeks of this gesture Harvard was rocked by scandal over the threat by Major Clarence Wiener of London, a quondam Harvard undergraduate in the class of 1900, to "cancel" a testamentary bequest of ten million dollars to Harvard unless "I receive a written assurance from the faculty that the German doctor [Münsterberg] has been removed from your list of professors." Wiener's original letter of threat was sent to the Dean of Harvard College and several newspapers. Later he told Lowell that he chose to make his letter public in order to alert Americans to the menace of Münsterberg.[15]

Rumors reached both Lowell and Münsterberg that Wiener was "not quite sane," had "purchased a captaincy in England," was immoral and, most significantly, did not have ten million dollars. In any event, Lowell made no response to Wiener. While some of his colleagues appeared to treat the whole affair as a joke, Münsterberg for his part took it gravely. On October 13 he rose in a faculty meeting to announce that he was prepared to resign in order to secure the much needed funds for the university. He had "hardly any doubt that the Corporation will not force me out," and a "clean conscience . . . that I have never violated the spirit of American neutrality." But he attached a condition to his resignation:

I feel that the sacrifice of my position would be vain and absurd, if from the other side nothing but major Wiener's present vague offer were in question. He will give ten million dollars after his death; but Mr. Wiener is a young married man and may still change his mind and his last will often after the war. Moreover, he may lose or even waste his capital during his lifetime. His disreputable career in Harvard in Dunster Hall and his record of scandals afterward do not suggest confidence in this direction. If Mr. Wiener is really anxious that I withdraw immediately, he also ought to give at least half of the money he offers at once. I understand that he is now amply able to do so.

After Münsterberg's speech to the faculty, Lowell curtly proceeded "without comment . . . to the next order of business." A shorter version of the speech was sent the same day to the President and Fellows of Harvard, and this time drew a sharp rebuke from Lowell: "Your letter was presented to the Corporation this morning, and at their suggestion I now return it to you, feeling sure that hereafter you will regret having written anything which could be supposed to show a lack of respect for the University."[16]

Münsterberg, of course, had good reason to believe that Wiener was *not* "amply able" to produce half of his bequest at once. A *New York Times* editorial on October 16 perceptively observed that he had cut "the ground out from all other protests" against his activities and effectively headed off other gathering pressures for his removal from Harvard. Lowell, on the other hand, was convinced that Münsterberg had tried to maneuver the administration into making him a martyr to the cause of pro-Germanism. He was also quite aware that Wiener was "a weakling and had been sent away from College. His recent letter . . . shows well his type of mind. Obviously what he is after is notoriety, for the offer of a bribe certainly would make it impossible for the University to take steps against Professor Münsterberg, even if it were otherwise inclined to do so."[17]

Thus the Harvard Corporation refused and Münsterberg withdrew his resignation. But unhappily for Harvard, there were sufficiently ambiguous circumstances in the case to leave doubt in some quarters, according to the *New York Times,* as to how Harvard would have reacted under other conditions. Lowell himself was quite clear on the underlying issue of academic freedom, even though he did not choose to spell it out publicly until two years later, after Münsterberg was dead. Nevertheless, he responded privately to frequent complaints about Münsterberg and other German professors at Harvard with a form letter explaining that the University could not take responsibility for the public words or deeds of its faculty members.

But certain influential Harvard alumni did not see the fuller implications of the Wiener affair as Lowell did. Intensely frustrated by its dénouement, William Roscoe Thayer, a member of Harvard's Board of Overseers, railed against the publicity seeking of "the Prussianized renegade Jew" and hoped that "his latest piece of effrontery may recoil on him in a way he does not expect." *Nation* editor Oswald Garrison Villard wrote to Thayer that he, too, was "hopeful that Cambridge can be made so hot for him that he will be compelled to retire." Thayer promised darkly that although Münsterberg had "cunningly increased his hold on his chair here" for the time being, it might be possible after the war to "see whether there are not some valid reasons—valid legally, I mean—for getting rid of him."[18]

Neither Eliot nor Lowell joined in "the demand for Münsterberg's scalp" which was, at Harvard, "the first issue raised by the war." But Münsterberg met suspicion, hostility, and abuse from almost everyone in the community, except for a small handful of pro-German faculty colleagues—Hans C. G. van Jagemann, John A. Walz, and Kuno Francke—and a few close friends. "Even the pigeons that the Professor's daughter customarily fed in the professorial backyard became, in the imagination of Cambridge neighbors, carrier pigeons taking messages to spies!"[19]

As early as March 1901 Münsterberg was the object of charges that he operated as a German secret agent in America. Emil Witte, the main author of these accusations, was a press attaché in the German embassy in Washington during the Spanish-American war. Fired from his job by Ambassador Holleben, he believed himself unjustly persecuted, and threatened German officials with exposure of their "secret" activities at the time of Prince Henry's visit in 1902. He claimed that Münsterberg was the head of a secret bureau that directed the German press in America and frequently supplied material for the use of embassy officials. This charge was picked up by the English *Fortnightly Review* and the *Boston Herald* in February 1915. According to them, Münsterberg received $5000 a year for secret service rendered to the German government. Münsterberg flatly denied the charge and stated, "I have never in my life received a single cent from the German government." A letter in the *Herald* claimed that he participated in "mass meetings in which they instruct Americans as to their duty as neutrals." He never supported mass meetings, he replied, never signed "any public political utterance, nor have I spoken a single word in such political meetings, nor have I participated in any political action. Yesterday I wrote the 154th declination to make a speech on the war." Nevertheless his critics persisted in the belief that he was deeply involved in "very shocking" activities for the German cause.[20]

These and other suspicions took a deeper hold in the summer of 1915 when Frederick William Wile, a journalist with whom Münsterberg had tangled during his Berlin year, published a sensational exposé, *The German-American Plot*. Purporting to reveal "The Campaign to Capture the Sympathy and Support of the United States," Wile dubbed Münsterberg the "Professor of Kultur" and cited his cultivation of a variety of influential Americans as evidence that he was a German agent. According to Wile, Münsterberg performed undercover work, serving as the chief propaganda adviser to German government agents based in New York. He was held to be a prime mover in the launching of *The Fatherland* and the equally pro-German *Vital Issues*. Wile claimed that Münsterberg intimidated anti-German news editors and boasted of his "confidential relations with American politicians."[21]

Although the case against Münsterberg was substantially exaggerated, he was not innocent of the general charge of collaboration. In the fall of 1914 he began to take a private hand in the formation of pro-German propaganda activity. This secret enterprise was undertaken neither for personal gain nor at the instruction of the German government, but in the belief that any publicly organized propaganda work in support of the German cause would become a target of hostile criticism.

Sometime after the war broke out, German embassy officials in New York together with interested German-American leaders and sympathizers began to meet at the Manhattan Hotel on Forty-second Street. Münsterberg attended the first gathering of this "propaganda cabinet." Although he was not an official member, preferring "to play a lone hand in purely intellectual circles," he came often enough to be known by the hotel doorman as "Professor." The cabinet itself was run by Bernhard Dernburg, a banker and German government official, and Heinrich Albert, a German lawyer. Within it were two sets of propagandists: "a more aggressive group" consisting of Viereck, Frederick Schrader, and Alfred Rau; and a group "defensive [in] character" under the initial leadership of M. B. von Claussen, former publicity agent for the Hamburg-Amerika Line. Rau acted as treasurer of the first group, which received funds from private benefactors and the German government. Münsterberg aided them by raising money from wealthy German-Americans. In a letter to prospective donors stressing the need to counteract unfair treatment of Germany's cause, he wrote:

the time seems to have come in which a reorganization of the whole political situation from the inside is possible. We can push the levers which reverse the country's attitude. But . . . this needs two things, secrecy and money. The secrecy prevents me from giving the names of those who will directly spend the money collected. It is really in the interest of the cause that such names shall not be mentioned and that confidence in the honesty of those who collect the fund be requested.[22]

To keep the matter private, only a small number of potential benefactors were approached. A total of $50,000 was set as the goal. Although he encountered some resistance from German-Americans who believed that the American press was increasingly balanced, Münsterberg succeeded in his money-raising effort. Rau warmly commended him for his "splendid work" as he forwarded checks from late September through November 1914. According to Rau, these funds covered part of the publication and distribution of free pamphlets to newspapers, magazines, and government officials.[23]

Münsterberg's contact with German agents in New York was not limited to fund raising and the planning of pro-German propaganda. In December 1914 he wrote to Theodore Roosevelt describing a meeting at the Plaza Hotel

where Dernburg, Albert, Viereck and I had with us fifteen Germans engaged in writing for German newspapers. We were to talk over in a private room the ways in which the American attitude could be presented to the German public without waking too much hostility in Germany, as we were fully aware that ample quotations from the American press would stir up much anti-Americanism. We had arranged the dinner to pour oil on the waves.

Münsterberg had long considered himself a friendly adviser to the German government on American affairs. The war situation now sharpened his sense of duty to Germany and made more urgent his concern for enhancing the American image there. In January 1915 he sent a wireless message to a German newspaper reporting a visit to his home in Cambridge by Theodore Roosevelt: "Expresident Roosevelt guest political dinner in Professor Münsterberg's house. Leading Harvard Professors present. Significant for increasing friendliness."[24]

Partly to promote the German cause and partly to protect his own interests at Harvard, Münsterberg undertook an independent fund-raising effort in December 1914 to pay the way of a Belgian professor invited to lecture at Harvard. He feared that the émigré from Louvain would be nothing "but a source of mischief . . . [stirring] up public opinion concerning German vandalism . . . [unless] he comes paid by German money."[25]

In addition to his private support of propaganda work, Mün-sterberg played a role in the attempts to revitalize the National German-American Alliance as an instrument for coordinating and expressing German-American sentiment. The idea of refurbishing the Alliance by attracting the wealthy, educated class of German-Americans apparently came from Harry Rubens, "the leader of the Germans in Chicago." Prodded by Rubens, Münsterberg wrote to Alliance president C. J. Hexamer arguing that the present organization of Alliance "membership by clubs and societies gives to the individual very little consciousness of his duties as a member. Moreover, this very system . . . has kept hundreds of thousands away from active participation . . . bankers and captains of industry, engineers and doctors, teachers and lawyers and what not who simply have never been drawn into any public activity for German-American interests." He proposed to Hexamer that about a hundred of the leading German-American political, financial, and intellectual figures join together in soliciting new members among their own class. This effort would be supplemented by an advertising campaign seeking "several thousand life memberships at $50 and many smaller direct contributions." His hope was that the new money and influence would enable the Alliance to be a force "in Washington politics in the interest of a really neutral policy." The plan never materialized on the grand scale that Münsterberg envisioned, for many nationally prominent German-Americans resisted public association with the Alliance.[26]

In addition to advising German and German-American leaders, Münsterberg continued to play a familiar role as a self-appointed liaison between the German-American community and the national government. On August 5, 1914, he wrote to Wilson describing the "rapidly growing indignation of the German-Americans over the anti-German partiality in the whole country" and warning him "not to underestimate the strength of [the] pro-German feeling." Yet he offered his assurance to Wilson "that I use my little influence to the utmost not only to stop absurdities but to relieve the tension." Three months later he advised Wilson that "thousands" of German sympathizers "have turned to me . . . to organize . . . widespread dissatisfaction" with the administration's lack of neutrality.[27]

Wilson replied that he was doing his utmost to keep the country neutral and "I would consider it a favor if you would point out to me what are considered the unneutral acts of which this Administration is thought to have been guilty." Münsterberg fired off a telegram to Viereck in New York: "Friend has asked me confidentially to write to him in respect the Germans feel that Administration is not really neutral in its decisions and attitude. Will you kindly help me by letter furnishing details on this point and anything else which I might include in my letter to my friend." Replying to Wilson a few days later, Münsterberg professed to give a résumé of the views of American citizens. His letter recited a litany of familiar complaints, the substance of which was that the American government repeatedly knuckled under to British bullying.[28]

Whatever Wilson's motive in making the initial inquiry, Münsterberg failed to win the President's confidence. Within a week the *Boston Herald* and *Transcript* printed a rumor—of which Münsterberg is the likeliest source—that Wilson had asked for Münsterberg's advice on how to retain the support of German-Americans. The rumor was damaging both to the administration and to Münsterberg's hope of acting as a government consultant. Nevertheless he continued to give unsolicited advice to Wilson on subjects including German-American opinion, English intrigue in the United States, and the innocent intentions of the German government. On the latter point he assured the President:

If there is anyone living in the United States who knows the German political activities behind the scenes, it is I. I have been on intimate terms with the German government through all the changing generations in the Foreign Office . . . [and] with the different Ambassadors and their staffs. I have planned their campaigns to win the friendship of America for Germany, just as I have helped men like David J. Hill in Berlin to win the Germans for America. I also did much secret work for Germany in the sense that I wrote the speeches which Holleben or Sternburg made . . . it would be entirely improbable . . . that secret plans of spylike character should have been carried out in America without my being involved or at least hearing about it.

But Münsterberg was not, in fact, privy to the "secret plans of spylike character" carried out by German agents in the United States. The effort to convince Wilson of his influence was betrayed, at the very least, by this naïve assertion.[29]

In the early months of the war Münsterberg got on far better with Theodore Roosevelt, who was inclined to think it "possible" that both sides were morally right in their war positions. Roosevelt's chief interest was not in assigning guilt to one or another of the combatants but in discrediting "the present Administration and its pacifist supporters." Even after he perceived German guilt in the invasion of Belgium, Roosevelt willingly conceded that ninety percent of the German people "acted primarily from an honorable fear . . . that German civilization would be wiped out if they did not strike their foes." Although disagreements over Belgium and the character of German leaders stood between them, Roosevelt and Münsterberg shared the belief "that the smashing of Germany would be a great calamity, and would result in the entire western world being speedily forced into a contest against Russia."

What appealed to Münsterberg (and to other German sympathizers) about Roosevelt was that he seemed not to favor one side over the other and that he was willing to listen to pro-German arguments. On November 11, he invited Münsterberg to visit him at Oyster Bay and to bring Edmund von Mach, "who has also written a first-class book [*What Germany Wants*] on behalf of Germany." Roosevelt's nationalism was as passionate as Münsterberg's. He never concealed his disgust for "hyphenated" Americans. But when Münsterberg wrote of his deteriorating personal relations in Cambridge, Roosevelt expressed a genuine solicitude: "I am really distressed at what you tell me . . . I am absolutely at a loss to understand any American feeling hostile to a German."[30]

Münsterberg's second war book, *The Peace and America*, appeared in April 1915. His earlier work had dealt primarily with the underlying causes of the war; the new volume concerned itself with the question of how the war might end. Once again Münsterberg uses the personal essay form and claims to record issues and events objectively as a man skilled in detecting the unintentional distortions of others. Only "calm judgment and sober will" can show the way to peace, he warns his readers.[31]

The themes of his earlier book are reiterated and developed in greater detail. In a conflict of national ideals, no partisan can be morally faulted—except that German ideals are more noble than others, and England does not know where her true interests lie. On the critical issue of the invasion of Belgium, Münsterberg examines "all the technical arguments." No "binding" treaty between Germany and Belgium existed, and even if it did Belgium herself abrogated it when she "swallowed the gigantic Congo State and was thus transformed [from a small state with meager resources] into a rich world power." Besides, the Belgian government schemed with England and France "for the coming of the European war . . . I have tried my life long to remain intellectually honest, even where my sympathies interfered," he assures his readers. "I should not hesitate to confess it, if I thought that Germany was in the wrong."[32]

All of the rhetorical devices at Münsterberg's command were brought to bear in his presentation of the English "case": the patronizing "understanding" of "mixed motives" on the part of Allied leaders; the disingenuous confession of an "instinctive admiration" for English willfulness and sympathy for those clear-headed Englishmen who recognize the truth about their venal government. Proof of the superiority of Germany's ideals lies in the fact that her enemies were led into war by ruling cliques. Germany, in contrast, achieved a "new rededication" in the war, a "oneness of mind" that is symbolized in the extraordinary person of the Kaiser. For Münsterberg the Kaiser is a paragon, a man of cultivation and simplicity endowed with humor, charm, "real insight," and "true scholarly knowledge." Possessing an ideal family life, this "genial human being" stands as a "sacred symbol" of German moral dedication; he is a "mighty soul" who is forced to speak through battles although his true end is peace. Insofar as militarism and German Kultur aim to develop the "national soul," they stand opposed to the acquisition of non-German subjects or territory.[33]

The Allied powers hold a monopoly on malevolent aggression; Germany is the exclusive repository of idealism and nobility. But in fact America is the main subject of the book.

Münsterberg's impatience had grown along with his belief that all hope of peace rested with America. True, he accuses Americans of hypocrisy, prejudice, "arbitrary egotism," rushing "into the wildest accusation[s] of . . . turpitude," betraying their moral mission, and playing the judge. But it is "the historic duty" of America "to become the only truly neutral arbiter and helper" in the current world crisis, to harmonize the national ideals of the belligerents. Eschewing the idea of a supranational league, Münsterberg sees the best prospect for Europe in the free cooperation of sovereign nations—a family of vigorous siblings free of the constraining influence of paternal authority. Germany, of course, will lead the way by focusing her energies on her "inner development." Throughout the book, he holds up his own role as a nonpartisan "witness for the truth" as the only proper one for the American government and its people. He hopes that Americans will change their erroneous views, and he claims to detect signs that although "the so-called society layer of the nation will be the last which will give attention to impartial evidence, the great thinking middle-class" will not be fooled for long.[34]

This shift of admiration from the Anglo-American elite to the "thinking middle-class" prepares the way for Münsterberg's eulogy of German-Americans. Deploring the "unspeakable moral misery of the twenty million [sic] German-Americans," he identifies himself with their trial: "to fight with words and to stand courageously for one's conviction when it means to be despised by one's fellow-workers and to be intrigued against and to lose the social position for wife and children which has been slowly gained through a lifework and to be deprived of all the little success which has been won in faithful service—that demands more courage than the battle-line." In the past, he claims, German-Americans were exemplars of the American ideal of cultural pluralism. Through them German culture "has given many of the best impulses to American life through half a century." Germany itself has "ceaselessly aimed toward cordial friendship with America"; yet "we who have devoted every heartbeat of our energy to this friendship from land to land" are rewarded with ingratitude. Despite his evident bitterness, it is not Münsterberg's style to dwell on rejection and defeat. He advises German-Americans "to advance their cultural mission" by a new political unity based not on a policy of counter-accusation and revenge but on the determination to understand and forgive the "pitifully perverted" course of American opinion.[35]

Anti-German critics rushed into print to attack the book as "misinformed," "prejudiced," and "against America's best interests," although some of his sharpest detractors charitably allowed Münsterberg his "sincerity." Without doubt, Münsterberg hoped to reconcile partisan positions. But his own aggressive defensiveness, and his need to exalt his German attachments (the book was dedicated "to my brothers"), worked against his goals. One reviewer noted that it was a "curious" thing to behold a professional psychologist employing arguments fated to affect the reader in a way opposite to his intentions.[36]

During the first winter of the war it seemed possible that pro-Allied and pro-German "neutralists" might be brought together to formulate useful peace proposals. A Chicago lawyer, Salmon O. Levinson, wrote to Charles W. Eliot suggesting the formation of a Committee of Ten. At first Eliot was cool to the idea, believing that no headway could be made until there was a "restoration to reason and sanity of the German leading class." He required "evidence of a change of heart in respect to their national ambitions, the sanctity of contracts, and the wrongfulness of making war except by public forces." But Levinson persisted, arguing that a recent interview with Dernburg in New York indicated that the Germans were indeed prepared to shift their position. A committee was set up to include Eliot, Andrew D. White, Cardinal Gibbons, Charlemagne Tower, David J. Hill, James J. Hill, Justice Edward D. White, and others. Eliot sent a letter to the *New York Times* laying down essential areas of agreement for peace negotiations. He advised Levinson against consulting Münsterberg or Dernburg, "for no confidence is to be placed in either of them."[37]

But Levinson had already asked Münsterberg to formulate

what he took to be the German position on specific issues. Münsterberg was unable to secure a place on the committee for any "German sympathizers like . . . [Charles] Nagel or [John W.] Burgess"; Eliot had even vetoed David Starr Jordan because of his "extreme pacifist opinions" and was certainly not prepared to work with German sympathizers. In a letter to Woodrow Wilson, Münsterberg described his effort to reduce Eliot's "preposterous" beginnings to a "reasonable" program that represented a "minimum which might be gained for all nations." This included (1) no territorial changes in Europe; (2) indemnity to Belgium from all three belligerents; and (3) neutralization of the open seas—without opening the Dardanelles or the Kiel canal. Sensing how far this was from Eliot's formulation—which, for one thing, demanded reparations for Belgium from Germany alone—Münsterberg scorned the Committee of Ten as a group of "self-appointed dilettantes" and, playing to Wilson's vanity, denigrated their efforts as "private men . . . [to] reach for a goal which would appear to the world as naturally yours."[38]

Nevertheless Levinson hoped that the German government would receive Eliot's proposals generously, for Dernburg apparently promised to prepare the way. But all parties suspended their efforts when in May 1915 a German submarine sank the British steamer *Lusitania* causing a loss of 1,198 lives, including 124 Americans. Eliot reaffirmed his belief that a military victory of the Allies must precede peace negotiations. Much chastened by the whole experience, Münsterberg refused to attend a planning session in June 1915 of the group that was to become the hard-nosed League to Enforce Peace, even though he was urged to do so by the Executive Secretary of the German University League in order to keep it from falling into the hands of anti-German "jingoes." By this time he knew that it was precisely his German interests that rendered useless any genuine effort to meet with pro-Allied partisans.[39]

The energy and concern that Münsterberg focused on the war put him under considerable strain. He jumped into the propaganda battle on behalf of the German cause, only to find himself rejected and abused in a number of roles central to his prewar life. In the early months of 1915 it came as a particularly stinging blow when the efforts of leading German-Americans to take a united stand on an important political issue were "sabotaged" by his close friend and Harvard colleague Kuno Francke.

Francke, Professor of Germanic Languages and a distinguished historian, had come to Harvard several years before Münsterberg. Despite minor professional disagreements through the years (over such matters as the introduction of the *Privatdocent* system at Harvard and the Exchange Professorships), and a certain amount of jealousy on Münsterberg's part, the two men had much in common and were together the leading representatives of German culture in the United States. There were differences of style and temperament between them—differences that Münsterberg's daughter alluded to in a perhaps wistful reference to the Franckes as a "very *American* family."[40]

But when the war broke out in Europe, they shared in a difficult situation that seemed, said Münsterberg, to bring them "truly close" together. Responding to that situation, Münsterberg gave high priority to activities aimed at restraining American involvement. Francke, on the other hand, though he did his part in publicly defending Germany, was torn by doubts about the compatibility of political activism and "my duties as an American citizen and as a Harvard teacher." In a letter to the *New York Times* in February 1915, he publicly repudiated a conference of German-American leaders who were meeting in Washington, D.C., to develop a political program featuring support for an arms embargo. In making his point that German-Americans ought not to form a political bloc, Francke also denied that there was any widespread discrimination against German-American citizens.[41]

Münsterberg vigorously disagreed on both points. He knew, for example, that while Harvard was "officially neutral" it was certainly "as a social organization . . . anti-German," and often crudely so. On the larger issue of German-American separatism, Münsterberg reminded his friend that for twenty years he had opposed any "political split of the Deutschtum in this country . . . [or any] union with the Irish." He had always argued "that the Germans should merge politically with the Anglo-Saxon majority." But now he believed that

our formula has been tried long enough and has proven itself ineffective for the situation of the whole country. As much as I regret it, I must admit that those people have a sound basis, who now wish to try the opposite formula for once and make the Deutschtum as such, by means of a political alliance with the Irish and the Swedes and the not at all weak anti-English element of other origin, into a fighting power in the country.[42]

What angered Münsterberg most was that Francke had published his dissent "in the most vulgar anti-German yellow-press paper in order to be the first to denounce the union of leading German allies as a crime against the Amerikanertum. The glee which your letter excited among the worst enemies of Germany can teach you best what monstrous harm you have done." The effect of Francke's statement was to stir animosity among Germans toward the "Boston clique," to encourage them to draw even further apart from other Americans, and to gratify their enemies. Since it was he who had suggested that Francke be included among the conferees in the first place, Münsterberg charged Francke with a betrayal of personal confidence.[43]

For his part, Francke held to his conviction that a political organization of German-Americans not only would be "harmful and unnecessary from an American point of view but make trouble for Germany herself." He believed himself to be "a good German" and one deeply concerned about Germany's well-being. For this reason alone he ventured to express his disagreement with German-American leaders: "My only comfort is that it is me who suffers, not the German cause."[44]

Francke's dissent, couched in pragmatic and moral terms, called many of Münsterberg's efforts into question. Münsterberg had believed that they shared in a spiritual dual citizenship. He refused to ally himself wholeheartedly with the German agents in New York—he advised and assisted them but would not participate fully in their inner councils. Yet unlike Francke he remained a Germain citizen and was not willing to admit a conflict or make a choice between his American and his German obligations. Instead he clung to his belief in a dual allegiance, and condemned Francke for seeking "the applause of the anti-German papers and to swim in the social stream." Francke's position offered a rallying ground for disparate German-American elements, one that eschewed the activism of the Alliance (and other pressure groups) and yet supported the German cause. But Münsterberg claimed that Francke had ruined himself among the Germans. In fact, the quarrel considerably shook Münsterberg's own self-confidence.[45]

The sinking of the *Lusitania* in May 1915 dramatically brought to a close the initial period of Münsterberg's political activity. At this point his loss of confidence, resulting from the ambiguity of his position and his sensitivity to the hostile climate around him, led to a temporary withdrawal into silence. But silence could not ensure a safe retreat. Three days after the *Lusitania* catastrophe Professor Josiah Royce, a longtime friend and colleague, packed up and returned a few books which Münsterberg had lent him during a period of illness. With them went a covering letter which remarked that "at a time like the present, it would be deeply unworthy of my debt of gratitude to the kindness you showed me in my time of illness . . . if I kept longer these documents of your friendship." In closing, he offered the stingingly sarcastic "hope for the health of your family, for your prosperity, and for that of all who are dear to you who travel by land or by sea."[46]

Münsterberg was deeply hurt by Royce's words: "I think nothing in recent months has reminded me of [the] deep change in the world more than your kind letter of yesterday in which you began with an address [My dear Professor Münsterberg] which I had not heard from you through two decades of friendship and in which you close with a reminder of the danger of travel by sea." Royce defended his actions on the ground that he could no longer respect his correspondent's defense of a country capable of such "a wanton and willful assault upon all that humanity rightly holds dearest." Münsterberg had not said a word in public about the tragedy, and was indignant that Royce should assume he would defend such an act. "I have never done anything but work for fair play. I have never abused or vilified the opponents of Germany," he wrote. His public position on the war had been to explicate German intentions, not to defend them or to place blame elsewhere. Now, suddenly, Royce was behaving "as if your home would be desecrated if you were to keep the books of one who sympathizes with murderers." He tried to convince Royce that "exactly those feelings against wanton violation of the laws of humanity which today fill every American's thought of Germany have since about Christmastime filled every German's thought of America" because of America's munitions shipments to the Allies.[47]

Münsterberg concluded that the most significant difference between Royce and himself was neither ideological nor moral, but the fact that he was a "foreigner." In America "the sympathy with the foreigner is so superficial that not only grave tension like the present but even the slightest tension is sufficient to make everything forgotten which the foreigner may have done for the country in which he lives." The charge was unfair to Royce, who had long been a devoted and admiring student of German literature and philosophy and a sympathetic friend to Münsterberg. Both men were capable of passionate outbursts and both were deeply depressed by the *Lusitania* incident. Royce had been working for five years on his theory of world community. If the *Lusitania* incident appeared to him as a crime against mankind, so Münsterberg's defense of war as an instrument of national expression must have seemed to support it.[48]

He had deliberately chosen a course of silence, Münsterberg told Royce, because

it would [not] have been tasteful or tactful if I had rushed into print with interviews about the sad occurrence. Everyone would have indignantly said this is not the time in which the Germans ought to talk much. Moreover, it is clear that I could not have spoken about my deep regret for the German action without coupling with it references to that indignation of the Germans with the American violation of humanity in the past months. And if I had done so the readers would have given more attention to my criticisms of American action than to my accusation of German deeds. In short, even with the best intention my words would have brought more irritation than healing influence. I considered

it carefully and became fully convinced that the only tactful and digni-
fied way for me . . . was to keep silent . . . trusting that my friends
. . . would understand my silence.

In the end, Royce came to regret the "misunderstanding" between them and the flow of tragic events which clouded the
friendship of so many years standing: "you are not *merely* 'a
lonely man in a hostile land' so long as you need or desire any
friendly service which I can do for you," he assured Münsterberg. His correspondent, however, was less forgiving:

in these last few days ever so many members of the community have felt
. . . that my life here has really turned into a tragedy, and I was deeply
touched by many proofs of sympathy. There have never been such beautiful flowers sent to our house as in this last week from Anglo-Americans,
and some of the finest women came to my wife and everyone tried to
show that there is a point where politics ends and human understanding
begins. Most others, of course, kept silent. You were the only one who
went out of his way to use this particular moment for a most surprising
act of unfriendliness.[49]

During the summer of 1915 Münsterberg went into relative
seclusion at his summer home in Clifton, Massachusetts, seeking a needed rest from "the great arguing, fighting, maligning
world." Since the beginning of the war he had written only
two short nonpolitical essays; his last professional publication
had appeared in August 1914. In the course of this summer he
revived his interest in popular psychology again, writing four
articles and laying the groundwork for an ingenious study of
the psychological aspects of motion pictures (which appeared
in April 1916 as *The Photoplay*). He spent much of his time in
the welcome anonymity of local movie theaters and indulging
his amateur interest in photography. Later he told Lowell that
one of the motives behind his film studies was that "my name
was so much connected with the war noise . . . I wanted to
break that association by a new connection with a popular interest. It seemed to me that this was desirable from the Harvard standpoint."[50]

But the book served deeper and more private purposes as
well. Münsterberg defined art as the showing of things and
events in perfect isolation, "freed from all connections which
lead beyond their own limits." In contrast to the scientist and

scholar, who pursue the connections and relations of given facts, the artist creates objects that are "delivered from these ties." Harmony, unity, satisfaction: these are the values that distinguish the aesthetic realm from the experience of worldly life. Münsterberg's technical analysis of the photoplay emphasizes the creative power of the self or mind. The salient mechanisms of this new art form, he argues, are akin to "the forms of the inner world, namely, attention, memory, imagination, and emotion": "The massive outer world has lost its weight, it has been freed from space, time, and causality, and it has been clothed in the forms of our own consciousness. The mind has triumphed over matter and the pictures roll on with the ease of musical tones. It is a superb enjoyment which no other art can furnish us." From the contemplation of motion pictures he draws a heightened "feeling of vitality" and emotional restoration. The great maligning world is not so much abandoned as "overcome" by a sense of self-sufficiency.[51]

By the end of the summer of 1915 Münsterberg had become a contributing editor to *Paramount Pictograph* magazine, edited the fourth volume of research reports from the Harvard Psychological Laboratory, and written a high school text on business psychology. In the ensuing year, he began to give popular nonpolitical lectures once again. But the public debate over the war continued, and he was far too emotionally involved to stay out of it. He published three articles that placed him at the very center of controversy.

The first of these, "The Impeachment of the German-Americans," appeared on the front page of the *New York Times* magazine section on September 19, 1915. It begins with the assertion, "This is not written in my own defense." To support his claim, Münsterberg recounts the personal sacrifices he made to live in America as a cultural ambassador. He "never . . . participated in a political action of the German-Americans." It is precisely "because I stand entirely outside of German-American politics" that he now feels able to "testify on the witness stand in the solemn trial which the whole nation has opened . . . against those millions of American citizens who emphasize their German descent."

The first charge against them—that they too zealously protest against anti-German agitation—he dismisses as hardly serious. The second charge—that they seek to influence American politics by forming an alien party—he sidesteps with the observation that "men who were born on German soil" are themselves alarmed and reject the idea as a "crime against the spirit of true Americanism." Then, after denouncing the distortions of German culture by such men as Oswald Garrison Villard, Münsterberg develops his central theme. Far from wishing to inject "German principles of arbitrary government" into American life, German-Americans labor under a moral obligation to introduce their special virtues of self-discipline and thoroughness. For the real enemy of America is her "spirit of carelessness and recklessness." Neither personal profit nor foreign allegiance lies behind the mission of German-Americans. They are "thoroughly American" in wanting to "contribute . . . [their] racial ideals to the inner life of the American nation." Münsterberg advocated an ethnic pluralism that would conserve those "singularly German" virtues which he believed were his own.[52]

The article raised a storm of controversy. New York *Staatszeitung* editor Bernard Ridder called it "superb," and the editors of the *Literary Digest* printed a supportive interpretation of Münsterberg's main point. The *New York Times* also agreed with the thesis, but argued that not all German-Americans were concerned with rendering a cultural service to America. On the contrary, many were involved in destructive and divisive activities, and resentment against *these* "hyphens" was amply justified. A week after the article appeared, Professor Albert Bushnell Hart of Harvard published a blistering rebuttal. He charged Münsterberg with expounding a racial theory capable of "immense harm" and accused him of saying that German-Americans had come to America for the purpose of "raising" it ("for the sake of spreading Germanism . . . [rather than] to become American citizens"). He thought that Münsterberg's repeated interference in American public affairs was reprehensible and untoward.[53]

The article represented a significant shift in emphasis for its author. It defended Germany, but it glossed over the international crisis and, despite disclaimers, revealed a close identification with the plight of German-Americans. Before the war Münsterberg had scarcely ever found cause to extol their virtues; on the contrary, he had criticized them as inferior representatives of German culture. In July 1916 the young minister Reinhold Niebuhr published an indictment of German-Americans (written before the war) for their failure to live up either to the virtues of their race or to American ideals—an indictment Münsterberg privately supported. In contrast to the Germans in Germany, Niebuhr wrote, the German immigrants to America were largely ignorant peasants who perpetuated customs and attitudes long since discarded in Germany. They were stolid, self-seeking, conservative, and unenlightened, without a trace of progressive concern for the social, political, and religious issues of American life. Their indifference to all but economic well-being contrasted sharply with Germany's leadership in the development of liberal Christianity and social reform. The significant "failure" of German-Americans was that they "had given the American people an inadequate interpretation of the genius and the character of the German people," and thus contributed to the negative American attitude toward Germany.

When Niebuhr asked Münsterberg's opinion of the article he questioned only the timeliness of the indictment. But Niebuhr believed that it was worth the risk of stirring up anti-Germanism to force certain harsh truths upon those German-Americans who sinned even as they were sinned against. He was particularly irritated by their tendency to belittle "every American virtue and magnify every American evil." Though their sympathy for Germany was natural, they allowed themselves to fall into the hands of professional propagandists who abused the American government in the name of the average German-American and thus crystallized a social and political group "both in its own eyes and in the eyes of the nation." Niebuhr apparently was not aware that Münsterberg's own efforts tended that same way.[54]

Münsterberg's second controversial article appeared in *The Fatherland* late in December 1915. In it he addressed himself to the political choices facing German-Americans in the coming election year. While it does not disparage Wilson, the article is close to a brief for Theodore Roosevelt, suggesting that German-Americans forget his anti-German lapses and realize that his personality "makes him a pro-German in all that is best in him, and only his temper and his perpetual desire to be with the masses made him a pro-Ally."

Münsterberg's idea that German-Americans might put Roosevelt back in the White House was treated as a joke by several American news editors. But German-American leaders were not amused. Resentful of their complaints, Münsterberg indignantly asked one critic if it was "really wise for those few Germans whose utterances are noticed throughout the land to criticize one another in insulting language?" He explained that his article was written to show Wilson that it was not impossible for German-Americans to rally behind Roosevelt. As a direct consequence, "a great speech which the President had planned and which was to be still sharper against the German-Americans than any of his preceding attacks was simply thrown in the wastebasket." His correspondent stubbornly maintained that Münsterberg had damaged the pro-German cause: "We have suffered tremendously in this country because we have given ground by our poor tactics for a large portion of the American people to believe that we were far more concerned with Germany's interests than our own."

Ambassador Johann von Bernstorff, whose concern for Germany's interest was primary and who always treated Münsterberg with wary respect, took an unusually critical line with him now. The last thing the German cause needed, he wrote, was a display of political activism among German-Americans. It merely aroused hostility and might even weaken Wilson's hand with Congress. Besides, he added with barely restrained anger, "whoever, like myself, will bear the huge responsibility before history should the United States enter the war against us, has an unconditional right to control all the levers [of political action]."[55]

Theodore Roosevelt was "dumbfounded" by the article in *The Fatherland*. He frankly advised Münsterberg that their views were "as far apart as the poles." He would continue to "set my face like flint against all hyphenated Americanism," and was pointedly critical of German-American opposition to preparedness. But he also boasted that "I have preached to my people the adoption of German methods and ideals to a far greater extent than I have preached to them the adoption of English methods and ideals." Münsterberg reiterated his support, but told Roosevelt that he "must carefully avoid any appearance of mixing into active politics. I have to keep the confidence of those who are lined up against you."[56]

By the time Münsterberg's third political article appeared in July 1916, his position among pro-German partisans was ambiguous. From the fall of 1915 a certain formality and stiffness characterized his relations with German officials in New York. In October 1915 he was approached by Karl Fuehr to oversee the translation into English of *Deutschland und der Weltkrieg,* a pro-German tract. Münsterberg estimated the cost of translation at $4000 and planned to farm out the work to others, but suggested to Fuehr that some of the money be raised from German-American sources. He was having trouble securing translators because "at present no one wants to risk being exposed in the newspapers as the recipient of German propaganda funds." Implying criticism of Fuehr and Albert, he suggested that the larger his own hand in the project the likelier its success; in locating a publisher, for example, "the negotiations . . . would probably have gone more smoothly if someone permanently on the ground like myself had undertaken them."

But Münsterberg had little luck raising funds on his own, and Fuehr, finding that he could have the translation done more cheaply elsewhere, reneged on the arrangements. In June 1916 Münsterberg received a more direct rebuke from Fuehr's superior, Heinrich Albert. He had been avoiding Albert for some time and questioned his judgment on specific German-American affairs. After a meeting with Münsterberg, Albert wrote:

I was very happy to have met you once again after a long time. An occasional discussion seems so much the more desirable, as such false conceptions easily gain footing on the side. I have heard subsequently among other things, that you have hesitated to discuss the milk-provision question [a campaign to raise funds for the shipment of milk to German mothers and babies] in my presence. I really should cherish hopes that my absolute objectivity and practicality are beyond doubt, and that there-

fore the pros and cons of every affair can be discussed with me purely
impartially.

Whether from jealousy or prudence, Münsterberg was concerned about the involvement of official German agents in
German-American activities, and the distrust was mutual. Nevertheless, he continued to make monthly trips to New York
through 1916.[57]

When Münsterberg published "The Allies of the Future" in the
summer of 1916, he had come to the end of more than a year
of intermittent public controversy and personal anguish. Hostility toward him, particularly in Cambridge and Boston, had
deepened and spread since the early months of 1915. Late in
December 1915 there was a substantial government crackdown
on German agents. Officials of the Hamburg-Amerika Line were
convicted of using false manifests, the German military and
naval attachés were recalled at the insistence of the U.S. government, and eighty-nine agents were arrested for inciting
strikes. Six weeks later Münsterberg complained, "About one
fourth of my Harvard colleagues no longer bow to me on the
street. About one half bows, but everyone does it with a face
either frozen or filled with disgust distinctly mixed with a fear
that someone might see him in the reprehensible act of recognizing me . . . among my colleagues surely three-fourths do
their best to force me out of the University." Members of the
Harvard Corporation, he claimed, were so convinced of the in-
sincerity of his resignation in the Wiener affair that he dared
not offer to resign again. But there was more than self-pity on
his mind. In April he inquired into State Department plans for
the incarceration of "all Germans living here" in the event of
war: "Are there not certain reasons suggesting that such a
wholesale rule would be inappropriate in my case? I feel that
I have earned the right to consider myself an invited guest in
America . . . [who came for] the upbuilding of scientific psychology . . . [Having sacrificed preference to duty, he was not
in the same category as] all those who came here to seek their
fortunes." He had retained his German citizenship for several

reasons: "my mere desire to help here in a piece of academic work could not be a sufficient reason for a moral man to change his nationality"; "the effect of my American books in Europe would have been greatly diminished if I had simply become an American"; "I could serve the Americans much better if I remained a German citizen. Am I now to be punished for all this by being treated like an intruder from the enemy's camp?" Finally, he offered his word that if he were allowed to remain in his home he would limit his excursions to a "certain radius" and pledge himself not to "communicate with Germany."[58]

Written at the nadir of his despair, this letter marked a turning point for Münsterberg: the assertion of an instinct for survival that would soon lead numbers of German-Americans to repair their bridges to the larger society. His every effort to reformulate a pro-German position acceptable to the American public had created opposition. "The Allies of the Future," an antiwar "meditation" appearing on the front page of the *New York Times* magazine section in July 1916, was a major attempt on his part to convert defeat into victory. Two years of war had left a legacy of unrestrained hatred; mere blunders had been "denounced as moral wrongs . . . every unintentional homicide was branded a murder and every munitions sale was abused as hypocrisy and violation of neutrality." Mistakes were made on all sides, he admits. He praises the compensating virtues of each belligerent. "Those who really know are sure that the strongest mental effect of these two years of war is a new mutual respect of the belligerent nations for one another," a respect that indicates that the present hatred cannot last. "However much the press, the priests, and, alas! the professors have sinned [in whipping up moral indignation] in all three lands," Münsterberg argues, growing mutual respect will provide a basis for peace. Inevitably, the "three Teutonic master nations" (England, Germany, and the United States) will form a new alliance, committing their national powers to its enforcement. Germany, he asserts, is ready to "initiate the coming age" by sacrificing some of her military gains in the war. She has achieved her purpose in breaking the "encircling ring of jealousy" and is prepared to negotiate a reasonable exchange of colonies. "The Allies of to-day," already restive with one another, must surely see that Germany and not Russia belongs among the "family" of the physically and morally strongest nations. The article concludes with vigorous praise for Wilson, through whom the "aesthetic ideals of harmony, of unity, of beauty, of perfection, have for the first time in history radiated from the White House."[59]

A letter to the *New York Times* lauded Münsterberg's essay as "intelligent," in marked contrast to the shrill and futile propaganda of the New York German group. But the *Times* also quoted an editorial from the London *Chronicle,* which argued that Münsterberg's soft line was merely an attempt to cushion Germany's imminent fall. Bristling at his interpretation, the New York propagandists were furious with Münsterberg. Viereck disingenuously told him that it was a "most remarkable and important document" but that the "German-Americans are not ready for it." Karl Fuehr was more direct: "I can say confidentially and privately that . . . in my circles there was quite divided opinion over it; it is just always feared that statements of that sort should be interpreted as a mark of slackening . . . You will not be surprised when I inform you that I am now occupied with the publication of an English edition of the extremely anti-English book, *Der Vampyr des Festlandes.*" Fuehr, however, was reluctantly willing to condone Münsterberg's performance on the ground that such a conciliatory gesture *might* "find a certain response among the intellectuals." But other German-American leaders, in the midst of mounting an anti-Wilson election campaign, were less generous. A German-language newspaper editor complained bitterly that Münsterberg's earlier backing of Roosevelt and his current support for Wilson allowed "the supposition to form that [the German-American group] . . . is internally split," and thus diminished its political leverage.[60]

Convinced of the wrongheadedness of his critics, Münsterberg replied to one of them:

The German-Americans in general, especially in the east, and the Germans in America at all times have shown an unusual lack of political insight . . . If I were to speak and to write before the public for the purpose of satisfying those cliques of Germans in New York whose views seem to you the fountain of true politics, I should indeed speak and write differently . . . While I have been sharply criticized and wildly hated by those groups, with occasional relapses . . . into cordial friendship, I have [gone] my own way without caring for praise or blame or accusations . . . I write and speak exclusively for the Anglo-American population, and as I am practically the only German who is really heard throughout the country and whose every line is read by the President and the other officials, I must do my duty as I see it even if some of my German friends bitterly disapprove.

He knew better than the militants where the best interests of German-Americans lay, he warned his correspondent. And what he wrote for one group was not for the other to read: "politics is politics."[61]

By this time the large German-American community was riven by factionalism. Münsterberg's alienation from the extreme pro-German wing enabled him to speak to the considerable company of those who—along with Anglo-Americans—supported Wilson's precarious pursuit of American neutrality and world peace. He attempted to ingratiate himself with Wilson by reporting that "however much I have been attacked by the anti-German press, I have been ten times more assailed by the German-Americans on account of my persistent Wilsonism." He advised the President that he had been "assailing the shortsightedness" of German-American opposition to Wilson since the summer of 1915: he had "carefully refrained from saying in public that I consider . . . [their] agitation . . . a suicidal act . . . [but] I have sufficient connections to make my views influential without expressing them publicly."[62]

Ironically, as Münsterberg's relations with the German agents and pro-German stalwarts deteriorated, so did his already painful position in the pro-Allied community of Boston and Cambridge. Early in 1916 he described the rudeness of his colleagues and alluded to their wish "to force me out of the University":

They are backed in [this] . . . by a large majority of the so-called Back Bay people of Boston. The social club which I enjoyed in Boston, the Thursday Evening Club, of which I was a member for fifteen years, has expelled me this winter; leading people who owe everything to me have cut their connections entirely; and the one man [Royce] who almost forced me to stay here . . . [and] promised me his most intimate friendship and assured me of the loyalty of Harvard in every possible life situation, has been first in line to treat me brutally.

At the time, most of these plaints were exaggerated. The Thursday Evening Club dropped him from its active list for lack of attendance; he was not, in fact, expelled from any group or association. As if to cancel one overstatement with another, he added that "only Boston and Cambridge has become hysteric . . . [The rest of the country] treats me just as two years ago." In any event, he drew some comfort from the belief that his persecution was impulsive and unjust, that it rested on his foreignness and his defense of an unpopular cause.[63]

On April 26, 1916, he was "staggered" to be called into Lowell's office for chastisement over his behavior toward the university. The confrontation was precipitated by the action of Edwin B. Holt, a former student and friend, and translator of Münsterberg's *Die Amerikaner*. Holt turned over to Lowell a series of abusive letters that Münsterberg had sent him during the preceding month. In March Herbert Sanborn, a friend of Münsterberg's, had reported that Holt was spreading malicious gossip to the effect that "you were no scientist and that you frequently falsified results in order to make them come out all right." Still fuming over what he took to be a vicious reference to himself as "one of the most unconscionable liars who ever lived" in Holt's recently published book *The Freudian Wish*, Münsterberg demanded an explanation. Holt denied that he had spoken behind Münsterberg's back or intended any reference to him in the book. But his evasive, sardonic letters only fed Münsterberg's wrath. Unable to secure satisfaction directly, Münsterberg shifted to an indirect attack. Expressing sadness over Holt's ingratitude, he offered a mocking "analysis" of the other's behavior. Holt, he argued (in Freudian style), suffered from a "repressed wish for the death of your mother." Unconsciously, he fixed on Münsterberg, "the man to whom you owe your career," as a mother substitute, and thus devised a way to express his hostile wish.[64]

Münsterberg tried to acquit himself of the charge of undignified behavior toward a colleague by advising Lowell that Holt had started the whole affair with "an outrageous attack against me . . . in public print." Furthermore, Holt had been an intimate friend as well as a colleague, and their exchange was meant to be "a man to man affair and not one settled in the president's office." Finally, Münsterberg told Lowell that he had been concerned for some time about Holt's "flickering mind" and that Sanborn's letter "forced me" to "risk open speech with regard to . . . [his mother] complex." His own sincerity in the matter could not be doubted. Münsterberg considered Holt's to be the least of the charges brought against him.

More serious was the allegation that he attempted to use his position at the Psychological Laboratory to "strangle" research projects of which he disapproved. The specific case behind this charge was Münsterberg's bitter opposition to the appointment of Leonard Troland to do psychical research in the laboratory. Lowell had informed him that Troland would be working entirely on his own, in no way under the supervision of the director of the laboratory. The very idea of psychical research was anathema to Münsterberg. Nevertheless, he claimed that he had made only helpful and cooperative suggestions regarding Troland's research design, in order to protect the reputation of the laboratory. "Throughout thirty years," he told Lowell, "I have done my utmost to strengthen the independence of those who worked with me." Münsterberg could not have chosen weaker ground on which to defend his record as research director. From the beginning of his tenure at Harvard he had evidenced the rank consciousness, authoritarianism, and favoritism that marked the worst aspect of personal relations among scholars in the German academic community. And it was known that he had tried—unsuccessfully in the cases of Holt and Robert Yerkes—to hold his younger laboratory associates in place as subordinate research assistants.[65]

According to Münsterberg, the next charge leveled against him was that he neglected laboratory work in order to indulge "in popular writing and speech making for self-advertising," and that his failure to produce disciples was a great disappointment to Harvard. In his defense, he stood first on the record of his five scholarly volumes; then he argued that even his popular books were a "valuable contribution to scholarship." Against his German scholarly inclinations he had yielded to the persuasion of "the leading men at Harvard [James and the geologist Nathaniel S. Shaler] not to closet my science but to make it popular." He had joined and led the new movement in applied psychology out of a sense of duty to the university and to "the country which had invited me." As for his speechmaking (which "was not in the least in my habit or inclination") and his social and political writings, he undertook them all for the benefit of others, with the assurance of President Eliot that they were "an asset for Harvard." Despite the strain of these popular activities, he never stinted the "six or seven hours a day" devoted to his laboratory work. As for the lack of disciples, he informed Lowell that "no effort of mind could overcome the latent opposition which is created by the American conditions." The structure of higher education in America worked against the recruitment of first-rate students for productive scholarship. There was no doubt in Münsterberg's mind that Lowell's charges against him were the direct result of distorted information "received . . . [during the past two years] of anti-German passion."[66]

Finally, Münsterberg claimed to "understand" why Lowell gave credence to the whole set of "fantastic" charges. The situation was "suddenly illuminated" for him during the last moments of their interview when reference was made to the Wiener affair. According to Münsterberg, Lowell harbored resentment over the episode because he mistakenly believed that Münsterberg's resignation had been a grandstand play. Recalling that period as a time of intolerable tension, when "I never left my house without fear of being shot down," Münsterberg argued that he had presented his resignation in public, before the assembled faculty, so that the public would know he was prepared to act in Harvard's interest and it would not look as though he had been dismissed if, in fact, his resignation was accepted. But Lowell imagined that the gesture was a "stab in the back" and

as soon as this idea took hold . . . it was only natural that you fancied that I tried to strangle my younger colleagues, and that I neglected my duties for my popular writings and that my whole university work has been a disappointment. I beg you to give up once and for all this entirely erroneous conception of my action at the beginning of the war, and you will then see that all the other reproaches are also entirely ungrounded.

"I know the limitations of my efforts very well," Münsterberg concluded in his seventeen-page response to Lowell, "but I [also] know that I have always been sincere and that I was guided by the purest motives."[67]

While it is certainly true that Lowell was furious with him for his behavior during the Wiener affair, it is also true that he had repeatedly resisted pressure to fire Münsterberg. The Holt correspondence provided a legitimate reason for chastising Münsterberg; and Lowell was under some compulsion to force him out as research director on the basis of the Troland complaint. But the general substance of the other charges had been floating around in Harvard circles for years. Eliot and Lowell had taken a firm hand with Münsterberg on specific issues in the past, but no one had seriously confronted him with such a full account of misbehavior or such a gross undervaluation of his professional achievements. It was not unreasonable for him to blame the war, and once he found this rationale he forced Lowell into inaction.[68]

Inevitably Harvard's grievances against Münsterberg became further entangled in the issues raised by the war. A *Report of the Committee on Philosophy, Psychology and Social Ethics to the Board of Overseers of Harvard College* on June 21, 1916, stated that the Psychological Laboratory was hampered in publishing its research by lack of funds, and that "the complications arising in current international politics, unfortunately affecting the personnel of the Department of Psychology as at present officered, render any effort to obtain considerable funds for its special requirements at present . . . inadvisable." Writing to the chairman of the committee, Münsterberg denied that his directorship had in any way exacerbated the shortage of funds. The department had been short of money for eight years, and had in fact been intermittently aided by two of his German friends "whose willingness to give to the laboratory 'as at present officered' would certainly not be hindered by the international situation." Münsterberg noted that neither the effective work nor the influence of the laboratory had suffered from the shortage of publication funds.[69]

The committee chairman, Reginald C. Robbins, stood by his

original statement and bluntly informed Münsterberg that there was a widespread feeling among Harvard graduates

that a German, however gifted, who engaged in public utterances or writing which favors Germanic culture in America, would be far more wisely and appropriately placed if educating Germans in Germany than Americans in America . . . No one can regret the apparent loss of your friendship more than I do; no one more regrets what I feel to be the loss of your academic value at Harvard. But the German invasion of Belgium changed a good many things in the world. And the position of Germany and the Germans in the eyes of civilized people is altered irrevocably.[70]

Despite the bitterness of this correspondence, Münsterberg's deepest humiliation was public, not private. On October 10, 1916, a letter from Münsterberg to the German chancellor, Bethmann-Hollweg, which had been written the previous May and intercepted by British agents, was released to the press. It was the kind of advisory letter that Münsterberg often wrote (without solicitation) to both German and American government officials. It was filled with expressions such as "my chief work" and "my main task" that made it sound like "the report of a subordinate to his chief." Münsterberg had written a dozen letters to Wilson in the same vein since the beginning of the war. In his letter to the German chancellor, he observed that

the widespread fear that he [Wilson] would be too pro-British as mediator I consider unfounded . . . Hitherto he has been wholly a party man; but if he once works himself into the idea of being the arbitrator of the world, he will be so intoxicated by the joy of playing a historic part that he will give himself up to it with his whole soul and without rest. He will remain strictly neutral, less out of moral conscientiousness than from an aesthetic pleasure in his unique role.

Münsterberg went on to say that there had been a "slump" in the German cause in recent weeks because of a "wave of patriotism" among German-Americans that swept the "weaker elements along with it." Even German-American leaders had succumbed. He himself was doing everything possible to aid the peace movement, and "all this peace material naturally appears without my name."[71]

The press release created a sensation. At Harvard Professor

William E. Hocking, a friend and former protégé of Münsterberg, demanded an explanation. In a open letter to the *Boston Transcript*, he accused his senior colleague of cynically supposing "that the American public could be fed on German-made propaganda without realizing either that it came from German sources, or that it favored Germany's cause." He further accused him of holding "that the Germans in this country who have declared their citizenship and loyalty here (as you have not) . . . shall still be first Germans at heart." Fixing on the reference to unsigned articles, he asked Münsterberg to state unequivocally whether he was acting as a German agent.[72]

Caught off guard, Münsterberg's immediate response was to strike back. He privately accused Hocking of printing "nothing but an arbitrary and uninformed misrepresentation of an illegally appropriated and miserably translated" document. But publicly he restated his belief that German-Americans should support America's interests first. His reference to the "slump" in the cause following a "wave of patriotism" was meant to describe the "regrettable . . . [fact] that many German-Americans have begun to be afraid to show their German sympathy." Furthermore, at the time of his writing to Bethmann-Hollweg he had intended to publish a series of essays without using his name so that they would "not be discounted by anti-German prejudices." But he had changed his mind and never "published a single line anonymously," even though it was the argument and not the name that was important. As for the accusation that he purveyed a "cry of peace [that] is a cry made in Germany," Münsterberg pointed out that precisely the opposite was true: that it was he who wrote to the chancellor arguing that Wilson should be trusted to mediate a peaceful settlement and not Bethmann-Hollweg who put the idea to him. "The very fact that I felt moved to write this to Germany indicates rather that the Germans did not feel as I did and that I made the cry in America . . . it is not for Germany but for the whole civilized world that I repeat and repeat: Let us have peace!"[73]

Unfortunately for the strength of his defense, Münsterberg went on to accuse Hocking of personal malice and to claim that he had tried to protect "the true honor of America" during the war years far more than the honor of Germany—although in the interests of the country he could "not go into details as to the way in which I have helped." This allusion to the Mc-Combs affair sounded like a mixture of insult, evasion, and boasting. Münsterberg came off badly in the public press, giving the impression of "colossal . . . conceit," of "slipperiness," and of making a desperate case for his good intentions. In the aftermath of the affair, the executive committee of the Boston branch of the superpatriotic American Rights League (led by William Roscoe Thayer) passed a resolution calling for Münsterberg's dismissal from Harvard. They were joined by editorial writers in several newspapers. Certain faculty members petitioned the Board of Overseers to request his resignation. But other Harvard professors announced that they would oppose an ouster move if it were brought up officially, and the Board of Overseers refused to take any action. Hocking, too, though he was convinced that Münsterberg had abused his position at Harvard "to a degree that exceeds good faith," opposed dismissal because it would inevitably appear to be for the wrong reasons.[74]

Through the later months of 1916 Münsterberg withdrew as much as possible from public controversy. Early in September he complained to Lowell that his health was failing and that he began to think of "the possibility of my sudden death or of a brain disease" which would render him incapable of providing for his family. When Josiah Royce died in the middle of September, Münsterberg's failure to attend the funeral was interpreted as a gesture of contempt rather than a precaution lest "the presence of a German colleague might possibly be embarrassing to some near him." But Münsterberg's moments of doubt and depression were quickly set aside. Putting the best face on his situation, he professed a "complete indifference" to signs of "unfairness, ingratitude and rudeness": "I have not the slightest rancor, understand completely why these good people act and must act as they do, and if they do not bow to me or do write letters like Hocking, I am sometimes a little disgusted and sometimes a little amused, but never irritated. That will have to go on until the war is over. Moreover, the students are splendidly loyal to me and so is the public at large."[75]

His final book on the war, *Tomorrow*, appeared late in October 1916, in the unfortunate format of a series of nine letters ostensibly written "To a friend in Germany." According to Münsterberg, when the letters failed to reach their destination he decided to publish them in the hope that "some stray volume will slip through." This small charade was undoubtedly meant to show that his letters to Germany contained "no indiscretions and no secrets" and to fend off any criticism of his political activity, for "while I should never meddle with political questions here, no one can blame me for speaking frankly to an old friend beyond the sea." Once again he adopts the role of "the psychologist who simply tries to understand" as he ponders the "common future" of the nations embroiled in war. Not surprisingly, what he sees in his crystal ball is his own reflection. The postwar world will witness a new birth of nationalism; each nation will foster its unique character and influence. Within the nations, individuals will renounce their petty pleasures and selfish interests in order to serve national ideals. The paradoxical result will be "the Germanization of the world."[76]

Almost on the eve of a period of frenzied patriotism in America, Münsterberg saw signs of a new day of idealism and internationalism; in advance of the most bitter defeat in German history, he foresaw that "whatever the cannons may say, the war will end with the spiritual triumph of the German nation." Only months before German-Americans began to lend their hands, if not their hearts, to the war against Germany and to eschew their hyphenate identity, he developed the thesis that after the war "thousands" disillusioned by "the pogrom of the hyphen" will make "an exodus [from America] like that of the Huguenots from France." But the "overwhelming majority" of German-Americans, undivided in their political loyalty to America, would lead the way in the postwar world to an idealistic redefinition of Americanism.[77]

Münsterberg's optimism was supported by his skill at shifting roles—and with them, perspectives—in order to deny or avoid unpleasant facts. A lengthy letter about the "pathetic suffering" of the German-Americans since 1914 stresses that he himself is a German citizen who did "not come here at my own desire." "Whatever I did was frankly done as a German. The rebuke

of the Americans of German descent has not even any reference
to me personally" and "I personally am not touched by it." It
suited him to underscore this point at a time when international
tension between Germany and the United States was lessening
(during the summer of 1916) but when "hyphenism" was developing as a major issue in the fall election campaign. His
pretensions fatally slipped, however, when he observed that
"nowhere have the Americans of German descent been harassed
as about the Charles River."[78]

Tomorrow represents Münsterberg's attempt to escape from
a painful present through the contemplation of a satisfying future. In this sense it is a companion piece to the autobiography
he now began to write. "Twenty-five Years in America" never
progressed much beyond outline form. But what was done provides a record of his perspective on past social and intellectual
achievements, including his wartime work "against corruption"
and his life's great moral mission. According to his daughter, he
planned to write a book on the psychology of war at a later
date. In his private correspondence he was already beginning
to shift from propagandist to psychologist. Writing to George
Sarton about the Bryce Committee report on war atrocities, he
claimed authority as an expert on the psychology of evidence,
not as a German. "Nine-tenths" of the "evidence" in the Bryce
report, he said, was untrue—not because it contained lies but
rather because it was not corrected for subconscious distortion.
Most atrocities were "products of illusions." He sent Sarton a
copy of *The Peace and America,* commending its first chapters
for their discussion of the psychological aspects of the war. "The
later chapters," he admitted, "were written in the heat of controversy, and they no longer fit the more peaceful atmosphere
of today."[79]

In his final writings, Münsterberg deliberately restrained his
unproductive bitterness. He shifted to an optimistic outlook and
an inner accommodation, dwelling on past glories and stressing
the positive aspects of his present situation. His activity in the
early months of the war had been aimed at winning "all possible sympathy for Germany in the United States." He had
played a vigorous role on the American scene, however ill-
calculated, in attempting to reconcile partisan positions on the

war, to guide German-Americans in finding self-expression, and to aid America in cleaving to a neutral course. His language was sometimes intemperate, his methods often devious and egotistical. The last months of his life, when doctors warned him to reduce the strain on his heart, were devoted to "preaching peace, and preparing the world for a friendly intercourse with Germany after the war." He kept his German citizenship as a symbolic expression of his uniqueness in America. But it was his sense of uniqueness and not his German allegiance that ultimately dominated and informed the various roles he played. In the end, he was sustained through his greatest crisis by the whole configuration of his American life: by his vision of an international mission, by his status in the larger American community beyond Boston, by the challenge and rewards of his professional work, and by those friends and students who continued to offer loyal support. By 1914 he had spent most of his adult life in America and raised and educated two daughters there. The single published chapter of his autobiography described his first years in America in idyllic terms, reminiscent of his earlier poetry. Selma Münsterberg recalled, too, that "the best part of my husband's life was devoted to Harvard . . . my own happiest years were spent in Cambridge before the great debacle."[80]

On December 16, 1916, Hugo Münsterberg made his way through snow-filled streets, in bitterly cold weather, to deliver a classroom lecture at Radcliffe College. Shortly after he began to speak he was seized by a swift and fatal heart attack. The news spread quickly. "That night," reported Selma Münsterberg, "it was President Eliot who was the one great supporting pillar that seemed to hold up my life structure . . . [He came] in my darkest hour . . . not only to offer me help but to bring some light into my darkness. He made me feel that warm personal friendship can continue even through the keenest political differences." George Palmer, Robert Yerkes, and Herbert Langfeld also gathered around the stricken family.[81]

Münsterberg's death, according to one old friend, "is a happy relief from persecution and malignant attacks, which have been a disgrace to American scholarship and civilization." The gen-

eral tenor of the obituaries confirmed the observation of Dean
Hodges of the Harvard Episcopal Theological Seminary that
"death make a difference . . . The way we feel about Professor
Münsterberg today is the way we ought to have felt about him
the day before yesterday." "It was only natural," the *Rochester
Herald* commented, "that Professor Münsterberg, German that
he was, should have been a partisan of his country, but there
was never any reason for assuming that he was a German spy."
George Sylvester Viereck solemnly announced that "he was the
leader of all those who fought the battle of German culture in
the United States. He falls, a victim of war."[82]

Rumor battened on the dramatic circumstances of Münsterberg's death. He had in fact suffered intermittently from a heart
condition first noted in 1891. But a secretary of Viereck, who
had come to know and admire Münsterberg in the course of
his many business trips to New York, later reported that Selma
Münsterberg and others believed he had poisoned himself in a
fit of depression and fear. She thought he had found himself in
an untenable position, boxed in between growing anti-German
sentiment on the one hand and pressure from the pro-German
group in New York on the other. The latter group, angered by
his independent actions and withdrawal from their councils,
allegedly threatened to make a public revelation of the extent
of his work for them. The official German line, however, was
that Münsterberg had been "killed" by his "ostracism" at Harvard. Three years later, testifying at a parliamentary inquiry
into the German defeat of 1918, Count von Bernstorff challenged the report of an "expert" on the propaganda contest in
America who implied that Münsterberg had been killed by
calumny for his "great service in representing German interests." "I don't believe that," Bernstorff asserted: "I believe he
simply succumbed to a stroke in the midst of his activity because of overwork or other exhaustion . . . it is true that Professor Münsterberg suffered unfriendly boycotting in Boston
and Harvard during the whole war period. But that was in fact
the case for all of us."[83]

Münsterberg's body was cremated and, as his will directed,
his ashes were shipped to Danzig. But his wife and two
daughters remained for the rest of their lives in the country

that had become their homeland. Beyond doubt, Hugo had shared their practical conviction that the family's future lay in America. There was never an opportunity for him to secure a position in Germany remotely equivalent to the quasi-patrician status he enjoyed in the United States. His devotion to Germany was distinctly one-sided; it is questionable whether his credentials as a German national would have been as fully accepted in Germany as they were in America. His fatherland was for him far more a symbol than a practical reality, representing a host of private feelings and associations. Germany, like his father Moritz and the august Kaiser, stood for authority, moral rectitude, and strength—the professed values of his inner life. The conscious rules he adopted to cover his behavior —absolute loyalty and devotion to duty—served at least two further psychological needs: to repress and deny hostile impulses toward authority (by exalting it to a status beyond question) and to justify his passive, submissive tendencies (by associating loyalty and duty with the "manliness" of authority and moral virtue). "A strong character," he wrote, "is one in which the idea of a goal . . . has such a strong determining tendency that every idea which would lead to opposite behavior is inhibited and suppressed and remains ineffective. The strong character overcomes a temptation and remains loyal to the ideal."[84]

The whole configuration of Hugo's childhood relationships reappears in his adult involvement in the war controversy. Ambivalence toward his father had been resolved by idealization and identification with Moritz's authority. In this way he was able to share in the moral blamelessness (and loveworthiness) he attributed successively to Moritz, Germany, and the Kaiser. The issues raised by the war pressed on Hugo's vulnerabilities, the residuals of his childhood experience. His self-identification with Imperial Germany led him to champion Germany's blamelessness from the first days of the war and to respond with fury to charges of German mendacity. He projected his own ego defenses onto the embattled fatherland, arguing that Germany's military aggression was both self-defensive and part of a moral impulse to place national self-interest above all else. His discussion of rivalries among the family of European nations also had a personal referent in his early jealousy and resentment of his competitive siblings.

America functioned as a far more complex and less coherent symbol in Münsterberg's inner life. On the ego level his American life supplied him with rich rewards of status and influence. Subconsciously, America functioned as a mother figure, drawing to itself the contradictory idealization and denigration that marked his feelings toward his mother and toward the female sex. As an abstract ideal, America signified to him a high order of integration: the fusion of diverse national strains. So Münsterberg's inglorious yearnings for place and power, as well as his personal achievements, were legitimized through the rationale of service to the ideal of America and the building up of her science and society. Service to this ideal America enabled him to see the "real" country "with the eyes of love." Still, the "real" America bore a host of traits characteristic of the female —and lesser—sex. She was frivolous, impulse-ridden, vain, "suggestible," and promiscuous; she was easily manipulated by propaganda and disposed to give herself to the highest bidder. He could put no faith in this America, for she would betray him as a "foreigner" at every opportunity. Furthermore, her mental traits were those he refused to admit in himself. The pleasures of direct gratification—the pleasures associated with mother—were those that "manliness" required him to renounce.

In the conflict between his negative and positive attitudes toward America, the latter had a crucial staying power. In an oration delivered at his funeral, Harvard Professor George F. Moore observed that Münsterberg had believed it his duty to explicate the German point of view on the war. This sense of duty had cost him dearly; his spiritual burden, in the end, was not vilification but isolation. To be sure, he was always dependent on the approval of others and he suffered greatly from his loss of status and influence through the war years. But the impending collapse of his moral mission—the symbolic glue that held his life together—was the more serious catastrophe. His international ambassadorship was the key to his sense of singularity, and it was a central inner goal toward which his behavior—skillfully or not—was directed. In his increasing isolation and anxiety over his failure to hold the disparate interests of his life together, he shared in the precarious situation of most German-Americans. Within months after his death, the life went out of German culture in America as well. Once war was declared between the two countries in April 1917, few German-Americans could sustain a painful double identity or allegiance. The new demand for consensus and conformity disallowed the special interests of ethnic group and unique individual. Overwhelmingly, German-Americans chose to emphasize their American ties and to repudiate those suspect group activities from which even Münsterberg had finally tried to dissociate himself.

It is in the light of Münsterberg's personality that one must scrutinize the role conflicts that troubled his life. From his earliest days in America he struggled to keep his various roles congruent. But his central ambition to serve as a scholar-ambassador beguiled him into pretentious plays for influence that elicited the censure of President Eliot and his Harvard colleagues. His efforts to reconcile pro-English and pro-German partisans and to shape and inform German-American responses in behalf of neutrality drew fire from all sides. To the German government he posed as an expert on American affairs; to the American government he posed as a German expert, an influential leader of German-Americans, and a professional analyst of testimony and evidence. To sustain these roles he had to maintain a variety of contacts without total personal commitment. A loner by inclination and habit, he set a lifelong pattern of marginal relationships that demanded enormous inner coherence from him. Lacking this as he did, he courted danger by the range of his roles as a German and an American, a scientist and a philosopher, a scholar and a popularizer, a politician, a teacher, and an ambassador.

As if in fear that the roles could not be harmonized, he rigidly compartmentalized the various interests of his adult life. He drew inflexible distinctions between causal and purposive psychology, and he compulsively asserted a hierarchical system of values that plainly masked internal disorder. The supreme value that he attached to unity and harmony reflected his own yearning for emotional integration. It was not his interests or roles that were incompatible; rather, his personal style in performing the roles brought them into conflict with one another. Despite his extraordinary skill in making adjustments to maintain self-esteem, he could not adapt sufficiently to the style of American life and social relations. His most successful social role was that of the distinguished foreign scholar for whom others made allowance. His intellectual abilities and his capacity for prodigious labor fitted him well for a career in scientific research. But his assertiveness and his voracious status needs played havoc with his other roles and engendered the ultimate conflicts that so strained his resources.

It is fortunate that Münsterberg was spared the experience of American entry into the war. He was incapable of repudiating his idealized fatherland or admitting any doubt about its moral splendor. Yet on a practical level, his self-esteem depended heavily on his being a German *in America*. For all his uniqueness, it was this latter reality that he shared with German-Americans. His psychological and social experience during the war years provides a close parallel to theirs. All who identified themselves or their interests with the fate of Germany responded aggressively to the issues raised by the war and gave their energies, in large part, to defending the status of things German in America. It was precisely their own self-esteem that was on the line. But the mobilization of aggression through group activity only elicited further rejection by the larger society. If the German-Americans' conflict lay between ethnic singularity and "Americanism," and Münsterberg's between two national ties, both still preferred to see their dual allegiance as a multiplication rather than a division of loyalty. Intense involvement tended to blur the line, for each, between political argument and private need. Münsterberg experienced the factionalism that rent the German-American community when he separated himself from the German agents and militants. He risked the censure of certain German-American leaders by his support for Theodore Roosevelt in 1915, and he spoke for many rank-and-file citizens—against their leaders—when he championed Woodrow Wilson in 1916. When aggressive action failed to alleviate his sense of beleaguerment, he retreated from areas of controversy. After 1917 most German-Americans took the same course to its logical extreme: their sense of diminished worth encouraged them to renounce the unacceptable German component of their dual identity.

In the last year of Münsterberg's life, turning to autobiography to relieve his inner tensions, he chose to celebrate only that part of his life which he had spent in America. It was an effort not only to remind others of his contributions to American society but also to restore himself by dwelling on the triumphs and pleasures of his American life. While he drew succor from reliving the past, he recorded his final vision of peace and international cooperation in the future. In the national emergency that followed the American declaration of war, these were the memory and the hope to which most German-Americans would cling.[85]

Part Two

George Sylvester Viereck . . . THE MAKING OF A GERMAN-AMERICAN MILITANT

■ ■ ■

George Sylvester Viereck—or Sylvester Viereck, for he preferred the exotic "Sylvester" to the nondescript "George"—was a man of many talents and enormous energy, profligately spent in an effort to create his own legend. He achieved precocious success as a young and "emancipated" American poet before the First World War. Entertaining no doubts about his commitment to America, he became during the war years a prominent and passionate spokesman for the most militant pro-Germans in the German-American community. Between the wars he made a name for himself as a journalist and novelist. In the thirties he became the major pro-German propagandist in the country, linking his cause to that of prominent isolationist groups. In the annals of American history, Sylvester Viereck ranks as a pariah—an uncongenial figure who gave wide offense on personal and historical grounds. A perpetual rebel against middle-class respectability, he took a perverse delight in notoriety. Supremely vain, he loved to be at the center of controversy. Indeed, he sought it out with the confidence of a true self-believer—a confidence that belied the many ambivalences characterizing his intellectual and emotional life. His pro-Germanism was, in effect, a lover's quarrel with America—which he sustained at such a level of intensity that it became unintelligible to others.

5 . . .

FAMILY AND CHILDHOOD

Sylvester's father, Louis Viereck, was born out of wedlock in Berlin in 1851. "His birth," according to a younger cousin, "furnished the conflict of his life." The only child of Edwina Viereck, a beautiful actress attached to the Prussian Royal Court, Louis was subsequently acknowledged by Louis von Prillwitz, an army officer and scion of Prince August of Prussia. Sylvester Viereck repeatedly gave currency to the rumor that Louis's real father was Emperor William I. Confronting Louis's denial, he disingenuously argued that he did not think the matter worth quibbling over, since "biologically the [Hohenzollern] strain is the same."[1]

As a result of his illegitimacy and his mother's early death in 1856, Louis held an ambiguous and precarious position in Berlin society. He "loved to be in noble circles." But despite his physical attractiveness, personal charm, and intellectual gifts, he remained a marginal figure. He joined the Socialist party in the early 1870s and quickly earned renown as a prominent "salon socialist." In 1878, when Bismarck outlawed the Socialist party, Louis lost his favored niche in the German Civil Service and was banished from Berlin for his alleged connection with a man who had attempted to assassinate William I. In 1881 he became the editor of a Socialist newspaper in Munich and married his American-born cousin Laura Viereck. Three years later he was elected to the German Reichstag. But in 1886 he again ran afoul of the government authorities—for attending a Socialist party meeting—and was imprisoned for nine months. During his term in prison, where he shared a cell with August Bebel, he became disillusioned with the extremism of the Socialist leaders, and upon his release he was expelled from the party. Several years of geographical and vocational drifting encouraged him to decide in 1896 to yield to his wife's "predilection for the United States" and to migrate to America in search of a home and a career in writing and lecturing. His wife and family followed him several months later.[2]

Louis Viereck became a naturalized American citizen in 1901. But he never abandoned his interest in German affairs, and in 1911 he returned to Germany to spend the remaining years of his life. For the fifteen years of his American sojourn he lived in New York City, writing works on German instruction in American schools and on German immigration to the United States, editing a German-language monthly, and serving as a correspondent for the *Berliner Tageblatt*. He was a strong-minded, active, and self-centered man, with marked intellectual ability and a seemingly insatiable appetite for public affairs. He enjoyed a wide reputation as a philanderer and, in his youth, produced an illegitimate child, Frank Viereck, who lived with him after his marriage.[3]

Laura Viereck was the American-born daughter of William Viereck, a younger brother of Louis's mother Edwina. A revolutionary who fled to the United States in 1849, William settled in San Francisco and established the first German theater there. After William died in 1865 his wife returned to Germany with her children. Laura Viereck was then almost eleven years old; fifteen years later she married her glamorous cousin Louis. She was a vivacious and intelligent woman who later worked alongside her husband, writing drama criticism for his German and American publications and actively involving herself in charitable German-American affairs. But she occupied a clearly inferior position in a marriage conducted in the European mode. In marked contrast to her husband, she was personally fastidious and "lacking in the low, enjoying power"; she was also a "devout though unorthodox Christian" while her husband styled himself a freethinker. Many years later a close relative recalled that Laura Viereck "hung on [her husband] with boundless love from the first glimpse, [and] . . . when in the course of a not all too quiet and comfortable married life she learned the shady side of his personality and fully admitted

it, a remnant was left of this younthful love even unto death."
Despite this lifelong bond—which at times appeared to be little
more than an empty habit—there were numerous disagreements and dissensions in the marriage. Louis lived in a world
of public and, occasionally, private affairs outside his home. In
compensation, Laura increasingly lavished affection upon their
first-born son Sylvester. Despite her huband's preoccupation
with German politics and culture she never ceased to nurse a
preference for America, the country of her birth, over Germany, the country in which she lived most of her life. "I like
the English language, the conception of [American] life and
ways of life more than the German," she wrote. "I cannot help
myself."[4]

George Sylvester Viereck was born in Munich on December
31, 1884. An aunt who was close to the family recalls that he
was a small and delicate child—his nickname, "Putty," was derived from Lilliput—who clung to his mother but admired and
imitated his distant father. Laura was an anxious and solicitous mother; Louis an impatient, authoritarian father. Parental
conflict over the boy's welfare may be surmised from the fact
that Laura arranged a secret baptism several years after Sylvester's birth "because his father was dissident and didn't want
to hear anything about it."[5]

Sylvester's preadolescent years were marked by the instability of his father's employment and political affiliations. He
was two years old when his father left home to spend nine
months in prison. After Louis's release and his subsequent expulsion from the Socialist party, a series of abortive business
ventures and geographical relocations kept the family in a
state of uncertainty. Louis's last post was as Director of the
Bath at Swinemünde. His son later recalled that "through all
kinds of intrigues, [we were] chased away from here too [by
the police], and we went to Berlin, from where Papa journeyed
to America, but we to Schöneberg." During these years Sylvester developed an ambivalent attachment to his half-brother,
Frank, whom he "ordered . . . around from the earliest times
[in imitation of Louis] but clung very much to [all the] same."
Sometime before 1896, Frank took a job with the North German Lloyd Line, jumped ship in Baltimore, and settled down

as a florist in America. Louis left for the United States shortly afterward.[6]

With his father and half-brother gone, Sylvester lived with relations in a country house in Schöneberg while his mother supported herself and his baby brother Edwin (born September 22, 1894) in Berlin by giving piano and language lessons. Late in 1896 the family followed Louis to New York, but reunion failed to turn the tide of hardship. They lived at first in a rooming house where Sylvester shared a bed with his ailing younger brother. "Little Eddy" died of spinal meningitis in March 1897. Shortly afterward, Laura was taken to the hospital with sudden appendicitis. A gift of money tided the family over the first winter, but without relieving the emotional strain on Sylvester.[7]

The boy had begun writing poetry at the age of eleven at Schöneberg, in part to court the attention of his cousin Erna Viereck, who presided over the household (which included several of her own children). It was a strategy he would later employ with his own mother. But once the family settled in America Louis Viereck became firmly convinced, from his own experience, "of the impotence of the Intelligentsia in its struggle with the material world," and insisted that Sylvester learn some useful trade. He made arrangements through Frank for the boy to be apprenticed to a gardener in Baltimore.[8]

Sylvester thus was separated from his family once again. He apparently spent most of his time discussing poetry with his employer, and was fired after six months at the insistence of the gardener's wife. Upon returning to New York, he enrolled in a public school, where his academic success was modest and his peer relations were clouded by his poor command of English. Yet there were compensating triumphs. In 1897 a German paper in Baltimore printed a poem by him on Bismarck, and in 1898 the Hearst-owned *Das Morgen-Journal* in New York featured a short verse he had written celebrating the American cause in the Spanish-American war. Laura and Louis were concerned about the boy's precocious and increasingly "erratic capricious qualities." But they were also flattered by the idea that they were raising a *Wunderkind:* "neither parent could understand the poetic temperament: but they could understand ambition, intelligence, verve."[9]

At the time of his arrival in America, Sylvester was on the threshold of adolescence. As we have seen, a series of extraordinary events occurred between his eleventh and fourteenth years. There was, first, the "disappearance" of his older half-brother Frank, to whom he was much attached. Then his father left for the United States. He was separated from accustomed intimacy with his mother while the new baby, Eddy, was kept at her side in Berlin. Once the family was reunited Little Eddy died under frightening circumstances, while Louis continued to be habitually absent on lecturing and business trips. So in effect young Sylvester had succeeded, in the course of these years, in removing all rivals for his mother's attention. An idealization of his dead sibling went into a fragmentary and childish memorial to Little Eddy that he wrote in 1900. Calling Eddy "the little sunray," Sylvester asserted that "everybody" had loved the child and that the child had "loved everything that was beautiful and good." The guilt inherent in his situation certainly was deepened by the fact that, in Louis's habitual absence, he had to wrestle with an idealized image of his father.[10]

After the brief separation from his mother that followed—at his father's command—Sylvester returned to an intimate relationship with her, thus being inordinately exposed to the regressive pull of childhood ambivalence and dependency. At precisely the time when adolescent development would seem to call for the establishment of nonfamilial bonds, he found himself thrown back upon his mother in an alien country. His developing sexuality ran up against his mother's cool "fastidiousness." A lifelong preoccupation with sex ensued.[11]

A wealth of evidence testifies to his modes of response to these unusual circumstances and relationships—modes that later became fixed characteristics of his adult personality. These included a narcissistic self-absorption and self-overvaluation (together with an exaggerated regard for members of his family, perceived as extensions of himself); the use of fantasy as a bridge to the outside world; unrestrained exhibitionism and self-dramatization; failure to integrate thought and feeling; and a sense of guilt which continually led him both to seek punishment and to justify his beliefs and actions. Egotism became his readiest defense against self-division and guilt. He also developed a characteristic ambivalence toward women he was fond of (mother substitutes) and both ambivalence toward and idealization of men with whom he identified (father substitutes). By the time he reached manhood, Sylvester seemed —according to the testimony of some of his friends and the judgment of history—to lack any developed moral sense, or any clear and steady goals other than to be rich, well connected, and esteemed. This moral poverty contributed as much as his vivid personality to Viereck's life history.

Certain themes emerged from Viereck's adolescent experiences that were to reappear throughout his life. His attachment to his father was crucial to his subsequent career, for it informed many of his adult acts. He himself later recalled that, in childhood, "mysterious whisperings about my father's romantic origin, while scarcely understood, nevertheless quickened my imagination . . . [and] wrought a halo of romance about his head." The better to identify himself with his father, he posed as a womanizer, played the role of a political insurgent, pursued a (collateral) career in journalism, developed an abiding interest in German culture and German-American community life, attached himself to the Hohenzollern Kaiser, defended and promoted the German cause in two world wars, exposed himself to charges of illegal political activity, and landed himself in prison. At the age of thirty he married a cousin-surrogate, Margaret Hein, whom he had first met when she was still a child and who looked upon him with inordinately adoring eyes. Even his understanding of his own emotional life depended upon identification with his father. Explaining his "bipolar" attraction to his parents, he wrote that "my father, too, was born under the baleful star of a double fixation, ever seeking vainly his beautiful mother and his dashing father, who passed from his life after his mother's death." That this identification often regressed to the more primitive level of *being* rather than *being like* his father is evidenced by Viereck's confession that he was not only attracted to older women (an imitation of his father) but "always attracted by [the very] women who played a part in my father's life"—a fascination that involved him in a doting relationship with one of his father's previous mistresses.[12]

Long after Louis Viereck was dead, Sylvester recorded a conversation with Sigmund Freud in his *Glimpses of the Great,* a book containing accounts of thirty-two interviews with famous men. Freud told him, "You have sought, year after year, the outstanding figures of your generation, invariably men older than yourself." "It is part of my work," Sylvester replied. "But," Freud insisted, "it is also your preference. The great man is a symbol. Your search is the search of your heart. You are seeking the great man to take the place of the father. It is part of your father complex."

In the course of his career, Viereck also developed strong filial attachments to Theodore Roosevelt, Hugo Münsterberg, and the poet and editor Edward J. Wheeler, as well as a sense of discipleship to Freud himself. None of these relationships satisfied his craving for an ideal father, and only one of them —abruptly cut short by Münsterberg's death in 1916—failed to produce evidence of ambivalence. There is much evidence, too, of buried guilt in Viereck's relationship with his father. He later observed that he had dropped his initial career as a poet for an involvement in German-American affairs "in atonement for . . . early rebellion" against his father's German interests. Significantly, he felt that he had to give up poetry—with which he courted his mother—in order to make this expiation.[13]

Recalling his father's long absences from the family, Viereck observed that "I concentrated my love upon my mother . . . I remember that long before Freud's Oedipus complex had passed into popular parlance my father once called me 'Oedipus' in jest." But his intense affection for her had to be held in check, for she might—and indeed did—betray it with one or another of his family rivals. A deep ambivalence toward his mother developed; later it would be transferred to America, the country of his mother's birth and preference. His exaggerated affection for his mother shines through the terms of childish endearment with which he addressed her in their correspondence. His anxiety and solicitude, especially during their

separation in World War I, were equally extreme. The very intensity of his regard was clearly compulsive in character, mask-
ing an unconscious hostility that constantly had to be overcome. Despite the fact that he often courted his mother's
attention with his poetry, Viereck understood that she instinctively "abhorred" everything he "wrote and stood for" as a
creative writer. To his last years he blamed her for the sense of
guilt that, he claimed, hampered his sexual life.[14]

At the end of his adolescence, then, Viereck's underlying relationships with mother and father remained unmastered. He
subsequently exercised life choices that would enable him to
work them through. At the same time certain childish modes
of response to mother and father and their symbols became
fixed in his character. Beyond the task of mastering these separate relationships lay that of experiencing his parents as a
unit—of reconciling and integrating their influence. Viereck
observed that "my father and my mother are the pole and the
anti-pole of my libido . . . [I wavered] constantly between
[these] two magnets of affection. The conflict between the
mother and the father fixation . . . may be the master key to
my soul." The marriage of Louis and Laura Viereck was, of
course, poorly integrated to begin with. Louis was self-centered, traveled much alone, and was unfaithful to his wife.
Laura increasingly centered her emotional life in her son. Yet
it should be remembered that Laura and Louis were blood relations, born with the same surname. Sylvester repeatedly tried
to bring them together symbolically through his thought and
action. He continually asserted the common interests of Germany and America and acted to unite the increasingly divergent concerns of the two countries. And he worked long and
hard to develop Freud's conception of bisexuality into a theory of the unity of the sexes.[15]

Viereck's preoccupation with sex is the final theme that re-
curred through his life. In the early years of his manhood he
may well have engaged in homosexual as well as heterosexual
experiences, and intense friendships with "brothers" figured
repeatedly in his life. Yet despite this affirmation of bisexuality, he seems not in fact to have mistaken his own gender.
His sexual liaisons appear to have been narcissistic exercises in

which he showed off to himself. The notion of bisexuality was for him a fantasy of sexual self-sufficiency, an excuse for his homosexuality, and a rationalization of his sexual failures with women. What he literally meant by bisexuality was the ideal perfection of being represented by the fusion of male and female components in one person. His constant dwelling upon the theme—particularly in his poetry and novels—seems to relate, beyond his narcissism, to his search for a unity of the parental polar principles. As for his sexual failures, he advertised himself as a potent libertine yet confessed to an inability to find lasting or meaningful sexual love. A psychiatrist whom he consulted at the age of fifty-five reports that Viereck's sex life was "a considerable bother to him. A sort of Casanova or Don Juan, he has travelled far and wide trying to find supreme sexual satisfaction and never quite achieved it." A few years earlier he had undergone an operation developed by Dr. Eugen Steinach to enhance potency, and this "seemed to give him some help for a while in his effort at finding the fountain of eternal sexual youth."[16]

6 . . .
FLIRTATION WITH THE
MUSE OF POETRY

Remembering his adolescent years at a later date, Viereck
wrote that "circumstances conspired to induce in me at all
times the feeling that I was an exceptional being . . . that I
was indeed a wonder child." Two records support the recollection. A diary kept during his seventeenth year is filled with
self-assertions, self-dramatizations, and the conviction that he
is destined for greatness. In this diary he recorded his admiration of Oscar Wilde—also something of an adolescent pos-
turer—and identified himself with the "deliciously unhealthy,
so beautifully morbid" English poet. "I love all things morbid
and evil," he wrote. "I love the splendor of decay, the foul
beauty of corruption." His diary "began . . . in the spirit of
self-esteem and it ended with . . . self-love. It displayed contempt for the ordinary usage of life and letters. It revelled in
high-spirited ignorance of mere facts. It gloated in triumphs,
petty and base."[1]

When Sylvester was sixteen years old William Ellery Leonard, a young American scholar and poet, boarded with the
Viereck family while attending Columbia University. Leonard
had just returned from a sojourn abroad during which he had
studied in Germany. He was anxious to maintain contact with
the Germanic culture he admired. Referred to the Vierecks by
one of his professors at Columbia, he quickly became an intimate member of the family circle. Although Leonard was nine
years senior to Sylvester, he held the young "cerebral elf" in awe,
sensing in him "the intensity of one destined for immortal renown." Leonard later described Sylvester's impatience when,
on first entering the Viereck household, Leonard failed to take
notice of the boy. Thrusting himself out from behind his moth-

er's figure at one point, Sylvester dramatically declared, "Ich bin ein Dichter; ich bin ein Dichter!"[2]

The incident and the association with Leonard are revealing. The sixteen-year-old boy, after hiding behind his mother's skirts, aggressively asserted himself to the outsider, in the role toward which all of his adolescent ambitions were directed. It was at the same time a childish gesture and an attempt to reject childhood. With his projected career as poet—frowned upon by his father and merely tolerated by his mother—the youth was grasping for autonomy. Leonard's awe of the boy is a measure of the degree to which Viereck's self-estimation prevailed in the household.

The association with Leonard grew in significance, particularly when Leonard introduced Ludwig Lewisohn, a fellow student at Columbia, into the household. For a while the three young men became intimate, the two students serving as beloved older brothers to Sylvester. They talked endlessly about poetry and life, and dreamed of the day when "we three will become the leaders of American literature." When Leonard left to return to Germany the friendship between Viereck and Lewisohn intensified. Lewisohn shared with Viereck the expense of issuing Viereck's collection of sixteen poems in German. Soon afterwards he spoke of the "mature and serious artist in this defiant, engaging and at times irritating boy. A slight affectation of cynicism and of worldly wisdom sits not ungracefully upon him, but one forgets and forgives it easily enough in view of the passionate sincerity of his best poems." Subsequently, both Leonard and Lewisohn publicly lavished praise on Viereck's poetry and contributed significantly to the early reputation he won as a poet. As for the young man himself, the two older men "were to me, on the slippery slopes of a new Parnassus, what Virgil was to Dante."[3]

Sylvester attended City College from 1902 to 1906, compiling an undistinguished academic record. During these years he regularly assisted his father with the latter's work for the *Berliner Tageblatt* and often wrote articles or short stories for the *New York Staats-Zeitung* and other German-language papers. But his aspirations centered upon a career as a poet, and he was resentful of attending long "German-American affairs" for his father's sake. By the time of his graduation he had published two volumes of German poetry and a collection of plays. *Nineveh and Other Poems* (1908), his first collection of poetry in English (translated from German originals), brought him instant and heady success. Already dubbed by Lewisohn "the only real German-American poet," Viereck now received wider recognition. Even his severest critic could "not . . . deny any of the gifts that experts of two continents have conferred upon this singing and sinning youth." Later Lewisohn would catalog him as "the most conspicuous American poet between 1907 and 1914," although he clearly exaggerated Viereck's "liberating influence on American life and letters." Whether or not Viereck was, as the *Saturday Evening Post* observed in 1908, "the most widely discussed young literary man in the U.S. today . . . [and] unanimously accused of being a genius," he certainly achieved a public acclaim, at the age of twenty-four, commensurate with his ambitions.[4]

At this point Viereck made a deliberate decision to continue writing exclusively in English. Although he believed that he had written some of his best work in German, he "suffered from the gift of two languages . . . My American heart was at war with my German heritage." He sensed the flowering of an alleged Hohenzollern literary talent in himself. But "I consulted with friends on both sides of the ocean, and it was finally agreed that America, being poorer than Europe, needed me more. I decided to become an American classic." With this good-humored egotism went more practical reasons for the denial of his German tongue. He wanted to have an American and not a German career. "The traditions of German poetry have affected me little," he wrote. Lewisohn, too, thought that Viereck had "passed those years of his life which really counted in his artistic development on this side of the Atlantic" and looked upon Poe rather than Heine as a literary model. The great personal model of his career in letters was Wilde, whose impudence, genius, and mask of conceit established a persona that Viereck tried to emulate throughout his life. He was interested, too, in Wilde's "bisexuality" and sympathetic toward the conflict between Wilde's "psychic exhibitionism" and his "British sense of propriety."[5]

Under a veil of intellectual speculation and aesthetic experiment Viereck deals, in *Nineveh*, with experiences of sin and salvation repeatedly presented in sexual terms. The young poet describes himself as a lover who has lost his soul to the irresistible force of sensual temptation, although he is still not insensitive to the higher bliss of virginal love. A poem entitled "Confession" poses the poet's knowledge of "a witch woman" whose dwelling place is a tropical forest:

> A ripe fruit hangs in the sultry place,
> For whose savour a man counts all but loss,
> Forgetting even his mother's face
> And the bleeding Head upon the Cross.

Opposed to this is "the cool green moss of the northern wood" where a virginal maid awaits him. He confesses that

> . . . I have walked where the sorceress dwells,
> Where poisoned blooms make the senses reel,
> And I have yielded me to her spells,
> And lost forever my soul's true weal.[6]

In *The Candle and The Flame* (1912), the poet has worked free of any guilt, has accepted evil as an "essential part of the cosmic scheme," and devotes himself to celebration of the many forms of love. "Love is the only theme of the poets," Viereck observed in reflecting upon his early verse. "God, patriotism and art may inspire the singer, but God and art and patriotism are merely sex in solution." In the course of exalting human passion, he dwells upon sexual perversity and nonconformity. He speaks of an eternal war between men and women, based upon the opposition of male and female principles and the conflict between these principles within each individual. His language is deliberately erotic. Later he would insist that the "maleness" of the poet always was dominant in him as he wrote, and that his poems were "lyric orgasms." Certainly they reveal his preoccupation with sex both as a struggle for mastery and as a quest for perfection. They reveal, too, his appropriation of the more pathological patterns of his father's behavior. His obsession with polarities appears in repeated declarations of simultaneous attraction to opposing female "types"; to Lilith and Eve, to the earthy Helen of Troy and the ethereal blonde

Marguerite, to the Eternal Harlot and the Eternal Woman. Each attracts him and yet each is rejected as insufficient. He seeks constantly to imagine a third figure, the Woman in Scarlet (later Salomé), who will reconcile the polar feminine types and thus transcend their limitations. It is only this woman who can be worthy of the vigorous poet who is torn by "that hunger beyond the flesh / That only the flesh can appease in me."[7]

If writing poetry became a way of adapting his sexual fantasies and regressive emotions to reality, his work during this period also stands as an aggressive critique of the puritanical strain in American life. The figure he cut as a poet and critic stood opposed to the genteel tradition in American letters, to its Victorian morality. In his typically flippant manner, he observed in 1907 that

Life in America . . . is one mad struggle after respectability. Our God is not Mammon, but Mrs. Grundy. Our poets would rather win a wink from her spectacled eyes than feel the kisses of the nine muses trembling on their lips . . . In the State of New York the penalty for adultery is half that for spitting on the street, and I can find no other explanation for the anomaly than the assumption that the temptation to spit is twice as overpowering.[8]

"I worked long and hard to acquire a bad reputation," Viereck later remarked, as if he were performing a social service by creating an image that would shock Americans out of their hypocritical complacency. Yet there was to his posturing and desire to shock a more than faintly literary, derivative quality. He was deeply influenced by the European decadents—particularly the German and English writers—and their passion for the exotic, perverse, and amoral aspects of experience. But his opposition to Puritanism derived less from moral principle than from the fact that Puritanism tended to cramp his personal style. Nor did the aesthetic freedom he demanded for the poet in America represent an internalized ideal, for he himself produced no more than competent imitations of Wilde and the German decadents. His need was to construct a personal identity out of the clash of the genteel and the radical. But the image of a vigorous and emancipated poet that he strove to project became, all too often, that of a mischievous, engaging boy saying lyric-naughty things to his mother. His intellectual radicalism served essentially psychological needs. He wanted to shock America in order to draw attention to himself, not to make room for new art. Viereck shared a commitment to self-expression and a flair for iconoclasm with the younger generation of poets who mounted the "Innocent Rebellion" in 1912. But he played no significant part in their movement, and just when they came into their *annus mirabilis* he decided to abandon poetry.[9]

In 1908 Viereck made a pilgrimage to Germany. Subsequently he wrote *Confessions of a Barbarian,* a best-seller in New York City in 1910, dedicated to his father and devoted to Germany. He declared himself uniquely fitted to interpret Europe to Americans because the process of doing so involved the exploration of his own "twofold racial consciousness." His book focuses almost equally on the shortcomings of American life and the virtues of German culture. In contrast to Münsterberg, who studied the German and American national characters as separate, external entities, Viereck placed his own divided self at the center of his analysis. This self he conceived of as a vigorous youth of royal blood, superior gifts, and exalted destiny. He personified the two nations as seductive women vying for his fealty and affection, and his own posture toward them is deeply erotic. "The German Empire," he wrote," regards me still as her subject. She clings to me with the tenacity of a woman. I think she accuses me of desertion. A uniform, spick and span, and with brass buttons, is waiting for me. But I don't want it. I'd rather wear my blue serge suit . . . I have politely informed Madame that I am an American citizen, and that she can not, can really not count upon me." Later, after returning to America, he saw himself as a "young Barbarian" who "having escaped unscathed from the Siren City, has returned to his pristine love. Marvellous tales he tells her, and circles her breasts with strange jewels. And only sometimes in the night when, listless and uncomprehending, she slumbers beside him, his thoughts wander back to perfumed women with painted lips and wise, far away beyond the watery hills."[10]

The book is shot through with polarities. Viereck presents himself both as a sophisticated aristocrat in his father's image and as a vigorous but crude representation of his adopted country. He spurns the insistent charms of a German seductress and yet he pays repeated fealty to her wisdom in the ways of life. He returns to She-America, to the source of his vigor and to his "pristine" mother love. But her shortcomings are an insistent theme of the book, and his mind wanders constantly from her bed to the person of her rival.

What Viereck found most attractive in Germany was the "superior" life of its arisocracy, bolstered by pervasive distinctions of rank and devoted to the highest ideals of art. He saw the German state as marvelously efficient and successful in purveying social welfare. He was impressed with the general level of manners and sophistication, and he believed the virtues of Germany to be superbly exemplified by the "individualism" of Kaiser Wilhelm II. He ranked among Germany's greatest cultural achievements the perception that passion rather than morality should govern sexual expression. Europe in general, he wrote, was far ahead of America in recognizing this truth. Nevertheless, he was not allowed to forget that he was inescapably an outsider: "My German friends tell me I am extremely American. They mean to imply that I am not an idealist. I admit that I have a bank account . . . Like most Americans, I am really a self-made man." While he freely gave half his heart to Germany, the other half was filled with nostalgia for the genuineness and "commonsense" of America. Viereck ended his hymn of praise for Germany with a description of a joyous gathering of Americans at "the German Waldorf-Astoria" to hear the 1908 presidential election returns:

That night I was unfaithful to Europe. My heart longed for America fiercely . . . Madame Europe, you are very wonderful . . . Columbia is very naive, I admit, but there is a certain charm in her inexperience . . . Thinking it over, I shall not keep house with you, Madame. Somehow, after all, my heart goes out to Columbia . . . I shall teach Columbia what you have taught me. I will not pose as a martyr. It really wasn't a matter of choice with me. I can't help being an American. I am a son of this soil. Whatever I am, America has made me. My feelings for her are deeper than gratitude . . . But I am not sentimental. I am like the lover who is not blind to the faults of his Mistress. I hate and I love her.

I was never comfortable abroad. I sometimes seem to myself a cha-
meleon—an inverted one. I always assume a color at variance with my
environment. There was an ever-tangible barrier between Europe and
me. The memory of home severed us like a sword.

If Viereck came to Germany to worship her as a prodigal son,
he quickly found that his credentials did not entitle him to re-
claim his full cultural patrimony. But this did not really trouble him, for he already knew that his was an American soul
and that his infidelity toward America was a characteristic
habit of mind, based upon a profound attachment. Europe—
Germany—was a fantasy he might pursue through the rest of
his life, but it never loosened the bonds that tied him to
America.[11]

Viereck's sensational success as a young poet and his growing reputation as a cultural critic fed his ambition and conceit.
He surrounded himself with a coterie of young admirers, including the intense neophyte poets Blanche Wagstaff and Elsa
Barker. One friend recalled at a later date that when he first
met Viereck during their college days, he found a rather "un-
couth" young man, "badly dressed and generally 'gauche.'
Within a short period he became a great dandy, foppish in his
appearance. He was then . . . [deeply into] his 'Oscar Wilde
admiration' period and liked to pose a great deal. He was extreme in his dress, wore velvet collars on his dinner coat etc.
Anything to be different." But this phase, too, receded as he
cultivated the friendship of the eminently respectable editor
of *Current Literature*, Edward J. Wheeler, and was taken onto
the magazine staff as Wheeler's personal protégé. He became a
close friend of fellow staff writers Leonard Abbott and Alexander Harvey, respectively seven and twenty years older. He
was advised and aided in his career by Richard Watson Gilder,
James Huneker, William Marion Reedy, and Hugo Münsterberg. Some of his closest friends afterward admitted that he
was a social climber, always pushing for significant contacts,
especially among the rich and well-placed. Speaking of Viereck
during these early days of success, Barker recalled, "Brilliant
though he was, he was under a nervous tension which fore-
boded some catastrophe . . . He had a unique but eccentric

character which would make him take strange and unaccountable attitudes." Like his idol Wilde, he presented a facade of
brazen self-confidence that concealed deep inner tensions.[12]

The years 1911–1912 were a turning point in Viereck's career. To begin with, his parents moved permanently back to
Germany and he took over the editorship of Louis's German-
language magazine, *Der deutsche Vorkaempfer,* converting it
into a German-language edition of *Current Literature.* Here
began his long career as a businessman-editor and his increasing involvement in German-American affairs. Prior to this time
Viereck had occasionally expressed "anti-German" attitudes
and opinions to his closest friends. He confided to his biographer that he now wished to atone to his father for his childhood "rebellion" against his German-American background. At
any rate he now began—in his father's absence—to identify himself strongly with the German-American community. At the
same time, the frontier of the "new" poetry had begun to shift
in the direction of greater experimentation, and Viereck's position as a pioneer quickly eroded. His second collection of
verse, *The Candle and The Flame,* published in 1912, was not
as well received as *Nineveh.* An edition of his collected writings
in five skimpy volumes, also published in 1912, revealed the
variety of his interests and talents but also how thin and diffuse
was his creative accomplishment. By 1912 he had played out
the role of poet for all it meant to him, without ever making a
total commitment of energy and resource.[13]

"The spirit of America has eaten into my heart," he announced in his preface to *The Candle and The Flame.* "Wall
Street is more interesting to me than Parnassus." The uneven
contest between ambition and aestheticism ended unfavorably
for the Muse of Poetry. His lyric emotions had run ahead of
the local poetic vocabulary, he rationalized, and he must wait
"for America to catch up." In calling it quits as a "lyric insurgent," he believed that he was assuring himself a niche in the
pantheon of art, for in America true "poets . . . [must] deny
poetry or leave the country." Nevertheless, some of the poems
in this volume were among his best. Most of them intone a
Whitmanesque affirmation of all things relevant to man's life,
with a special emphasis on sensual pleasure. The afterimage of

the book is that of the poet as a pagan piper full of inflated passion—a state occasionally modified by a note of gentle self-mockery. But Viereck obviously sensed a diminution of his "lyric libido"—which he would later argue "was diverted by the [First World] war." He also would claim that he had abandoned poetry because "praise began to bore me." In fact psychic tension had begun to wear him down. After his parents' departure he turned from this adolescent mode of singularizing himself and took up the task of succeeding his father.[14]

Seeking a new cause and a new role, Viereck attached himself briefly to Theodore Roosevelt's campaign for the presidency in 1912. He did some campaigning and ran as an elector on the Progressive ballot in New York State. But he was primarily interested in Roosevelt, not in politics, and his involvement subsided after the election. Meanwhile he cast about for a larger enterprise with which to merge his unsuccessful German-language monthly. In 1912 *Der deutsche Vorkaempfer* was absorbed by *The International,* an avant-garde "little magazine," and Viereck became chief editor of the combine. The finances of the venture at first were extremely tenuous, and Viereck instinctively turned for aid to the community of German-Americans, whose wealthy and socially prominent members he had long cultivated. Paul Warburg obliged with a pledge of $5,000, and additional support came from Mrs. Philip Lewisohn, Mrs. Randolph Guggenheimer, Mrs. Samuel Untermeyer, Adolphus Busch, Gustav Pabst, and Otto Kahn. Both Roosevelt and Münsterberg assisted him in the raising of money. "I should have no difficulty in continuing the magazine as a purely aesthetic literary journal," Viereck boasted to Münsterberg, "but I cannot continue it with its present strong pro-German policy unless I get some German support." The general idea behind the new publication, however, was "not to make it purely a German-American magazine, because in that case its influence would be limited, but to make it a vital American periodical, with strong German affiliations." By the end of 1912 Viereck had found the material and spiritual vocation that would dominate his life. He would be a writer-businessman, an influence on culture and politics, and a "vital" American publicist with inviolable ties to Germany.[15]

At the beginning of 1914 the magazine still was financially insecure. It had only 2,000 paid subscribers, and some of those who furnished copy also contributed expenses out of their own pockets. Low on funds himself, Viereck considered abandoning it when he left for Europe in May 1914 to visit with his parents. When he returned in late July, the threat of war hung heavy in the air. The German invasion of Belgium shocked and dismayed most Americans, and placed German-Americans almost instantly on the defensive. Their need for skilled spokesmen was evident. Viereck's financial and emotional interests lay with them, and his special talents answered their greatest need. His energy and resourcefulness came into sudden focus as he met this extraordinary opportunity. Between 1914 and 1917 Viereck achieved a position of some influence because the political expression of his psychological needs significantly appealed to other German-Americans beset by a crisis of divided loyalties.

7 ...
DOMESTIC CRISIS
AND WORLD WAR

The First World War offered Viereck an opportunity to play
out the conflicts of his emotional life in an arena larger than
his personal relationships or creative abilities alone could provide. His attachment to Germany always had figured conspicuously in his fantasy search for a father figure. Now, he wrote,
"in fighting for Germany I was not merely defending the
Fatherland but my father's land." Here, then, was a chance for
triumphant atonement to his father. At the same time he could
emulate his father as a political rebel, expand his own contacts
among German officials residing in the United States, and hope
to be rewarded for these efforts with prestige and money.[1]

But the same ambivalence that had marked his feelings toward his mother underlay his attitude toward America. His
earlier love-hate for mother was now transferred to the motherland, and as American sentiment began to crystallize in favor
of the Allies the alienating hate component of his attachment
necessarily rose to dominance. When the German-American
crisis began in 1914 it was not a question of choosing between
his loyalty to Germany and his loyalty to America. He could
not turn his back on his German fatherland. Yet his dependent
attachment to America was equally insistent. The negative
aspect of his feeling toward America, enforced by a need to
play the rebel and by the increasingly hostile climate of public opinion, made him into a pro-German militant. His was not
so much a crisis of national loyalty as a crisis of psychological
adaptation. The strain upon him was deepened by his lifelong
need to reconcile, in his own person, the two countries for
which his parents stood.[2]

The Fatherland, a weekly newspaper Viereck founded in

August 1914, details the progress of his militant pro-Germanism to the time of America's entry into the war. Together with
each of three German-American friends, he put up an initial
stake of fifty dollars to launch a newspaper that would hold
up the German end of the war issues. There was no expectation of financial profit at the outset, but a first edition (August
10) of 10,000 copies was snapped out of the hands of street
vendors (mainly German reservists) by news-hungry New
Yorkers. Circulation mounted to a spectacular 100,000 by October. A small office on Lower Broadway, donated by Mrs.
Randolph Guggenheimer, was quickly abandoned for a suite
of rooms housing thirty employees. Soon Viereck began to see
himself as the "mouthpiece" or leading "representative of the
Americanized—assimilated—German-Americans." Besides expounding the German point of view, *The Fatherland* took upon
itself the tasks of exposing the malfeasance of the Allied countries, revealing the prejudices and distortions of the American
press, and rallying German-Americans in their own defense.
In a letter to Münsterberg in early August 1914 Viereck presented the paper as "a weekly of protest and information."
After the war he spoke of its "undiluted pro-Germanism,"
claiming that it arose "spontaneously in response to a world-
wide need" and "became the spokesman in the English language of pro-Germans everywhere."[3]

Viereck's early affiliation with the propaganda cabinet set
up in New York by German agents under the leadership of
Dr. Bernhard Dernburg, a German banker and government official, and Dr. Heinrich Albert, a German lawyer, supplied rich
rewards of money and status. As holder of the "German-American portfolio" in the cabinet he received about $40,000 be-
tween 1914 and 1916. In addition, German agents bankrolled
the various enterprises of his Fatherland Corporation to the
amount of $100,000, fully covering the cost of printing and dis-
seminating pro-German books and generously purchasing advertising space in *The Fatherland* to purvey these wares. They
also underwrote the paper's free subscription list. Not satisfied with ad hoc subventions, Viereck entered upon negotiations with Albert in 1915 for a regular monthly payment of

$1,750 in order to expand the size of *The Fatherland* and increase the circulation of *The International*. In a letter to Dernburg, he argued, "I have certain knowledge of the psychology of the American public and certain connections which may make my advice of some value. In fact, I am of the opinion that *The Fatherland* and I have been able to place more facts before the American public from the German point of view than the entire German Information Service." Lest he seem to be selling himself as a mercenary, Viereck was careful to add that his motives in giving aid were entirely patriotic: "I am personally of the opinion that this country is drifting into war with Germany . . . [and] as a patriotic American I would like to fight against any [such] policy . . . For that reason I would like to influence anybody whom I could possibly reach." He may have added this note to impress Dernburg with the risks Germany was running. Or perhaps he meant, by emphasizing his own Americanism, to counter the suspicion that *The Fatherland* had limited usefulness because it was widely held to be an "organ of the [German] Embassy." At any rate he emphatically presented the paper's position as a truly American one, which merely happened to coincide with German interests.[4]

Albert and Dernburg were not ready to come to an agreement over additional aid without taking over the financial management of the paper from Viereck and reaching an "understanding regarding the course of politics which you will pursue." When the *New York World* ran an exposé of Viereck's negotiations with the German agents, he claimed that nothing had come of them. In the course of a later investigation Viereck admitted that it had been the German agents who were reluctant to go through with the deal (which, in its final stage, involved the purchase of stock in The Fatherland Corporation). But when he wrote his "impartial" study of war propaganda in 1930 he described the situation very differently, recalling through his own selective processes that "the editor of *The Fatherland* refused to submit to such control." In point of fact the German agents, often embarrassed by Viereck's excessive zeal in the German cause—particularly his attacks on Wilson—were undecided whether their best way of controlling

The Fatherland was to limit or to expand their financial support. The *World's* exposé, not Viereck's independence, ended the negotiations.[5]

Nevertheless, in the early days of the war Viereck worked closely with members of the propaganda cabinet in New York. He attended meetings two or three times a week with Albert, Dernburg, Fuehr, and others to advise the German Information Bureau on matters involving American psychology and the molding of American opinion. He was assigned to the "aggressive" group within the propaganda cabinet, furnishing editorial matter and giving public interviews on a variety of subjects—especially the shipment of munitions—that were of special interest to the pro-German strategists. In the fall of 1914 he provided personal services to the German officials as they began to assemble in New York, securing office space and staff personnel for them and arranging salary payments. He set up introductions to prominent German-Americans and acted as a "go-between with the German-American wealthy class in the city of New York and throughout the country." At the same time he kept a finger in several other propaganda operations, serving as a director of Jeremiah O'Leary's American Truth Society, a militant anti-English organization which received a $10,000 subvention from the German government, and using his many connections with pro-German partisans to distribute printed propaganda material. Defending himself later against charges that he had "sold . . . [his] favors for German gold," Viereck argued that "fighting, almost singlehanded, against the greatest combination of political power and finance ever aggregated in one camp, I turned for assistance to those to whose interest it was to help me. Is a reformer insincere because he accepts campaign contributions?"[6]

Despite a mounting complex of involvements in the pro-German cause, Viereck's chief vehicle of expression remained *The Fatherland.* In contrast to *The International* it provided a platform that could be used exclusively to air the international and domestic issues raised by the war. Strategically located in the news capital of the country, *The Fatherland* served as the primary English language outlet for the militant pro-German views that Viereck shared with many editors of German-language newspapers and leaders of the National German-American Alliance. His editorials were widely reprinted in local German-language papers throughout the country.[7]

The announced purposes of *The Fatherland* were threefold: to give the German side of the war story a fair hearing; to review the events of the war on a weekly basis, without bias or embellishment; and to expose the "misstatements and prejudices" prevalent in the American press. In its early issues *The Fatherland* hammered away at the alleged misrepresentations and distortions of the "Germanophobe press." A series of articles by German-American scholars such as Münsterberg, Julius Goebel, and A. B. Faust warned readers that foreign correspondents feeding the American press were overwhelmingly Anglophilic, that certain American editors were deliberately "malicious" in treating pro-German views, and that there existed a conspiracy of silence about German intentions and successes. *The Fatherland* attempted to right this wrong by running a weekly letter from Louis Viereck in Berlin and other less regular correspondence from prominent German intellectuals.[8]

Under Viereck's guidance the characteristic tone of the paper was belligerent and aggressive. A master of the art of insinuation, Viereck typically reprinted from a London newspaper a social note announcing that Secretary of State Bryan's daughter had just married an English army officer involved in war relief work: the intention was to imply that Bryan himself was personally enmeshed in the British cause. Nor was Viereck above taking direct and deliberate liberties with the truth. On one occasion he ran an article in which the English poet Aleister Crowley—posing as pro-British—admitted on behalf of his country that it had the lowest of vengeful motives in entering the war. The article, he alleged, was suppressed in England.

The paper recurrently exhorted German-Americans to political unity. Late in December 1914, coeditor Frederick F. Schrader wrote that if America did not become truly neutral then German-Americans must "pledge ourselves to stand together to visit political retribution upon those in our eyes guilty of such evasion and infraction of the ethics of neutrality, regardless of party." A cover page editorial on January 27, 1915, enjoined German-Americans to "Organize, Organize!" so as to "break the power of England upon our government" and to secure neutrality, an embargo on arms, the election of sympathetic public officials, the restoration of the German wireless service, and the end of Allied loan flotations. Despite these calls to unity, Viereck considered a similarly militant weekly, *The Vital Issue* (later *Issues and Events*), to be a rival publication, probably because it competed with him for German government funds.[9]

A series of favorable articles in *The Fatherland* on current German life was supplemented by Louis Viereck's letters depicting the kindness of German soldiers in France and the bravery of the Kaiser. The "facts" about the war, reported in a regular column by an unnamed "military strategist" (probably one of the German attachés), told of repeated German victories. These aspects of the paper strictly adhered to the German propaganda line. But the review of American press opinion reflected Sylvester Viereck's particular relationship to American life.

While Louis Viereck told a mass meeting in Germany of widespread German-American support for the cause of the fatherland, his son was blaming pro-Allied "hate sheets" for forcing the German-Americans to consolidate as an ethnic group and "go into the arena of politics . . . to beat [pro-English warmongers] at [their] own game." According to the younger Viereck, "We have no interest in the German government. In fact, the German government has often treated us shabbily. The German Empire as such is nothing to us. We are with America, right or wrong, at all times. We now propose to set America right . . . [Many] have ridiculed the hyphen. We shall make it a virtue." Sylvester Viereck's advocacy of the German cause was shaped by his peculiarly ambivalent attachment to America. His pro-German columns exalted the moral integrity of the Central Powers in an attempt to give the lie to English propaganda. But underneath their layers of purpose rested a fundamental commitment to America. "Celebrate George Washington's Birthday," exhorted an advertisement in the paper, "by subscribing to *The Fatherland*."[10]

Through 1915 *The Fatherland* increasingly sounded three leitmotifs with domestic political implications: anti-English propaganda, ethnic nationalism, and American neutrality. As part of its campaign against the British Empire, the paper dwelt on British seizure and detention of American ships and featured stories about Anglo-American conflict in the past. It urged a boycott of British goods and vigorously pursued pro-English partisans whether they were "sinister advisors of the President," agents of the English government poisoning the American press, or "pathetic" cases like former Harvard president Charles W. Eliot.[11]

The Fatherland sought to develop a sense of group solidarity among German-Americans. To this end it fixed on both parts of the hyphenate designation:

The love of Germans for the Fatherland is unquestioned, deep and abiding. Germany is the "Holy Land" of their faith and reverence, of undying affection and devotion. Loyalty to country is not merely fine sentiment to the German, it is a precious and universal privilege. This is not because of inherited nationalism or racial superstition. It is because of what Germany is and of what she has done . . . The German . . . rejoices in [Germany] because she represents to him the best in thought and action that has been attained among men.

German-Americans thus were reminded of their superiority to those who chose to "dissolve their racial characteristics and ideals in a solution of colorless New England Puritanism." Viereck argued that they made better Americans than their Anglophile compatriots because their sole interest in the war was to protect America through neutrality.[12]

Having incited ethnic nationalism among German-Americans, Viereck was quick to cash in on it. *The Fatherland* began to carry regular advertisements for enlarged photographs of German political and military heroes, offered a variety of German souvenirs for sale, and promoted the numerous pro-German books and pamphlets published by the Fatherland Corporation. Viereck pictured himself as a young David "trimming" Goliath. He announced that pro-Allied newspapers were losing circulation in New York City while pro-German papers were gaining. He attempted to secure lists of the German-

American clients of New York City banks, insurance companies, in order to mobilize protest against investments in Allied loans and munitions manufacturing.[13]

The policy and practice of American neutrality was a central concern of *The Fatherland* from its beginnings to the time of American entry into the war. Viereck addressed the subject from two different angles, concentrating a major portion of his energies on a muckraking critique of the "money trust" and on the alleged pro-English bias of the President and his cabinet. Joined in its efforts by a number of peace advocates, Viereck's paper hammered away at the "Morgan Ring." He raised the already clichéd charge that the ring ran Wall Street, adding that it wished to protect its investment in Allied war loans by ensuring Allied victory and hoped to profit even more by financing an American war effort. And he found evidence of a munitions trust that further compromised American neutrality by placing profit from the sale of munitions above all other considerations. So vehement were his diatribes that in July 1915 the *New York Tribune* accused Viereck and *The Fatherland* of inspiring a bodily assault on J. P. Morgan, Jr., by a mentally deranged man of German birth.[14]

Woodrow Wilson was the other major object of Viereck's hostility. Charging that "in every controversy that has arisen during the war the decisions of the Administration, no matter on what grounds they are based, have invariably been injurious to Germany," he laid the blame directly on the Chief Executive: "President Wilson is a modern Janus. His neutrality has two faces. One, smiling, apologetic, is turned to Great Britain; the other, scowling, malevolent, glowers upon the Germans." Although *The Fatherland* occasionally criticized Wilson for excessive firmness in dealing with the German government, it concentrated its fire on his weakness toward Great Britain, calling him "The Most Hyphenated American" because his background, education, and general orientation were English. Predicting a wholesale repudiation of Wilson's leadership by German-Americans, Viereck argued that they were concerned not so much with Wilson's anti-Germanism—they did not want to install a pro-German administration in Washington—as with his failure to act in the best interest of America. A poll of German-American news editors conducted by *The Fatherland* in June 1915 revealed that 92 percent of those who had previously supported Wilson now were hostile to him.[15]

Muckraking journalism and the thrust and parry of personal attack on Establishment leaders thus constituted one aspect of Viereck's quarrel with the conduct of American neutrality. He gave his support as well to another, more positive approach, which originated among the German-American leadership: the movement for an embargo on arms. He believed that the participants in the Washington Embargo Conference in January 1915 represented "moderate" German-American opinion. When Kuno Francke repudiated the ethnic separation implicit in the conference, Viereck bitterly criticized him. It was not that he disagreed with Francke on the inadvisability of a separate German-American party, he claimed, but rather that Francke harmed the pro-German cause by exposing it to public misunderstanding. In this sense, Francke was a renegade.[16]

Crusading on its own for arms embargo legislation, *The Fatherland* tapped a deep stratum of support among German-Americans. It seized upon a genuine issue in the public debate over neutrality and presented a reasonable case with conviction. But on the other great issue of the first war year—the sinking of the *Lusitania*—the instincts of its editor were out of step with those of other German-Americans. To begin with, Viereck participated in the decision of German Embassy officials to place a public advertisement in the *New York Times* warning Americans of the danger of traveling on the high seas. Just before the disaster occurred, he wrote an editorial in *The Fatherland* alluding to the sunken American tanker *Gulflight* and predicting that "before long, a large passenger ship like the *Lusitania*, carrying implements of murder to Great Britain, will meet with a similar fate." In the face of these coincidences it was hard to convince an outraged American public that he was not guilty of foreknowledge of the disastrous event. Instead of taking refuge in silence, Viereck joined the militants in defending the German action. He argued that the United States had neither legal nor moral grounds for protesting the sinking of the *Lusitania*, since it carried contraband as well as reserve troops. Furthermore, he charged that the American passengers on board the ship had been exploited to cover the true purposes of the voyage. He called for the immediate impeachment of Secretary of State Bryan on the ground that he had been negligent in protecting American lives after sufficient forewarning. After bitterly castigating Bryan for the language of the first *Lusitania* note, he had to reverse his stance quickly when Bryan himself broke with the administration over its second *Lusitania* note. He now hailed Bryan as a hero—and, perhaps self-consciously, extolled the German government for "not losing its head" in the first round of exchanges.[17]

Meanwhile, a broad representation of pro-German partisans rallied in support of the President's diplomatic conduct. Considering the frequency with which Viereck claimed to put American interests before all other considerations, he was strikingly remiss in failing to see either the serious threat that submarine warfare posed to American interests or the tragic dimension of the loss of lives involved. His own emotions were too closely bound up with his pro-Germanism for him to promote it consistently at a rational level. Nor did he serve the interests of the German government on all occasions. Together with other militant spokesmen of the German-language press and the National German-American Alliance, he supported the agitation for an arms embargo well after the German government admitted the legality of the arms trade, and publicly criticized the principle of war loans at the very time when the German government itself was trying to raise money in America.[18]

On August 11, 1915, *The Fatherland* celebrated its first anniversary with self-congratulations for the work of the year gone by and a firm resolve to extend its influence in the year ahead. In a public letter to Viereck, Münsterberg observed,

The voice of *The Fatherland* has been heard from the Atlantic to the Pacific. You have not expected that its message would be approved in the turmoil of this hysteric year. If the world around us had been ripe for approval, your courageous work would have been superfluous. You must be satisfied with the fact that everybody recognized your sincerity and strength . . . The time will come when true American patriots will see not only your sincerity, but also your wisdom, your fairness, and your great service to America's future.

But the celebration was short-lived. On August 15, the *New York World* covered half its front page with revelations of German undercover activity that deeply implicated the editor of *The Fatherland*. The story of the capture of a briefcase belonging to Dr. Heinrich Albert is typical of the bad luck and fumbling indiscretion that dogged German agents and of the way in which they were outmaneuvered at every turn by British Intelligence and the American Secret Service. On July 24, an agent followed Viereck and Dr. Albert aboard the Sixth Avenue El in New York. After Viereck got off the train, his companion apparently lost himself in reverie. Startled when the train drew into his station, he hastily made an exit, leaving behind a briefcase containing plans and proposals for German propaganda and sabotage activities. Shortly thereafter these documents were turned over to the *New York World*.

Although the documents contained no evidence of activity liable to prosecution, they did contain several wild and improbable schemes, which Albert claimed had come to him without solicitation and which he could not have taken seriously. The documents created a protracted sensation as the *World* launched their serial publication. Viereck and Albert protested vehemently that no lawbreaking had been exposed, only propaganda efforts aimed at securing fair play for Germany. Viereck's response to the revelation of his attempt to win additional financial support for *The Fatherland* from Albert was that he had done nothing incompatible with his American citizenship. *The Fatherland* had been a going concern before either Dernburg or Albert arrived in America, he argued, and their subsequent subventions neither influenced nor controlled its policies.[19]

British Intelligence scored another coup in August 1915 when it captured documents that included a letter implicating Austro-Hungarian Ambassador Constantin Dumba in fomenting strikes among Hungarian munitions workers in America, and detailing the involvement of German attachés Franz von Papen and Karl Boy-Ed in sabotage activities. Although they did not involve Viereck directly, these revelations too had the effect of discrediting his pro-German activities. He came to the defense of Count Dumba, arguing that the ambassador was only trying to get Austro-Hungarian nationals out of munitions work, and decried the ambassador's subsequent recall, claiming that he had been dismissed on a pretext because he was "too skill-ful."[20]

As the unsettling year of 1915 drew to a close, Viereck took steps to refurbish his "pro-American" position by supporting Wilson's version of preparedness, submitted to Congress in December. He drew solace from the prospect of German-American influence to be wielded in the forthcoming presidential nominations. It was "inconceivable," he announced, for any nominee to win the election in 1916 without the support of German-Americans. And despite the bad publicity he received for his connections with the German propaganda agency in New York, he continued to work in close cooperation with German agents. In March 1916, Viereck, Albert, and Fuehr jointly hired a Washington correspondent who sent Viereck weekly letters about "the probable policy" of the government and the plans and opinions of government officials. This information, reworked by Viereck, was printed in *The Fatherland* and ultimately transmitted to Berlin. In addition, Viereck and Bernard Ridder, president of the New York *Staatszeitung*, jointly distributed a semiweekly letter offering "confidential" information to the editors of the German language press.[21]

Washington and the contest for the presidency drew increasing attention from *The Fatherland* after the party conventions in June 1916. Just prior to the Republican convention, Viereck and Schrader announced their opposition to Roosevelt. But their pleasure in the nomination of Charles Evans Hughes was cut short when Roosevelt mounted a hyphen-baiting campaign on Hughes's behalf. At the same time, Bernstorff put pressure on Viereck to abandon his attacks on Wilson. Despairing of the "rabid" German-Americans, Bernstorff argued that their virulent assaults on the President embarrassed him in his dealings with the State Department. Viereck softened his stand to such an extent that some were convinced *The Fatherland* actually supported Wilson. But deep-seated hostility toward the Chief Executive finally prevailed for Viereck as for most militant pro-German partisans. He later wrote that "I was sorry for the Ambassador, but I could not permit my regard for him to interfere

with my civic duty." Despite the Republican candidate's refusal to commit himself on the issues of most concern to him,
Viereck gave his support to Hughes.[22]

On the day of the election Viereck expressed supremely
hedged confidence in the power of the German-American vote:
"Whoever is elected, it has been a triumph for German-
Americans. If Mr. Wilson is defeated, the hyphen is the hatchet
that has decapitated his hopes. If Mr. Hughes is defeated, he is
defeated because he permitted his Machiavellian adviser,
Theodore Roosevelt, to drive the German-Americans into the
Wilson camp." The major issue in the election, as Viereck saw
it, was whether or not Americans would allow Great Britain to
blacklist their merchants, to loot their mails, and to block their
commerce with neutrals and their noncontraband trade with
belligerents. It was, of course, entirely wishful thinking to
imagine that this was the central issue. Viereck so perceived
the election out of a need to stir his own indignation and thus
keep dominant the hostile component of his adjustment to
America. His political alienation found constant expression
through the first two years of the war in the belligerent tone of
The Fatherland and in freeswinging assaults against America's
fealty to the British Empire, America's money and munitions
trusts, the American press, and the Anglophile President. He
approached all issues aggressively. Rather than urge leniency
toward Germany on Wilson in the *Lusitania* crisis, he attacked
Wilson for being soft with England. On the day of the 1916
election, when most Americans responded to the widespread
desire to keep out of the war, Viereck dwelt on England's aggressiveness and spoke of "decapitating" Wilson's hopes. His
need to pick a fight expressed itself too in fantasies of intellectual and moral potency. It was he, he claimed, who most effectively championed the cause of the underdogs at home and
abroad, and it was he who singlehandedly cut the pro-English
press in New York City down to size. He believed that he
could take Albert's money and hold Bernstorff's influence at
bay because he was fundamentally incorruptible. His dreams
of German-American political power—with himself as leader—
appeared in vengeful threats to punish enemies of the pro-
German cause. Once the results of the 1916 election were in, he

found it impossible to relinquish his belief in German-American power and, in a quick reversal of position, argued that the German-Americans themselves had elected Wilson in response to the Democratic slogan "he kept us out of war."[23]

After the election as before, Viereck used every device he could to stir his readers to political activism. Early in February 1917, just after the United States broke off diplomatic relations with Germany, Viereck mounted a special plea to his readers to wire the President and members of Congress on behalf of peace rather than to remain quiet in the face of this potentially tragic turn of events. Through February he experimented with new names for his weekly paper in an effort to find the right words to convey the Americanness of its position and to avoid misunderstanding as to the priority of its allegiances. *The New World* lasted for only one issue, because it was discovered that a Catholic periodical published in Chicago had the same name. Next he tried *Viereck's New World,* and settled finally upon *The American Weekly.* At the same time he changed the name of his book-distributing agency from The Fatherland Corporation to Viereck's Library. This agency employed about eighteen traveling salesmen who carried booklists of some variety, including Shakespeare, among their essentially pro-German war books. Later it was alleged that these salesmen functioned as distributors of German propaganda, that they were not self-supporting as salesmen, and that sixteen of them were aliens.[24]

Late in February, Viereck's paper carried an article by William Ellery Leonard that constituted its last vigorous avowal of a strictly pro-German position. Leonard argued that pro-German sentiment at this time was in the best American interest because it aimed to keep America out of the conflict; pro-Allied sentiment, on the other hand, would give the country over to war. On March 1, publication of the Zimmermann telegram—a message from the German Foreign Secretary proposing an alliance with Mexico and future territorial spoils if war broke out between Germany and the United States—evoked indignant disbelief from Viereck and the editors of the German-language press. He declared it to be a British forgery: "It is impossible to believe that the German foreign secretary would place his name under such a preposterous document." When Alfred Zimmermann himself confirmed the telegram, Viereck realized the severity of the blow that had been dealt to pro-Germanism:

The friends of Germany lie on no bed of roses, and not all the thorns are planted there by the Allies. If the German government allies itself with our foes, then, no matter how earnestly we may be convinced of the fundamental justice of the German cause on the original issue, we have come to the parting of the ways . . . When Germany, even tentatively, proposes an alliance against the United States to Mexico, she deals a cruel blow to Americans of German descent.

Yet he went on to argue that Germany had every right to preserve herself first and that the intent of the telegram was to "provide a counterstroke to meet a declaration of war" from an increasinglly bellicose United States government.[25]

After the United States formally declared war on April 6, 1917, Viereck continued to avoid condemning Germany and to dwell on the original sin of the Allies in starting the war. German-Americans, he wrote, would enter the war on the side of America and not in support of the Allies: "We shall . . . register a dissenting opinion, and then prepare ourselves to serve our country to the best of our abilities . . . under no obligation to include the Allies in our prayers." His support of American involvement was qualified by the cluster of critical opinions and interpretations of the nature and origin of the war that had characterized his pro-Germanism. At the moment when a final commitment to America was required of him, he chose to emphasize that his allegiance did not include a dependency component—in the guise of either Anglophilia or unqualified patriotism. Less militant pro-German sympathizers at this point developed their own rationalizations of support for the war in terms of a distinction drawn between the worthy German people and their "evil" rulers.[26]

Viereck continued to think of himself as the leader of a group whose special interests persisted into the postdeclaration period. In May 1917 he announced the formation of Viereck's Agricultural Bureau for the Unemployed and solicited donations from his readers in order to help find farm work for unemployed aliens. In a letter to his parents in Germany he boasted that "in this way [Germans and Austrians can be] . . . of the greatest aid to the United States without undertaking any kind of work which, from the point of view of the Father- land, can be construed as lending aid to the enemy." He also set up Viereck's Legal Information Bureau, which offered free legal advice on subjects related to war conditions.[27]

Again pleading the special interest of German-Americans, Viereck repeatedly asked that they be granted the right of con- scientious objection to military service. They would be glad to serve, he asserted, as farm labor, in the Red Cross, in home or coastal defense, or in Mexican patrols, but should not be re- quired to serve at the war front. Basing his position on the men- tal anguish that conscription caused German-Americans, he cited stories of suicide attempts by young German-American men faced with the prospect of fighting their German kin. He opened the pages of *The American Weekly* to a discussion of the issue of German-American exemption, claiming the support of such public men as Senator Charles Thomas of Colorado, Congressman William L. LaFollette of Washington, and Wil- liam Jennings Bryan, as well as leading German-American fig- ures such as Theodore Sutro, A. B. Faust, Kuno Francke, J. A. Walz, and August Heckscher. According to one unfriendly observer, Viereck boasted that he had arranged for an exemp- tion resolution that Congressman Frederick A. Britten of Illi- nois planned to introduce in the spring of 1917. The proposal was widely criticized in the American press, and a number of irritated German-Americans, among them Bernard Ridder, be- lieved that it reflected exceedingly poor judgment.[28]

Viereck carried a number of his predeclaration themes into the war period, finding evil in the actions of Great Britain, criticizing American vassalage to England, and recalling the virtues of German life. He also published feature stories on prominent isolationists and explained that the new slogan of his weekly paper, "America first and America only," meant that "we are for America, but not for the Allies." But increasingly he dwelt on the persecutions and restrictions of free speech suffered by German-Americans. Dramatizing himself as an ex- ample, he continually reprinted news items that abused him.

The idea was to show how far above insult he was—and to revel in the notoriety he had achieved.[29]

The American Weekly experienced little censorship; only one issue was withdrawn from circulation under pressure from the Post Office Department because of an article criticizing "entangling alliances" and describing Wilson as a hypocrite. But Viereck himself was expelled from the Authors League in July 1918, and from the New York Athletic Club in August 1918. After the passage of the Espionage Act in June 1917, his offices were raided and copies of the pro-German publications of Viereck's Library confiscated. In April 1918, when Senator Gilbert M. Hitchcock of Nebraska came up for the chairmanship of the Senate Foreign Relations Committee, a letter he had written to "My Dear Viereck" in connection with plans for an arms embargo was used to discredit him. The Deputy Attorney General of New York State and the congressional committee investigating the National German-American Alliance documented Viereck's financial and advisory connections with agents of the German government, giving rise to a "campaign of unprecedented violence" against him in the spring and summer of 1918.[30]

New York Deputy Attorney General Albert Becker revealed that in addition to the more than $100,000 paid to Viereck before 1917 by German and Austrian officials, he had collected over $100,000 through his Agricultural Labor Relief Bureau. According to Becker, Viereck had agents traveling through the country raising money on a 25 to 40 percent commission basis. These agents' records showed gross receipts of over $100,000. Becker charged that only a "handful" of aliens were actually aided by the bureau and that most of the money went into Viereck's pocket. According to the testimony of May Binion, Viereck's secretary, he took $700 per month in salary as head of the organization and paid $400 to $500 per week to *The American Weekly* from bureau funds for advertisements. She also contradicted Viereck's claim that he had assisted in relocating five thousand aliens by reporting that he "rarely had the people who wanted jobs." Viereck denied these charges but could produce no records in his defense. He did admit, however, that $26,000 of the money raised was used to publish books and pamphlets. Despite evidence that he had personally drawn off large sums, Viereck insisted that the bureau operated at a loss.[31]

An investigator for the congressional subcommittee conducting hearings on the National German-American Alliance charged that Viereck's bureau was actually a refurbished version of one founded earlier by Hans Liebau to oversee the withdrawal of German aliens from war industries. It was also claimed that the Alien Women's Relief Bureau, which Viereck had established through the offices of *The American Weekly*, was a front for the continuation of German information-gathering services. Later Viereck attempted to ridicule these charges by reporting that some people believed his Agricultural Bureau functioned as a training center for spies. But the clear indication was that he had been devious in writing a four-page declaration of loyalty to Wilson on April 17, 1917; that he was far from "through" with the Germans and had not "burned his bridges," as he claimed, once the United States entered the war. A "Mama and Papa" letter which Viereck wrote to his parents in May 1917 was introduced into the hearings: its compromising statements included one recommending that the elder Viereck, now living in Germany, call upon Albert or Fuehr if he needed any help because both of the German officials were "under obligation" to the younger Viereck. He was, of course, swaggering, but a number of newspapers mistook the swagger as evidence of a continuing and sinister liaison with the German government.[32]

The congressional subcommittee heard testimony linking the Alliance to liquor interests and alleging that its leaders fostered racial separatism and foreign allegiance among German-Americans. Having worked closely with Alliance leaders, Viereck was tarred by the general charges. Following a precipitous decline in branch membership, the National Alliance voted to disband in the spring of 1918. Viereck began to feel seriously the effects of adverse publicity. His papers were boycotted at newsstands; his verse was dropped from anthologies and his name from *Who's Who*. He allegedly was refused life insurance by forty different companies, and his writing commissions dwindled. He claimed that his employees were approached by investigators and tempted "to bear false witness."

In Mount Vernon, where he moved into his father-in-law's home with his wife and two young sons, a real estate broker sent a letter to the local newspaper saying that the community did not want a resident who thought America was barbaric and the Kaiser a hero. According to Viereck, an angry mob menaced the family in August and caused him to flee into hiding in New York City, leaving his family behind. He registered at the Hotel Savoy, only to be asked to leave after one week because of complaints from other guests. This misadventure was repeated at the Hotel Netherland, and he finally took refuge again in Mount Vernon. While in hiding he requested police protection for visits to his family. During the first few years of the war Viereck had taken delight in the notoriety accruing from his unpopular pro-German position. In 1917 his pleasure stiffened to obstinacy. He wrote to his anxious mother, "I can take jolly care of myself. I can snap my fingers at . . . [my persecutors], because I am independent intellectually and financially."[33]

But Viereck was deeply affected by his expulsion from the Poetry Society of America. Ostensibly he had quit his career as a poet after the publication of *The Candle and the Flame* in 1912. Nevertheless he published a third volume of poetry, *Songs of Armageddon,* which met with a frigid reception in 1916. The volume contained three groups of poems: love lyrics, memorials, and political pieces. The latter group, praising the German people and their Kaiser and charging the United States with an ugly betrayal of its German-American citizens and a silent complicity in the war, stirred considerable hostility. Where the book was not received with contumely and abuse it was ignored, to Viereck's chagrin. Later he blamed "the war psychosis" for its reception, but he confessed that his wartime experiences destroyed his ability to write poetry by straining his self-confidence and causing him to lose faith in his own immediate responses to the world—responses on which his poetry was based. Yet he was not prepared to abandon either the psychological autonomy or the social status among American peers

that his successful career as a poet had won for him. Membership in the Poetry Society had been central to his identification
of himself as a significant figure in American literary culture.
He saw little difference among his roles as literary insurgent,
social critic, and political rebel, and he could not understand
why the two earlier roles had been rewarded with sophisticated
appreciation while the last met with implacable disapproval.
He was prepared to forgive popular anti-Germanism as a wartime aberration and expected a quick restoration of his stature
on the American cultural scene. He had, after all, been a
founding father of the Poetry Society and nursed a "filial affection" for its president, Edward J. Wheeler. This double rejection—of his own fatherhood, and by an admired father figure
—"lent an emotional color to [his] quarrel with the Poetry Society" that seemed disproportionate to the event itself.[34]

After the public disclosure of Viereck's involvement in German propaganda, the Executive Committee of the Poetry Society requested his resignation at the behest of forty of the
society's members. Viereck refused to leave; instead he demanded that the Executive Committee itself resign and ran
short items in *The American Weekly* heaping ridicule upon the
society leadership. He was encouraged in his antics by a small
group of sympathizers within the society. Shaemas O'Sheel led
an ill-starred insurrection on Viereck's behalf at a full meeting
of the society in November 1918, but he could muster no more
than six votes to condemn the action of the Executive Committee. A subsequent vote of the membership showed an overwhelming majority in favor of expulsion. Viereck claimed that
a "band of literary war profiteers"—referring to Hermann Hagedorn's Vigilantes—engineered the whole affair. "I am con-
soled," he declared, "by the fact that our greatest American
poets, Edgar Allan Poe and Walt Whitman, were not members
of the literary coteries of their day." His primary concern was
to present himself as the object of persecution even as an
American poet.[35]

Public repudiation of the German-American Alliance and the
threat of suppression of the German-language press broke
down the centers of German-American organization. The arrest and detention of German aliens spread fear within the com-

munity—a fear considerably enhanced by private and quasi-official acts of violence. For German-Americans, the experience was chastening. Straining to prove their loyalty to America, they disengaged themselves from public controversy and gave their support to the President.

Viereck, too, was deviled by these concerns. Whatever emotional and material opportunities the war offered him, the years from 1914 to 1919 exacted a toll. He had been a young bachelor before the war, with a wide circle of friends and admirers, a respectable position as a poet, and the prospect of a new calling as a businessman-journalist. After the war he was a middle-aged husband, the father of two small children, with an unsavory reputation and a shattered career. Many former friends and associates severed connections with him because of his wartime activities. For almost three years he had spoken to many of the concerns that weighed upon German-American citizens. But the virtual collapse of the German-American community by 1918 left him without a significant audience.[36]

Separation from his parents was a constant source of anxiety —especially when, after 1917, communication became difficult. In February 1918, he wrote to them begging Laura Viereck to keep a diary of "her feelings and thoughts," which he might hope to read at a later date and thus not lose that sense of continual intimacy with her which he held so dear. At the war's end he could expect to reestablish this intimacy. But the reestablishment of his status in America seemed (at least to him) to require a lifetime of self-justification.[37]

8 . . .
PEACE AND THE
SECOND COMING OF WAR

On August 14, 1918, Viereck published the last issue of his paper as a weekly. Henceforward it would continue as *Viereck's American Monthly*. He cited by way of explanation the increased costs of labor and material as well as the lack of advertising. By 1918 the paper was operating at a loss. Obviously its financial base was weakened by the withdrawal of German funds and the loss of subscribers after America's entry into the war. But for nine more years Viereck persisted in his attempt to be counted as a leader of the disintegrated German-American community and in his war-born habit of using political symbols to express his emotional conflicts.[1]

Several months after the Armistice, Viereck was confidently professing pro-Germanism once again. The *American Monthly* was pro-German, he asserted, where American interests were not involved, but for America when American and German interests were in conflict. He proposed a Deutschland Irredenta Committee which would look to the redemption of lands taken from Germany in the war settlement. Playing to the one issue which continued to evoke widespread sympathy among German-Americans, he organized a Feed Central Europe Department through which food might be purchased and sent to starving Germans. The food enterprise, by Viereck's own admission, turned a handy profit on commissions from wholesale grocery houses.[2]

One measure of the fear and disarray of German-Americans in the postwar period was their notable passivity in the public debate over the peace settlement and the League of Nations. Viereck's was among the few German-American voices to protest against the Versailles Treaty. From 1920 through 1924 his

American Monthly worked over the old issue of the war's causes and the new one of its settlement. Viereck argued that Wilson was guilty of plotting American entry into the war from the very beginning; he ran an article by Edmund von Mach claiming that Germany had not lost the war on the battlefield but had voluntarily surrendered because of Wilson's false peace promises; he carried anti-British pieces by Shaemas O'Sheel and others and lashed out against the corruption of the French press. Beginning in April 1921, he attempted to exploit American racism by complaining that the French army used "negroid" troops in its occupation of the Rhine. He alleged that the French government condoned fraternization between black men and white women in order to demoralize the Germans. He printed an inflammatory picture of racial mixing and reported on meetings held to protest this "Horror on the Rhine."[3]

In 1920 Viereck refused to print an article by his father criticizing German anti-Semitism, on the ground that it would not be seemly for the *American Monthly* to publicize Germany's delinquencies. His major concern now was to combat the disunity of the German-American community. Criticism of Germany, however well founded, would defeat his purpose. Rejecting another article by his father, this time about the ex-Kaiser, Viereck explained that it was not favorable enough. Perhaps the German people were not ready to restore Wilhelm II, he suggested, but the readers of the *American Monthly* were.[4]

The disruption of the German-American community threatened Viereck. He believed that he had been "almost deified by the pro-German minority" during the war, and now struggled to hold his "following" together. He did so in two ways: by keeping vivid the memory of persecutions suffered during the war and stirring indignation through sensational revelations, and by promoting a revival of group organizations and appealing to the interests that German-Americans continued to share. According to him, one of the causes of German-American disunity was factionalism among its leadership. He himself fell into a bitter quarrel with Bernard Ridder, editor of the New York *Staatszeitung*, over the minor issue of whom to support for a vacant ambassadorship to Austria. He argued that it was Ridder who tried to scuttle a united front among German-

Americans, preferring to see leadership devolve on German-language newspaper editors rather than a developing central organization. In his jealousy of Ridder he accused him of being a "professional German-American," one who used his affiliation for his own purposes without being pro-German, and of informing on German-Americans to the Secret Service and the Justice Department.[5]

In February 1922 Viereck was called to testify at hearings connected with a $500,000 libel suit brought by Mayor William Hale Thompson against the Chicago *Tribune*. Thompson claimed that he had been falsely linked with German propaganda activities. In the course of the hearings many of the old stories about Viereck's financial dealings with the Germans were aired again. He seized the opportunity to defend his propaganda work during the war in the pages of the *American Monthly,* and to recapitulate his exposure to slander and character assassination. He said of *The Fatherland:* "Our little magazine was the rod upon which every storm of jingoism and anti-German hysteria discharged its lightning."

But Viereck could not live entirely in the past, though memory stirred his wrath and served up images of himself as a mighty David holding the forces of evil at bay. For a while he dwelt on the vindication of victimized German-Americans. There was the example of Edmund von Mach's lawsuit against the Macmillan Company—settled for damages out of court in 1921—for reneging on an agreement to publish a collection of official diplomatic documents relating to the war's outbreak. There was also the case of Henry Albers, who was arrested in 1918 for expressing pro-German opinions under the influence of alcohol. Under the Sedition Act, Albers was sentenced to two years in prison and fined $10,000. In April 1921 the United States Supreme Court set aside the lower court decision and dismissed the sentence, whereupon the *American Monthly* took occasion to proclaim the injured virtue of all German-Americans.[6]

But old grievances and new vindications would not suffice to rebuild German-American power and position, as Viereck well realized. In 1919 he became one of the founders of the Steuben Society, which championed the civil rights of German-

Americans. Its membership, according to Viereck, was open to those individuals who "never betrayed or denied their race." In 1920, Viereck and von Mach tried to organize a nationwide Committee of 96 to mobilize German-American political opinion. In 1921 he became a member of the Executive Board of the newly formed (and Chicago-based) German-American Citizens League, the chairman of its eastern branch, and the editor of its official English-language organ. The Citizens League intended to function as a national *Bund*, tying together other lesser organizations much as the National German-American Alliance had done. Its constitution called for efforts to revive German language usage and the dissemination of *Kultur*. But the special goal of the new organization was to involve its members in American politics. At a preelection convention in 1920—which Viereck attended—the league threw its support to Harding because of his opposition to the League of Nations. At the time Viereck wrote, "Between Harding and Cox we are for Harding. We do not hate Cox. We do not love Harding. But we mean to repudiate in no uncertain terms the party tainted by Wilsonism." Soon afterward Viereck privately confessed that he himself preferred Eugene Debs, for "as a man and as a fighter" Debs was superior to both of the regular party candidates.[7]

The *American Monthly* launched a variety of appeals to German-Americans in the hope of stimulating their shared interests. A regular column was supplied by Louis Viereck with notes, culled from papers across the United States, of particular interest to the German-American community. Readers were urged to boycott English and French goods, support the move for full restitution of property seized by the Alien Property Custodian, and protest against the relief work directed by Herbert Hoover—whose promise of eight million dollars for German relief had never materialized, according to Viereck. But such causes were not likely to draw a substantial response from a community heartily sick of the war and its domestic political repercussions.[8]

In 1921 Viereck began to launch other, less political appeals. He offered the *American Monthly* as a collection agency for funds to feed needy German babies and nursing mothers. He organized the Fatherland Freight Forwarding Department to send small packages to Germany and Austria by parcel post; Viereck's Wireless Service to purchase combination food packages for delivery in Central Europe; and the Fatherland Import Department through which his readers could aid Germany by purchasing imported gifts—including German police dogs with pure pedigrees. He continued to purvey books on subjects of interest to German-Americans and offered tie-in subscription deals with magazines published in Germany. He became, in his own phrase, a "professional German-American," for he was not above running articles predicting an industrial boom in postwar Germany at the same time that he operated an investment and security counseling service that recommended German industrial bonds. And his attacks on Hoover's European Relief Council were featured alongside advertisements for his own relief agencies.[9]

In 1919 Viereck published an extraordinary little book, *Roosevelt: A Study in Ambivalence*, ostensibly a study of Theodore Roosevelt but in actuality an extended apologia. As a personal confession it is notably lacking in any sense of culpability. It is, in fact, an act of aggression. In his thirty-nine-page introduction (the text itself ran only an additional ninety-two pages) Viereck spoke of a conspiracy by an "invisible government" of writers and reviewers to ignore and discredit him. What, he asked, was the source of this rancor? Recounting the many charges hurled at him in the course of his career, he dismissed them all. Had he defied too many conventions as a writer of verse and prose? Certainly not: "My sins against Mrs. Grundy are not held against me. Mrs. Grundy secretly loves me. She absolves me because she does not understand me." He saw no reason why his involvement in politics should have diminished his standing in the literary community, nor why his accepting German money for a cause he believed in should have disturbed anyone. It was not his pro-Germanism that brought him disrepute, for he was pro-German from the beginning of his career and no one had ever held it against him. The crux of the matter was his Americanism, his firm insistence on the independence of America from Great Britain. The "silent government" that now dubbed him a heretic held the

interests of England above those of America and bitterly resented his support for "America only." To the "vengeance of
the Invisible Governors" he attributed the rejections and persecutions he had sustained after 1917: "Officials were found
who, prostituting their brief authority for private political gain,
poisoned the public mind, not by prosecuting me—there was
no basis for prosecution—but by publishing piecemeal the distorted testimony of dismissed and discredited agents, of scoun-
drels and scalawags. Bureaus . . . burnt midnight electricity
at the expense of the public to encompass my ruin." But despite the slanders heaped upon him he had, like the martyred
Hugo Münsterberg, stuck with his principles to the end.[10]

Viereck then turned to a psychoanalytic interpretation of
Theodore Roosevelt. The format was a convenient one for re-
playing some of the major issues of the war period, and this
time coming out victorious. More important, it provided Viereck with an opportunity to project his own psychological condition onto his subject. He centered his analysis on Roosevelt's
"bipolarity" and emotional ambivalence:

He was at once the Progressive and the Reactionary. He was Sophist and
Rough Rider, Simple Simon and Machiavelli, rolled into one. He was
more English than George V., more imperialistic than the *London Times;*
yet he hated the English from the depth of his heart, he despised them,
and, to use his own phrase, he patronized them. He was at once the
faithful Patroclus and the treacherous Apache. He loved the Germans
and bitterly denounced them. His attitude toward Wilhelm II was
equally ambivalent. He admired the Hohenzollern, yet had no kind word
for him . . . We cannot explain [Roosevelt] without the theory of ambivalence.

Viereck argued that the deep ambivalence he himself felt toward Roosevelt was a function of the object rather than the
subject: "Every popular hero is both hated and loved by his
followers."[11]

His personal relationship with Roosevelt, Viereck revealed,
went far back into his past. His father had written about
Roosevelt's student year in Germany and had been an ardent
supporter of Roosevelt in the early days of Progressivism. He
himself at first had professed a youthful cynicism toward
Roosevelt's "championship of the Simple Life." But even then

his "dislike . . . arose . . . from a spirit of filial opposition."
Later on he warmed considerably toward the Rough Rider.
Roosevelt complimented him on his verse and lent a hand in
raising funds for the conversion of *Der Vorkaempfer* into a
German edition of *Current Literature*. In those days—or at
least on those occasions—Roosevelt appeared to have strong
pro-German and anti-English attitudes. Only through watching
and listening to Roosevelt, Viereck claimed, did it first dawn
upon him that "antipathy against Great Britain [was] . . . the
quintessence of Americanism."[12]

A fervent Progressive in 1912, Viereck continued to enjoy
the friendship of Roosevelt until irreconcilable differences of
opinion over the war intervened. Knowing that Roosevelt could
never be neutral about anything, Viereck expected him to
champion the German cause. His disappointment was profound. He complained bitterly to Roosevelt that "in spite of
your reputed friendship for the Kaiser, you did not have one
word to say for him personally when this obscene campaign
of vilification was started in the American press." Roosevelt,
annoyed at the charge of hypocrisy, replied,

You made it evident that your whole heart is with the country of your
preference, for Germany, and not with the country of your adoption, the
United States. Under the circumstances you are not a good citizen here
. . . As far as I am concerned, I admit no divided allegiance in United
States citizenship; and my views of hyphenated-Americans are those
which were once expressed by the Emperor himself, when he said . . .
that he understood what Germans were; and he understood what Americans were; but he had neither understanding of nor patience with those
who called themselves German-Americans.

Viereck's rejoinder was that under the circumstances his Germanism did not divide but doubled his Americanism, for "the
interests of this country are identical in this present conflict
with the interests of Germany. They are not identical with the
interests of England which now . . . has actually declared
war on American commerce."[13]

More than a year after this heated exchange, Viereck wrote
to Roosevelt again criticizing the latter's course, and offering
the advice that "those who oppose you now are probably better friends and citizens than those who . . . [have led] you

up a blind alley." Much later Viereck was to imagine that "my indignation solidified the German element against TR. The recognition that the German vote was lost to him deprived Theodore Roosevelt of the nomination in 1916. He now became my relentless opponent . . . he frequently attacked me, though suppressing my identity, for fear of making the welkin ring with my name." In the last chapter of his Roosevelt "study" he represented the ex-President as having inspired the persecution of German-Americans with "fanatical zeal" and "brushed the skirts of disloyalty" through his irresponsible words and deeds. Possessed by hatred, "the windows of his mind . . . filled with distorted shapes," Roosevelt ceased to be himself. Now Viereck became compassionate:

When I realized that he was blinded in one eye, when I remembered my glimpse of his pain-wracked face, I understood. Tortured and disappointed, grief-stricken by the loss of his son, goaded by false friends, his body in perpetual anguish, his mind in perpetual irritation, TR was himself no more . . . The preacher of race conciliation transformed himself into the Grand Inquisitor of Americanism, smelling treason everywhere, casting the eye of suspicion in every direction.[14]

Such was the picture of Theodore Roosevelt in Viereck's mind: a man bigger than life, with high spirits to match; a man of bipolar interests and contradictory emotions, like Viereck himself; a man with whom, before the war, he had shared a definition of Americanism as incorporating hostility toward England and admiration of Germany. When Roosevelt rejected Germanism as incompatible with Americanism, Viereck's response to the conflict thereby created for him was typically ambivalent: "I hated and I loved him, as Catullus did his mistress. His feelings towards me must have been equally contradictory. He was both my generous friend and my relentless foe. If I attacked him bitterly the arrow intended for him entered my heart. Praising him, I spoke in strident accents, in order to drown the secret misgivings, the latent hostility, the hidden distrust in my bosom.[15]

Viereck's study of Roosevelt clearly was designed to afford him psychological release. It had also the larger purpose of reviving his good name and position in postwar America. The last twelve pages of the book were devoted to favorable reviews of his prewar works of poetry and prose. His reputation as a writer, he argued, must be held separate from his involvement in politics. It was, after all, as a poet that his American status had been established and legitimated. By reviving that identity he hoped to reestablish his respectability. At the same time he was not prepared to abandon his conception of himself as a leader of the hyphenated community. The book summed up Viereck's attempt to vindicate his dual national allegiance on the ground that neither loyalty excluded the other.

To reestablish his repute as a poet he brought out two pamphlet collections of his earlier work, instructing his readers that in its time his poetry was "the lyric battering ram of the New Movement in American letters." Ineffectual as this attempt may have been, Viereck's public reputation benefited considerably in the twenties from disillusionment with the war and from the growing vogue for revisionist literature—which he featured in the *American Monthly*—on the origins of the conflict. He later appeared to some as a determined war resister who "refused to be stampeded by the hysterical propaganda of that time." Gradually, opportunities revived for his journalistic talents—especially his flair for sensationalism—and he became a popular writer for the *Saturday Evening Post,* the Hearst papers, and *Liberty* magazine, which he served as an advisory editor for ten years. He specialized in writing anti-Communist articles and interviewing prominent European figures.[16]

In 1928 he "aided" the Empress Hermine, who had married the Kaiser in 1926, in telling her life story. Together they produced a sentimental romanticization of the ex-Kaiser's marriage and exile. Out of his magazine writings he compiled books about the war and its heroes and, in 1930, a collection of interviews with thirty-two great men of Europe. In the same year he published *Spreading Germs of Hate,* a study of German, English, and American propaganda efforts during the war. Stressing "the authenticity of my data and the impartiality of my presentation," Viereck insisted on the essential Americanness of his point of view. Yet his criticisms of the German effort were merely technical. Defining propaganda as the attempt to put across a point of view regardless of the truth, he argued that there was no real German propaganda in World War I because

German agents were concerned exclusively with presenting the "facts." Written in the third person, the book suggested that its author had achieved an impartial position above the passions of battle. In his preface he stated that

> I fought for what I deemed the right.
> I saw the Truth. I was her knight.
> My foemen, too, were thus aflame,
> Blind chessmen in the obscure game
> Of some malign divinity.
> Now, with unfolding eyes, we see
> The paradox of every fight,
> That both were wrong and both were right,
> That friend is foe and foe is friend,
> And nothing matters in the end.

Viereck's "impartiality" consisted of admitting opposing views equally and uncritically. He apparently equated moral objectivity with moral neutrality.[17]

By 1928 Viereck seems to have abandoned his ambition to become a German-American leader. In the first place, the wartime community seemed unrecoverable. Its few self-conscious survivors did not turn to him for guidance. Viereck had seen in Robert LaFollette's 1924 presidential candidacy an opportunity for German-Americans to press their grievances. But his vigorous advocacy seems to have exerted little influence. Indeed, his celebrated intimacy with the German Kaiser irritated and embarrassed even those stalwarts of the Steuben Society who shared his commitment to LaFollette.

After 1924 he tried to broaden the circulation of the *American Monthly* by introducing a wider range of material with a less intensely German focus. But the result was only to discourage his old German readership without attracting a new following. In 1927 he sold the journal, declaring in his parting editorial that his battle for fair play had been won and that he wished to return from politics to his original calling, the literary life. At this time he was already making more money as a foreign correspondent and feature writer for the Hearst, MacFadden, and Lorimer publications than from his own journal.[18]

The next year Viereck published the best known and most widely sold of his creative writings. He had conceived the idea behind *My First Two Thousand Years: The Autobiography of the Wandering Jew* as far back as 1914. He dabbled with it through the war years but was dissatisfied with his partial manuscript and unable to bring it to completion. Essentially, the book was to be a psychoanalytic interpretation of Man. It would chronicle the significant and recurrent experiences of Eternal Man through the course of human history, revealing his attempt to surmount mortality and his search for an ideal fulfillment in bisexuality. Cartaphilus, the Eternal Man of the final version, is a gifted Jew, a contemporary of Christ, who has reached a stage in life (at the age of thirty) where nothing has meaning or purpose for him. He is cursed with immortality for taunting Jesus, and not until he perceives the task of finding an ideal synthesis of the male and female principles does life take on significance for him. The book consists of a series of loosely knit episodes recounting Cartaphilus' varied sexual adventures and his search through history for his ideal. He is presented as an image of the truly sophisticated modern man who understands and readily explores the female component in his own nature.[19]

For several years Viereck tried unsuccessfully to interest publishers in the project and to enlist the aid of a collaborator. In 1924 he finally met the man who would bring the book to fruition. Paul Eldridge was a few years younger than Viereck. He had lived abroad, was a teacher of Romance languages in New York, and had written minor verse, fiction, and plays. The two men formed an intense friendship. According to Viereck, he was " 'the father' in our intellectual relationship"; Viereck's were the "emotional and intellectual experiences," which Eldridge brought into focus and articulated. Their relationship was a critical device for releasing Viereck's creative energies, and he thought of the book as truly the "child" of its authors. "Somehow," he wrote, the book "needed a double parentage." *My First Two Thousand Years* was Viereck's first creative endeavor since the abortive *Songs of Armageddon* in 1916, and he pinned great hopes on its publication. Despite poor reviews the public was excited by its pornographic content. It was a bestseller in 1928, reached the half million sales mark in 1929,

and by 1930 had gone through twelve printings and was being
translated into several languages.[20]

Encouraged by this success, Viereck turned in 1931 to a
more direct contemplation of his inner passions. *My Flesh and
Blood: A Lyric Autobiography* consists of selections from his
earlier published verse, with elaborate annotations of an autobiographical nature. Part of its purpose was to present himself
as a poet of stature and historical importance. But it was fundamentally an exercise in self-exposure. Under the guise of self-
psychoanalysis, Viereck exploited the facts and feeling of his
private life to the point of exhibitionism. The primary image he
held of himself was that of a masculine poet preoccupied with
the transformation of libidinal energy into poetry. His "lyric
libido" had been merely "diverted . . . by the war": "I am
not, I never was, concerned in the question of war guilt. Irre-
spective of the rights or wrongs of the case, something in me
leaped instinctively to the defense of my race . . . I am surprised by the spirit of righteousness which pervades my war
poems . . . My righteous indignation represents an infantile
regression." Reflecting on his life history, he drew himself as a
personality split by "duality of affection" or polar tendencies.
He dwelt at length on his Oedipal relationship to his parents
and on his poetry as an exploration of his bisexuality. He re-
counted his sexual adventures, affirming that "nothing is evil
or shameful in itself" yet noting in himself certain "idiosyncra-
sies and . . . inhibitions . . . [that] dampen the ardor of
plural amours." He proclaimed the doctrine of sexual relativity
and libertinism, though in retrospect he found that he himself
had made a clear choice between the chaste "Blond Marguerite" (an allusion to his wife) and the amorous "Helen of Troy."
But even his single clear choice was not one-sided after all,
since he claimed that for him the Blond Marguerite represented
Eros and Lilith in combination. With these tensions went one
of another character, between the "constructive moods" of passion and the "destructive self-analytical attitude," between out-
going feeling and ingoing thought, which Viereck could resolve only by exhibiting himself in both postures at once. His
self-destructive antiintellectualism was to appear later as an

element in his sympathy for the Nazis and in his ambivalent attack upon the intellectual "liberators" of modern thought—Galileo, Luther, Rousseau, Darwin, Marx, Freud, and Einstein—who constituted, according to Viereck, *The Seven against Man.*[21]

In *My Flesh and Blood* Viereck speaks, too, of his search for an ideal father, of his filial affection for Roosevelt, the Kaiser, Münsterberg, and the poet Edward Wheeler. Throughout the book Viereck asserts the centrality in his own history of his "lyric" or libidinal life. He thereby succeeds in minimizing the import of his political activities in the war, by then long past, and in supporting his self-image as a gifted poet. The book ends with a selection from the best reviews of his poetry, including the introduction provided in 1922 by Professor Eduard Engel for the German edition of his poems. Ironically, that introduction paid greatest tribute to Viereck's political past. "The History of German-America," Engel wrote, "will accord Viereck a still higher place than Carl Schurz, who, after all, was not subjected to so hard a trial . . . In German hearts, Viereck will always be enshrined as the poetic exponent of the high courage, the unselfishness, and the loyalty of the race—in very truth a hero and a bard."

One measure of Viereck's success in redeeming his public reputation was the commission he received in 1930 from Colonel Edward M. House to use the latter's personal papers for a study of Wilson and House: *The Strangest Friendship in History.* Viereck's denunciation of Wilson in the immediate postwar period had been loud and bitter. But in the course of studying the Wilson-House correspondence, his attitude toward Wilson was "revolutionized." Where once he had seen a villainous Anglophile, he new perceived "a tragic and solitary figure," genuinely devoted to the cause of peace, and martyred —not unlike Viereck himself—by the course of events.[22]

Despite his apparent break with the past, 1933 found Viereck still privately concerned with German-American affairs. He wrote to House of the considerable German-American support for Franklin Roosevelt and of his feeling that "recognition would consolidate their support of the administration. It would probably help keep the German element definitely in the Democratic fold." And once again, Viereck went on the payroll of the German government. To Dr. Hans Dieckhoff of the Nazi Foreign Office he wrote, "There is . . . nothing that pleases me better than if I can serve the cause of world peace by interpreting German events to my own countrymen." Later, as his involvement deepened, he formulated his calling differently: "The son of a German father and an American mother, I always regarded it almost a consecration to interpret the land of my fathers to the land of my children."[23]

German propaganda activities in the United States from 1933 to 1941 bore little resemblance, in practice, to those from 1914 to 1917. If the Nazis hoped to organize German-American support for American neutrality once again, they did not reckon with the changes that had occurred in the German-American community. They were, in fact, unable to locate a significant German element in the United States. The prewar Germans had been largely assimilated. The German-language press, which numbered 750 publications in 1904, had declined to 225 by 1924. By 1940 there were only 118 papers; most were weeklies and monthlies with small circulations and all were undoubtedly bolstered by the postwar immigration of more than half a million Germans between 1920 and 1940.

Many publications were vocally anti-Nazi. Prominent German-American Jews such as Samuel Untermeyer, who had been active in or sympathetic toward the German cause before 1933, were alienated by the anti-Semitism of the Nazi regime. The German Ambassador himself reported in 1938 that "not more" than a third of German-Americans retained German traditions or participated in German-American organizations, "and of that number many were hostile to Nazism, a majority were indifferent to politics, and only an infinitesimal fraction were Nazis." The former German-American community neither publicly supported nor visibly aided Nazi propaganda work in any significant degree. Once burned, German-Americans looked with suspicion on any organization that would identify them with the interests of a foreign government.[24]

Nevertheless, propaganda efforts on behalf of National Socialism were initiated even before Hitler claimed the German chancellorship. The Friends of New Germany, under the leadership of Heinz Spanknoebel with the cooperation of Otto Kiep, the German Consul in New York, gained control over the German veterans' organization and the United German Societies of New York. By 1935 it claimed a membership of 10,000. But when a congressional investigation in 1934–1935 exposed its activities, the German government ordered all German nationals to withdraw from it. Sixty percent of its members accordingly retired, and it collapsed. In 1936, remnants founded the German-American *Bund* under Fritz Kuhn, a German-born adventurer who came to the United States in 1927, was naturalized in 1933, and was convicted of embezzling *Bund* funds in 1939. Although it became the most influential pro-Nazi group in America and received support from German agencies, the *Bund* did not take orders directly from the German Reich. It stressed the German language, German culture, and "militant practices," and claimed a membership of 25,000 at its peak. *Bund* activities provoked such criticism that it, too, proved an embarrassment to the German government. Public opinion in the United States—unleavened by any sizable pro-German sentiment—grew far more hostile to Germany by 1939 than it had been in 1917.[25]

Viereck met Adolf Hitler in 1923 and was "dazzled" by him. He found the Nazi leader to be a "widely read, thoughtful, and self-made man," destined for great things. Years later he saw him as the heir of the "Kaiser's party," the man who was saving "Germany from disruption and Europe from Bolshevism." The rise of Hitler offered proof of the insanity of the Versailles settlement and revived for Viereck the old issues of Germany's role in Western Europe—with the promise that this time his pro-German position would be fully vindicated.

But Viereck's interest in "interpreting German events to my own countrymen" and in aiding the cause of National Socialism served a more parochial purpose than saving the world from Bolshevism. Viereck had been all but wiped out in the stock market crash of 1929, and was severely pressed financially for several years thereafter. In 1931 he began to work on Nazi contacts in the German government and the German consulate in New York, encouraging them to launch a propaganda effort in America that would counter anti-Nazi sentiment. The German Consul in New York paid him $500 a month "for four or five months" to supply general advice and editorial work on pamphlets. He edited the statements of Nazi party figures on a variety of subjects, and later published them in a volume called *Germany Speaks*. And he administered "several thousand dollars" provided indirectly by the German government to facilitate the transport of American correspondents assigned to Germany.[26]

In 1933 he succeeded in engineering a contract between the German Tourist Information Bureau of New York (representing the German railways) and the public relations firm of Carl Byoir and Associates for the promotion of German tourism. Byoir's firm would receive $6,000 a month for eighteen months; Viereck's cut was $1,750 a month—of which $750 represented his commission for procuring the contract. For his thousand-dollar monthly salary Viereck would supply editorial advice. One of his chief projects was assisting in the publication of the *German-American Economic Bulletin*, whose ostensible purpose was to encourage trade between the two countries. For its first issue, Viereck put together a collection of American press clippings favorable to Hitler. He later claimed that, as far as he knew, the source of Byoir's money was the Tourist Bureau and not the German government. But it is virtually certain that he had direct knowledge of the tie-in between the Tourist Bureau and the German government, and he may even have been aware that several months prior to the Byoir arrangement Goebbels had written to the Tourist Bureau giving "detailed and explicit instructions specifying the political uses of tourist and economic propaganda."[27]

Viereck could not have been innocent of the implications of his work. By 1934 he had established direct relations with the German Foreign Ministry in Berlin. He filed numerous reports with the ministry, including detailed descriptions of the 1934 McCormack-Dickstein congressional investigation of Nazi activities in the United States. In January 1935 he traveled to Berlin to consult with Nazi officials about improving America's image of the German Reich and tried unsuccessfully to secure $50,000 to quiet Kurt Ludecke, an ex-Nazi agent who threatened to expose German propaganda in the United States. He continued to hide behind a mask of virtue by clinging to the literal truth that he "never received one penny from Hitler." To this evasion he added, however, "there is no one in the world from whom I would take money more willingly . . . [for] it is nice to be paid for doing the things you believe in."[28]

While Viereck was not a Nazi, he was strongly drawn to the "new men" of Germany and their "regeneration" of the fatherland. Hitler was only one of a long succession of strong men who attracted him. And his partisanship for Germany had such deep unconscious roots that it had become a reflex action. Once again he failed to perceive any conflict of interest or ideals between his fatherland and his motherland, and once again he devoted much of his considerable energy to reconciling and integrating their divergent concerns. In 1935 the renowned psychoanalyst A. A. Brill, who had known Viereck for twenty years and had heartily agreed with his position in the First World War, observed that his stand on "Hitlerism convinces me that he is a very neurotic personality, too tied to the past to see beyond very small horizons." Demonstrating that this involvement with Hitler's Germany went far beyond financial arrangements, Viereck published a short fictional parable in 1938 that contrasted the virtues of fascism and democracy. It expressed a preference for American democracy, to be sure, but extolled the "social welfare" and "order" of the German form of government as ideals for America to ponder and emulate.[29]

Viereck's support of the Nazis in the early thirties did not arouse any dangerous criticism or pose any moral dilemma for him. But he was soon caught up in a swirl of controversy over Hitler's anti-Semitic policies, a volatile issue in America. German-American groups such as the Steuben Society at first denied reports of Jewish persecutions and tended to see the organized boycott of German goods and the hostility of Jewish organizations as attempts to revive the anti-German hate propaganda of the First World War period. Pro-Nazi elements, increasingly on the defensive after 1933, tended to adopt the party line that Jews had brought persecution upon themselves, that they were identical with Communists, conspirators, and "enemies of God." The issue quickly became a matter of domestic controversy, which focused almost as much on the role of Jews as on Nazi policies.[30]

Viereck himself had never revealed prejudice toward Jews, but his involvement in the German cause was so deep that he went far in defending Nazi anti-Semitism. He convinced himself by 1938 that "there is now a Jewish-Communist reign of terror in this country." At first he tried to warn influential Nazi leaders that anti-Jewish actions alienated Americans and German-Americans and were therefore "impolitic." But soon he was arguing that the Jews had provoked Nazi reprisals and that American Jews were bent upon war with Germany. In a letter to Ambassador Dieckhoff he observed that the American government was overly influenced by Jews, and that anti-Semitism could not be too significant in Germany since only one percent of the population was Jewish. Thereafter his moral obtuseness and his willingness to believe in conspiracy meshed neatly to produce, in effect, an anti-Semitic outlook. Many of his Jewish friends and supporters of the First World War era had shared his views on Germany; when they later took issue with Nazi policies, they became part of the conspiracy to persecute him and the German cause.[31]

Viereck's need to justify Germany—and, by extension, himself—took precedence over all other attachments and commitments. He had often written of the Jewish "race" in the past, but largely to praise a quality of "psychic adaptability" which he saw in himself. He had a wide circle of Jewish acquaintances, among whom he numbered some of his intimates and idols—Alfred Rau, Ludwig Lewisohn, Paul Eldridge, Sigmund Freud. But he was not deterred by these friendships—any more than he had been restrained by the loss of pro-Allied friends in 1914—from freely defending German policies. Viereck's ultimate defense of Nazism was that "it is not a question of ethics; a great nation must live."[32]

From 1936 to 1940 Viereck was a "ubiquitous factotum" of pro-German propaganda. He lent editorial assistance to the head of the American Fellowship Forum, a pro-Nazi organization ostensibly devoted to American neutrality. He held a contract with the German Library of Information (sponsored by the German Consulate in New York), which paid him $500 a month to edit *Facts in Review,* a weekly newsletter that from 1939 to 1941 brought the Nazi version of European affairs to a readership numbering 100,000. He was cited as the "most valuable liaison agent" by the German Foreign Office's Information Section for a variety of services, including weekly reports on and advice about American opinion that were sent to Hans Dieckhoff in Berlin. And he served as "a principal intermediary for the [German] embassy in a host of matters," including the cultivation of isolationist senators and congressmen whose franking privileges were used for the distribution of propaganda (often written by Viereck) that had been inserted into the *Congressional Record.* He took over the fledgling Flanders Hall publishing house in 1940, using German government money for the production and distribution of anti-British and pro-Nazi books and pamphlets. A few of the texts were supplied directly from Berlin. He later admitted that he received $15,000 from the Germany Library of Information between January and July 1941 and a net income of $55,000 from German "principals" for an unspecified eighteen-month period. Through all of his connections, Viereck probably received close to $200,000 in German funds, a substantial portion of which he retained for salary and expenses.[33]

Viereck's deepening financial involvement with the German government started in the fall of 1939, a few months after a bitter quarrel over politics with Fulton Oursler, the isolationist editor of *Liberty* magazine. The magazine had been the chief source of Viereck's income as a free-lance writer. But Oursler's isolationism did not extend to sympathy for the Nazis, and he was reluctant to print Viereck's increasingly extreme views. Despite his emotional and financial involvement with the German cause, Viereck nevertheless continually insisted that he had not, in fact or in spirit, compromised his American citizenship. He denied that he was ever more than a consultant to Nazi propagandists, and argued that he was actually serving America by making his special knowledge of European affairs available to the public. His contract with the German Library of Information "explicitly stated that the relationship could be terminated in the event of a break between the United States and Germany, and that he would undertake no assignment which would conflict with his duties as an American citizen."[34]

Viereck survived a series of minor exposés of his activities during the 1930s and narrowly escaped interrogation by the Dies Committee in 1938. But in 1940 familiar restraints began to close in on him. He was asked to resign from the Overseas Press Club of America on complaints that he brought 'Gestapo and German-American Bund members" to its meetings. After a grand jury investigation into foreign propaganda in September 1941 he was indicted for failing to comply fully with the Foreign Agents Registration Act of 1938. He had described himself as editor of *Facts in Review,* and as an American correspondent for the *Münchner Neueste Nachrichten* (which was used as a cover for his weekly reports to Dieckhoff). But he had neglected to reveal his connection with Flanders Hall, or his behind-the-scenes role in establishing such agencies as the Make Europe Pay War Debts Committee and its successor, the Islands for War Debts Committee, front organizations that were used to disseminate isolationist (and pro-German) propaganda under the congressional franking privilege. Nor did he indicate that his ultimate employer was the German Foreign Office. For the first two omissions he was convicted in March 1942 and sentenced to a term of two to six years in prison and a fine of $1,500. He served one year under this conviction.[35]

While in prison, Viereck was indicted (along with twenty-eight others) under the Sedition Act of 1940 for conspiracy to undermine the morale of the armed forces, on the ground that much of his isolationist propaganda was subversive. In March 1943 the Supreme Court reversed his earlier conviction, admitting Viereck's claim that the jury in the case had been improperly charged and that the prosecuting attorney had delivered an inflammatory summation that was prejudicial to Viereck's rights. But a few weeks after his release from the Washington District Jail, he was again indicted and prosecuted by the Attorney General on the charge of being an agent of the German Foreign Office and failing to indicate the true extent of his activities. He was convicted in July 1943 and sentenced to a term of one to five years in prison. This time the Supreme

Court refused to review the case. Meanwhile, under a revised indictment for conspiracy to undermine morale, Viereck was brought to court once more in April 1944. The trial was a sensational one. Government prosecutors were determined to show criminal intent on the part of the numerous defendants; for their part, the defendants and their lawyers tried to make a mockery of courtroom procedure. A mistrial was declared in the fall of 1944, but the sedition charges remained. Until they were dismissed in December 1946, Viereck was ineligible for parole. He was not released from jail until May 1947.[36]

In response to the initial charges against him, Viereck steadily maintained that "my real crime is twofold: I am an American of German blood and I oppose the desperate and despicable attempt to catapult our country into Europe's war." He saw his indictment as part of a "perfidious plot to smother and smear all opposition to the arbitrary forces cunningly at work to destroy the America we know and love." After his second conviction, Viereck argued that none of his activities was illegal or improper, and that "over ninety percent of all registrants" had misunderstood the degree of specificity required by the registration form which had brought about his conviction. Admitting his pro-German sympathies, he declared that he had never done and would never do anything to compromise his primary allegiance to the United States. He simply did not see, nor was he capable of making, a choice between these conflicting interests. He had glossed over a similar conflict of political interests during the First World War by alleging that the moral failure lay with those who disagreed with him and persecuted him.[37]

So profound was his involvement with the symbols of Germany and America that it held fast even against his closest personal attachments. After his initial conviction and internment in the Washington District Jail, Gretchen Viereck, his wife of twenty-seven years, pleaded with him to repudiate the Nazis and confess his guilt in lending support to their reign of horror. Stern and unbending, Viereck turned aside her genuine anguish with charges that it was she who was "a Judas . . . Nothing I can say will penetrate the armor of your self-righteousness." He was preoccupied with the "travesty of justice" that had brought him to jail; he had "never espoused Totalitarianism" but acted only in the interest of world peace. He would continue to appeal his case because the real points at issue, as he saw them, were the Bill of Rights and the Constitution itself. After the death of their younger son, United States Army Corporal George Sylvester Viereck, Jr., at Anzio in 1944, the couple were permanently estranged. Gretchen Viereck converted to Catholicism and sought atonement in service to the church. Sylvester alternated between condemning her desertion and pitying her weakness, complaining bitterly on one occasion that she gave all of his money away "to Jewish refugee committees and the Catholic Church." [38]

After Viereck's first indictment, prowar spokesmen heaped abuse upon him. A letter from Upton Sinclair informed him that "if there is anybody in America who is doing Satan's work you are the man . . . if there is a Benedict Arnold of this war, you are he." But there were those who aided in his defense. Several prominent isolationist senators and congressmen challenged the original indictment and tried to get the Justice Department to set it aside on the ground that the government had used irregular methods in making its case. One of Viereck's most sympathetic lawyers was Daniel F. Cohalan, Jr., son of the Irish patriot and Tammany judge whose pro-German activities in the First World War had earned him the label of traitor. In September 1945 a movement to appeal for parole on Viereck's behalf won the support of the editor and pacifist Oswald Garrison Villard—himself repeatedly accused of pro-Germanism in two world wars—on the ground that Viereck had not willfully betrayed the American government or American laws but was the "victim of wartime hysteria." No one, of course, was aware in 1945 of the full extent of Viereck's association with the German government. Later Elmer Gertz summed up the sentiment of many former supporters when he wrote Viereck that "you should have been hanged for some of your sins, but you certainly did not deserve imprisonment for the matters charged."[39]

Released from prison in 1947, Viereck found it difficult to pick up his career. Nevertheless, he mustered the energy to publish three books between 1950 and 1952. *Men into Beasts*, a memoir based on his prison experience, was shot through with his insistent need to justify himself. Its sensationalist appeal brought sales to the half million mark. He fared less well with an autobiographical novel published in 1950. *All Things Human* concerns a sexually repressed man who is "intellectually . . . a hedonist" but has been victimized by "anti-sexual Judaeo-Christian morality." Stuart Kent, the hero, is married to a woman who, over the years, has turned from a "child-wife" into a mature society matron whom he can no longer love. He is impotent and seeks medical help to restore his vitality. He meets a young woman who releases his passion and confesses to her the lifelong guilt instilled in him by a priggish mother who "thwarted [his early] passional explorations." Shortly afterward, the young woman is murdered by a former lover. Stuart Kent is unjustly convicted of the murder and sent to prison. He is deserted by his wife, who divorces him, takes all his money, and marries another man. But in prison he meets a young man, Jack Reynolds, who arouses him sexually and reminds him both of a son lost in the Second World War and of his murdered mistress. Reynolds, it turns out later, is the very same man who committed the murder in a frenzy of passion. But Kent, in prison and afterward, has come to know many forms of sexual love and to discover, after Goethe, that "nothing human is alien to me." In the end, he finds fulfillment in his homosexual attachment to the son-figure, Reynolds, and in an erotic love affair with a new mistress. The autobiographical elements in the novel are legion and its reenactment of Viereck's Oedipal conflicts almost startling. Kent's first mistress, Edda, is slain by a rival lover with whom the hero later establishes a father-son relationship. Meanwhile, his years of imprisonment serve as an atonement for the son's crime. He finds eventual bliss in sensual love for a new mistress and a reciprocated attachment to his former love rival.[40]

In the early 1950s Viereck supported Senator Joseph McCarthy's anti-Communist crusade and kept in touch with a few neofascist friends, but on the whole he turned his back on politics. In 1955 he published a short apocalyptic poem, which professed to see in the use of the atomic bomb a symbol of the bankruptcy of Western civilization. His despair was held in check, however, by a lively and aggressive sense of persecution. He claimed that a prewar article about Russia that he wrote for the *Saturday Evening Post* aroused the "ire of Communists and Fellow Travellers" who then intrigued against him. "The tentacles of the conspiracy against me extended into the White House," he reported in a preface to an unpublished collection of verse written in prison. After pursuing this theme he launched upon a psychoanalytic interpretation of Franklin Roosevelt as a power-mad cripple who "lashed continents into war and shook the pillars of civilization." Viereck's "unintentional rebuff" of an alleged bid from Roosevelt for his support in the 1932 campaign, he asserted, "rankled in Roosevelt's mind" and provoked in 1941 a determination to "get" him. His subsequent trials were deliberately prejudiced by "hysterical appeals to mob psychology." He had been crucified "in order to intimidate every critic of the New Deal." He believed that he had been listed as "Enemy Number One by many American Jews" and gave his final statement against allegations of anti-Semitism: "I am not and never was, an anti-Semite, but I oppose professional Jews who, for personal profit or spite, keep racial antagonism alive."[41]

To a considerable degree Viereck's bitterness and hostility functioned to ward off a recurrent despondency, which grew out of his intermittent perception of his own failures. Elmer Gertz has noted this tendency toward self-dissatisfaction in the final chapter of his unpublished biography of Viereck. His subject had complained to him of the meagerness of his achievements, of the fact that he had "several scattered reputations, but not one great reputation." In 1933, at the age of forty-nine, Viereck reflected upon a happier time when he recalled being "forever young [and] forever in love with myself." But even then he had been haunted by a fear of approaching age and the realization "that what matters was not any love given to me, but my own inability to love others, or to love deeply even myself." The first shock to his self-esteem had come when he discovered that he was "not the greatest genius that ever lived." This had been followed by the equally unsettling realization that he "was not even the greatest American poet; perhaps not even a great poet at all." In the early thirties had come the final burden of financial insecurity. He had "wanted to be independently wealthy" and found himself weighed down by debts and obligations, thus losing his last shred of faith in his own powers. It is interesting to note that Viereck's allegorical poem, *The Bankrupt*, centers on a Christ-figure—representing Western civilization—who is declared "insolvent, bankrupt, spent" in the final Judgment Hall.[42]

Viereck died on March 1, 1962, after spending his last three years in ill health with his son Peter in Hadley, Massachusetts. Even then his self-assertiveness and need for self-justification persisted: he was still trying to publish a collection of verse written in prison and was working on a final apologia. But through all the vast display of his egotism, self-division remained his nemesis. His egotism functioned in part as a self-protective mechanism designed to cover over "polar attractions" and psychic ambivalences. He used politics as he had used a theory of sex, in order to integrate his own inner life. But the record of his life's work betrays a pattern of self-diffusion and moral anarchy.

Viereck's initial relationship to his parents set in motion a series of psychological, intellectual, and social adaptations that eventuated in a most remarkable career. His lifelong search for a father figure led him to numerous intellectual and emotional attachments, and his attempt to emulate his father significantly affected his election of a literary career, his interest in politics, his association with the German-American community, and his recurrent fantasies of sexual—later political—powers. The guilt that lay buried in his relationship to his father restrained him from ever turning against his father's land. His intense involvement with his mother was another fount of emotional ambivalence. In self-defense, Viereck would read his ambitendencies as an intellectual capacity to tolerate opposing views. Ironically, he attributed his "tolerance" to the example set by his parents in indulging his early aesthetic interests.[43]

Viereck's "duality of affection" brought the issues raised by the two world wars into sharp focus, and bore importantly on the question of his rival national loyalties. Among the most militant of American pro-Germans, he identified strongly with the German cause, persistently denying German war guilt. But his defense of that cause in the First World War was due in large part to the dialectic of his American allegiance. His militant response to the sinking of the *Lusitania* derived from both his need to defend Germany and his need to attack America. But in attacking America he never meant to reject it; his hostility was part of a larger, complex attachment. His aggressive demand for a showdown in the election of 1916 reflected his need to feel power more than any objective goal of affecting the course of events; whichever way the election went, Viereck could not have seen it as other than a vindication of himself.

Domestic hostility toward German-Americans also was turned to feed his psychological needs. He used it both to stir his indignation and to project his aggressivness onto imaginary conspiracies and the "war psychoses" of others. He was proud to be, if not a public power, then a public menace: "The hatred that raised its head . . . did not frighten me. In fact it fed my vanity. It was a tribute to my importance." So weak were his ties to the world outside himself that he could drift freely and without any sense of loss from one career to another and from one set of intimates to another.[44]

In militancy, Viereck sometimes spoke to the psychological, intellectual, or social strivings for self-respect of other German-Americans. But few of them could consistently follow his political course. So much did the German-American community change in the aftermath of World War I that in the 1930s Viereck was widely viewed as a crackpot. From the time of the revisionist movement in the mid-1920s his interests often coincided with those of other partisans critical of England, France, or the Soviet Union, and with antiwar, isolationist, and, finally, America First groups. But their concerns rarely centered on German revival, and Viereck was able to manipulate them only when he concealed his own purposes and worked behind the scenes. Driven by the same psychological needs and along the same course as in 1914, he met with small response from German-Americans. He appealed to isolated elements of the old

German-American community, who still remembered the tra-
vails of the First War. But Viereck, almost alone, looked to the
supermen of Germany to restore his power and influence on his
own home ground. This time, however, his fantasy world
touched reality only at its most peripheral points—points that
were of interest, perhaps, only to a grand jury.[45]

Part Three

Hermann Hagedorn . . .
PORTRAIT OF A PATRIOT

■ ■ ■

Hermann Ludwig Gebhard Hagedorn—poet, biographer, and passionate American patriot—stands in dramatic contrast to George Sylvester Viereck, a contrast heightened by remarkable parallels in their life histories. They were born and they died within two years of each other (Hagedorn, 1882–1964; Viereck, 1884–1962). Both began their careers as poets and achieved early recognition. Both pursued literary interests throughout their lives and supported themselves by writing. Both came from German-American families with strong ties to the fatherland. Severe personality conflicts, stemming from filial relationships, influenced their national identifications: each man transferred his intense mother attachment to America and identified his father with the German fatherland. Theodore Roosevelt for a time was a hero to both men.

The German-American crisis in 1914 brought them to the fore as militant publicists—but on opposing sides. After the war, Hagedorn and Viereck maintained their personal ties with Germany and criticized the harshness of the Versailles settlement. In the 1930s they shared a deep dislike of Franklin Roosevelt and a passionate hostility to Communism. Both lost sons in the mid-1940s. Both wrote poems about the bombing of Hiroshima, an event that each saw as a symbolic summation of his life's experience.

More than most men who share a given time and place, they faced similar issues and events. Yet their public careers could not have been more different. Hagedorn became a superpatriot during the First World War, an ardent champion of the Allied-American cause. Viereck became a paid propagandist—in effect a secret agent—for the German government, a role he repeated in the Second World War.

Rejoicing in notoriety, Viereck devoted himself to establishing his image as a brazen rebel—in art, politics, and personal morality. Hagedorn was a traditionalist in these spheres, applying his talents to the celebration of heroic ideals. The key to their differences lay in the realm of personality. Viereck, afflicted by an undeveloped moral sense, often set his course by the promptings of impulse and self-gratification. Hagedorn, obsessed with moral concerns through much of his lifetime, distrusted his own impulses and sought to place himself in the service of benevolent authorities. These psychic needs underlay their dramatically contrasting responses to the profound choice of national identity that the twentieth century demanded of German-Americans.

9 . . .
THE FAMILY

Hermann Hagedorn's assumption of an exclusively American identity came after a protracted struggle to resolve the rival claims of his German heritage and his American future. That struggle, rooted in family conflict that had begun well before his birth, tormented him until his death. A student of the Greek tragedians, he perceived that character is destiny; and it is in early influences on his character that we may find the sources of his adult behavior.

At the age of seventy, when he began to collect material for an autobiography, Hermann looked back to his grandparents for the starting point of his own life's story. His father, Hermann Anton Conrad Hagedorn, was born in Nienburg in 1846, the oldest child of Charlotte Gunther and Adolph Hagedorn. Adolph was an established young lawyer and a rising political figure. Charlotte Gunther Hagedorn was a proud, beautiful, strong-willed, and possessive woman who harbored a sense of social superiority—to which she may well have been entitled—throughout her life. When her husband died suddenly in 1859, she was left with three children in financially straitened circumstances. Relying upon the counsel of her two brothers—Ludolph had married into a prominent Virginia family and moved to America; Anton was a successful merchant in Hamburg—she took her brood to live in the city of Hanover. Her son Hermann was educated there until at the age of sixteen he was apprenticed to his uncle Anton in Hamburg. There the young boy met and had his imagination stimulated by two American cousins—sons of Uncle Ludolph, who were studying at a school for foreign youths. They were charming, cultivated, and spirited, presenting a marked contrast to the stern and unbending character of Uncle Anton, who saw it as his duty to instruct young Hermann in "that respect for authority, that awe of seniority, position and power, which [the boy] . . . retained throughout his life, and blindly passed on to his own sons."[1]

At the age of nineteen, faced with the prospect of military service and yearning to measure himself against the opportunities reported in the New World, Hermann Anton determined to emigrate to America. Taking leave of Charlotte was no small matter. Relations between the mother and son were intimate and ardent. After her husband's death Charlotte Hagedorn seems to have focused much of her passion upon the boy. She refused two attractive offers of marriage, allegedly out of a sense of duty to her children. She was not a person to relinquish control easily; her "word was law . . . [and] her temper was like the blast of an electric torch." Hermann Anton's ties to his mother, in return, passed the bounds of filial obligation. But he made the break nonetheless, perhaps—as Hermann, Jr., later speculated—giving assurances that he would "throw out no anchors" in America.[2]

In 1866 Hermann Anton found rooms in a German neighborhood in Brooklyn, New York, and settled into a clerical job with a German firm. He soon met the family of Friedrich Schwedler, a participant in the 1848 revolution who had emigrated to the United States in 1851 with two infant daughters. Schwedler had taken control of the *New Yorker Demokrat* in 1856 and devoted himself to pressing the cause of the new Republican party on his German-reading constituency. According to his grandson, Schwedler was an idealist who had come to America in pursuit of freedom. Abraham Lincoln was the "presiding genius" of his household, and for himself and his children American ideals became far more significant than German realities. They were unmoved by notions of "race or soil or blood": the *idea* of America took first claim on their loyalties. Though Friedrich Schwedler held firm convictions, he was a mild-mannered man whose gentleness shaded into meekness and ineptitude. His wife was by far the stronger personality of the two. A woman of some cultivation, Marie Schwedler was a thoughtful, religious person who loved poetry and practiced self-discipline. Her husband adored her and respected her opinions. Undoubtedly he shocked those of his readers who were bound by more traditional conceptions of the German woman's inferior and submissive role when he indited, in 1860, "an appeal to the women of German households to come out and take part in the fight against slavery."[3]

Young Hermann Anton was attracted by the family—and particularly by the eldest daughter, Annie—despite political disagreements with Schwedler. He was a conservative, a monarchist, and a German nationalist while Schwedler was a liberal, a republican, and an American patriot. Hermann Anton soon would be stirred by a vision of German glory in the Franco-Prussian war and look upon Bismarck as the hero of his age. But he was more interested in winning the favor of Annie Schwedler than in arguing with her father—and more successful. In 1870 he returned to Germany to secure his mother's permission to marry. Charlotte Hagedorn fought the prospect; she pressed her son to marry a German girl, but he was adamant. Again, according to her grandson, there is reason to believe that she exacted promises about Hermann's future resettlement in Germany. The young man was bound to his mother by conscience as well as love and she apparently was not above manipulating either. A cloying degree of devotion marks all of the extant letters that Hermann wrote to his mother. Each time he opposed his mother's will, it would seem, a rush of sentiment obscured his guilt, which then survived to work itself out on his own children.[4]

Hermann Anton Hagedorn married Annie Schwedler in 1872. They had five children in rapid succession. The fourth, born in 1876 and named Martha Washington by her mother, was renamed Elspeth—after one of Charlotte's daughters—at her christening several months later. Despite this intimation of conflict, the family settled down to a relatively happy and prosperous life in Brooklyn Heights, New York. Following the advice of Uncle Ludolph, Hermann switched his business interests from petroleum to cotton and began to enjoy considerable financial success as a broker on the cotton exchange in New York. Together with their friends they constituted an upper-middle-class "German set": "The attractive, socially congenial group was self-contained, and seemed to be content to have it so. The children who came to the heavy, sedate, handsome houses talked German as their native tongue, had German governesses and nurses, ate German food, played with boys and girls who were to all intents and purposes German."[5]

The impalpable presence of Charlotte Hagedorn in the household intensified its Germanness. Through weekly correspondence with her son she dominated the domestic life of the family, lecturing Annie on her proper duties and supervising such mundane details as the clothing the children might wear. She "kept her son tied to her apron strings," yet so fierce was her possessiveness that she could still ask Annie Hagedorn "how you can have a single quiet moment . . . knowing you have robbed me of my son?"[6]

For her part, Annie Schwedler Hagedorn was a model of the modest, understanding, and dutiful wife and daughter-in-law. She had been attracted by her husband's courtesy, liveliness, and cultivation. Amenable to a fault, she derived her "philosophy of non-resistance" from Friedrich Schwedler and knew instinctively how to get along with persons of stronger will. Like her own mother, she had learned to draw sustenance and wisdom from religious values. But also like Marie, she was an inveterate realist. Combining patience and courage, she learned to ride out the storms of hot temper that swept Charlotte and her son. Hermann, Jr., later ventured a rare criticism of his mother for submitting to authority on principle and failing to "let the steel that was in her flash out and thrust home."[7]

In 1880, after an absence of ten years, Hermann Anton Hagedorn returned to Germany to visit Charlotte, bringing his family with him. They remained for a year and a half while Hermann investigated various business possibilities for himself in Germany. He seemed unable to locate a promising opportunity, and in the meantime serious business reverses at home demanded his personal attention. Once more there was a strained leavetaking from Charlotte. Then, shortly after the family's return to New York, their eldest daughter, Annie, died of pneumonia. Hermann appears to have interpreted her death, on Christmas Eve 1881, as retribution for his defiance of his mother's wishes. The burden of financial disaster, wild grief, and guilt opened the "sluice gates" of a histrionic emotionalism in him. It was into this atmosphere that Hermann Hagedorn, Jr., was born in 1882. His first childhood recollection, of a family crisis in 1886 involving the "exile" of his older brothers, was in large part the direct consequence of his father's collapse into self-absorption.[8]

Annie Hagedorn had been particularly close to her firstborn. She seems to have transferred much of her special affection to the new baby, although the other children—Adolph (age 8), Fred (7), Elsie (6), and Irma (4)—felt no lessening of her regard. Four years later the relationship of mother and son was further cemented when Father Hagedorn took it into his head to send the two older boys off to their grandmother Charlotte, now in Göttingen, to attend the government-run Gymnasium there. His self-justification was that the public schools in America were a "slipshod . . . melting pot" and that he could not afford to send the boys to private schools. But on another level this act represented an expiatory sacrificial offering to Charlotte, after the precedent set by the admirable Uncle Ludolf, who had sent his own sons back to receive a German education. At the same time—and after twenty years of residence in America—Hermann Anton Hagedorn became a naturalized citizen "in order to give the boys the protection of the American flag." Ironically, according to Hermann, Jr., "he became a citizen at the moment when he was committing the act that would forever keep him from being wholly an American himself, an act that would alienate completely from his American birthright one of the sons he was asking the flag to protect, and leave the other plagued by conflicting voices."[9]

Hermann, Jr., grew up in a household abruptly contracted by the death of his oldest sister and the lengthy exile of his two older brothers. Wracked by conflicting emotions and pressed by financial adversity, Father Hagedorn became an unloving, willful, irritable, and moody man who alternated between capricious displays of power and "feminine hypersensitiveness." His very presence generated tension within the household. Irma later recalled that Father Hagedorn had two sides to his nature: he was "intolerant and strict," wedded to the rigid observance of convention, on the one hand; and "kind and loving" on the other. The children were further bewildered by the contrast of his tyrannical authority over them and his seemingly blind submission to the manipulations of Charlotte and her spinster daughters.[10]

Father Hagedorn was particularly mindful of his obligation to discipline the only son remaining in his household. Shortly before the boy's sixth birthday his father confided to Charlotte that there was "something so free about him, so vivacious in his manner and at the same time so unassuming . . . Don't worry, Mother, I can be stern with the boy, too, but when I have had to punish him, then it's a sorrowful day for me." For his part the child saw only excessive vigilance with respect to minor infractions of the rules of proper behavior. Resentment festered in him. Even in his late seventies, Hermann could vividly recall an occasion during that sixth year when his father had reprimanded him unjustly for playing some innocuous game on the parlor floor with a miniature dump truck. It was an instance of his father's "instinctive urge to command first, and think afterward, if then," he later wrote. And "one didn't talk back to fathers in the world I was living in. One merely felt crushed and bewildered and very small and weak."[11]

The boy sensed, too, the brooding presence of Charlotte Hagedorn in all of their lives, and he grew to hate her. He detested the empty formality of having to write regular letters to her in painfully demanding German script—letters in which the slightest sign of erasures brought paternal chastisement. While he inwardly resisted the arbitrary power that Charlotte and her son exercised over his life, he was made to feel the inferiority and insignificance that they deemed to be the salient characteristics of the young. At the same time, he was drawn to the happier atmosphere of the Schwedler household. There his elderly grandfather and vivacious maiden aunt made him feel like "an honored guest." His mother, too, gave and received a deep affection: she was "a darling, firm with us, yet tender and gay, soothing our bruises, laughing off our hurt feelings with her quiet sense of humor, smoothing down Father, avoiding conflict at any cost to herself, nursing no grievances." As a disciplinarian she took the more successful course of establishing a sense of "fellowship" with the children, thus encouraging them to obey voluntarily.[12]

Although the family moved from one rented house to another during these years—Father Hagedorn "would never buy a square foot of real estate in America"—they continued to inhabit an exclusively German world. In later years Hermann, Jr., looked back upon these German friends, German holidays, and German meals with strongly qualified affection:

All these were to the good. Unfortunately, they were not all. With them went a conception of human relations that ran directly contrary to American tradition and custom: an insistence, so continuous that I never dreamed of questioning it, on uncritical respect for the judgment and opinions of my elders . . . I . . . developed a sense of awe of my elders, especially when they had 'position,' a blind trust in their intelligence . . . Ridiculous as it may seem, I was actually in my thirties before I realized that a man with gray hair might conceivably know less of a given proposition than I.

Father Hagedorn himself obeyed the laws he imposed upon his household. But he stood revealed in the contrast between his deference to outsiders and his familial tyranny. It was his concern for rank and status, for appearance and protocol, that structured the children's social experience. Yet his performance made it all seem false and hypocritical.[13]

Young Hermann was five years old before he spoke English. His closest boyhood companion, Bernhard Rechnagel, came from a similar German home and belonged to the same Schermerhorn street (Lutheran) Church, which was the focus of the Hagedorn family's social and religious life. Both boys attended school at the Bedford Academy, where "a stiff Prussian with black hair, a black cavalry moustache and a left cheek heavily gashed as a result of students' duels in some German university" presided over an overwhelmingly German-American student body. At the age of seven or eight Hermann met and befriended two neighboring boys of Scotch-Irish background whose family was acceptable to the Hagedorns because they were clearly old-stock Americans. Through these boys he was introduced to American books "which carried my imagination out of my German environment into the American scene."[14]

For a few years before his twelfth birthday the boy spent country summers in the Catskill Mountains with his mother and sisters. It was there that he first "began to have a feeling for America when I became conscious of its physical beauties and experienced its freedom and its wildness." In later years Hermann deepened his attachment to America through travel across her wilder far western terrain. This orientation to America controlled, in part, the way he interpreted more frightening contacts with American life such as the encounters in the streets of Brooklyn with young Irish "Micks" out hunting "Dutchmen." He saw himself as a "nice, timid little German boy" who, unhappily, had not been taught to stand and defend himself. His attackers, he later wrote, were "probably perfectly decent youngsters, terrorizing me because I was easy meat and deserved to be terrorized." This extraordinary approbation of his tormentors suggests the depth of his sense of inferiority and his yearning to be accepted by his antagonists. It reveals, too, a streak of self-destructiveness, which lay below the surface of his outward affability throughout his lifetime.[15]

Meanwhile, his older brothers Adolph and Fred were finishing their course of studies at the Göttingen Gymnasium. Father Hagedorn now began to reap the harvest of his decision to send them abroad. The first issue arose over Adolph's interest in pursuing a business career. His father was looking around in New York for an appropriate position for the boy when Charlotte's "devastating possessiveness" asserted itself. She could not bear to part with her favorite grandson. Adolph, for his part, wanted to come home. Once again, Hermann Anton stood up to his mother and once again she gave him reason to suffer profound guilt. Three years later, on May 17, 1894, Charlotte Hagedorn committed suicide by jumping from the window of a sanitorium where she had gone on a brief holiday to soothe her nerves.

The reason Charlotte chose to end her life was never fully determined. But the fact that she did so on the anniversary of her son's marriage was lost on no one. "Father went all to pieces," reported Irma Hagedorn. He collapsed into a state of moodiness and self-absorption, which the children resented for the unreasonable demands it placed upon their mother. His mourning was excessive and flamboyant, casting doubt upon the character of his grief. Hermann, Jr., thought him a hypocrite; Father Hagedorn's intense professions of love were not to be trusted, for his feelings were not "true" like Annie Hagedorn's.[16]

Before she died, Charlotte had secured a victory of sorts— though she may not have known it. Fred Hagedorn had set his heart on studying law at the University of Göttingen. The implications of such a course of study were deeply unsettling to the American Hagedorns, for inevitably it would bind his future career to Germany. In the same year that Charlotte died, Fred came to the United States at the bidding of his parents to look into legal studies in America. He had not seen his mother in eight years. He felt a stranger in his own family, and recoiled from the unfamiliar structure of American universities and the alien ways of American life. "Try as he might . . . he could not see himself in the American picture. He had been away too long, and had, in his thinking and feeling, become definitely German." A few months later he returned to Göttingen. This act forged a new and indestructible link in the chain that bound the Hagedorn family to Germany. Father Hagedorn's behavior toward Charlotte had always borne the mark of ambivalence; his affection was genuine and ardent, yet he missed few opportunities to leave her side. Under the changed circumstances, he could now transform his devotion and sense of obligation to Charlotte into fealty toward Germany. Having done so, he no longer needed to fear dependency or suffer guilt as before.[17]

On the conscious side of this fealty were a wish to hold on to Fred and a sense of duty toward his two spinster sisters in Göttingen. Having recouped his fortunes on the cotton exchange by 1894, he would henceforward bring his entire family there to spend their annual summer holidays. "That year that I became twelve," Hermann, Jr., wrote, "our family life took a new direction." He and his sisters likened Göttingen to an "arid wilderness, unfit for human habitation," and were bored to distraction at first, considering these summers as "punishment for imagined sins." But gradually, as they came to know the town intimately, to enjoy walks on the promenade and visits to the

marketplace, they softened and followed their mother's example in making the best of it. They discovered comrades among
their peers and warmed to the indulgent affection of adult family friends as well as the company of Fred's companions at the
university. The two maiden aunts seemed grim characters,
given to self-importance, hypocrisy, and incessant hypochondria. But distaste for them was mixed with wicked delight in
their pompous and stuffy posturings—which the children des-
ignated as *"Tantentheater."* Hermann, Jr., came to know Göt-
tengen better than he knew Brooklyn, and felt that each of his
friends "was a vine, growing out of the German soil and fasten-
ing itself to me. If one could imagine a Laocoön with vines
instead of serpents coiling about his limbs, the picture would
have been true of me." He surrendered part of himself to the
German world—in Göttingen as in New York—so that by the
age of sixteen he felt that he was "German in all the deeper
areas of tradition, character and personality." Yet he held another part of himself aloof, largely under the influence of his
mother, who "saved me . . . and kept me integrated; Mother,
pronouncing to Father, one day, the only words resembling an
ultimatum that I can remember her ever muttering. They were
these: 'I want one of my sons to be an American.' "[18]

To be sure, Adolph, the oldest son, had returned and made a
life for himself in America. But his feelings, like his father's,
were drawn in two national directions. Into its second generation the family continued to live in a "hyphenated state that
was neither American nor German but was accepted as natural
. . . by the men and women of German background." What
Annie Hagedorn held out for was "something deeper than conformity to the outward pattern":

When in her early childhood, the word America had entered her consciousness, it came in a radiance of a dream to which a man might gladly
give his life. The dream had come true in the form of a home, free from
the menace of Authority . . . She was seeing me in relation to her
father's love of freedom . . . What she meant, when she said that she
wanted me to be an American, was that she wanted me to be possessed
by the American idea.[19]

When young Hermann reached the age of sixteen his parents
decided to send him to an American boarding school. They were

influenced in part by considerations of health. He was "less than robust" and it seemed wise to provide him with more fresh air and exercise than he would find in a city school. The boy suffered from Saint Vitus's dance, a minor brain disorder characterized by irregular, spontaneous, and abrupt muscular movements. In a household in which Father Hagedorn's own pronounced hypochondria set the tone, there was much concern over this condition. The year was 1898 and Hermann, Sr., felt a "newly surging ardor for America" in the midst of the Spanish-American War. Thus Annie Hagedorn had special leverage in appealing to him to release his youngest son to the larger American world. Father Hagedorn had already surrendered authority over two sons out of "weakness and sentimentality." Of this surrender Hermann, Jr., later observed that "the thought that his sons might have needs which these women [Charlotte and the aunts] could not meet seems never to have occurred to him." Crisply, and without apparent emotion, he noted that in his own case Father Hagedorn "accepted Mother's ultimatum with surprising docility." The adjective "surprising" carries ironic weight in its implied charge of weakness and betrayal with respect to himself.[20]

Hagedorn's attendance at The Hill School in Pottstown, Pennsylvania, was a critical factor in the formation of his ideals. The Hill was, first of all, a totally "American" school, and it was there that he gained entry into the "brotherhood" of American boys. It was there, too, that he came under the sway of headmaster John Meigs, who had "Power, as I knew it in my father and would know it again, long after, in Theodore Roosevelt." Meigs taught him to value a combination of physical stamina and spiritual purpose, which were the hallmarks of the heroes Hagedorn would later admire. Even more significant was his friendship with the headmaster's wife, Marion Meigs, who left upon the impressionable youth the lasting mark of her moral earnestness. She had a "passion for souls" and a driving social conscience. It was her mission to teach the boys in her charge to "make the world better for [their] having lived in it." "She had a nation on her heart . . . she knew that the nation could be redeemed only by the 'remnant' that had God at their lives' center." Marion Meigs's "blazing religion of service" offered

Hermann two important things: a congenial spiritual ideal to which he could devote himself, and a style of expression—moral uplift—that would serve as a device to channel his aggressive needs and to counter his habitual self-distrust and low self-estimation.[21]

At first, Germanic young Hermann Ludwig Gebhard Hagedorn was handicapped in his relations with the other boys at school. They talked a "language of quips and banter that I understood only vaguely and could no more talk than I could talk Arabic." In the course of his first year he was the butt of a harmless practical joke that took advantage of his "unhumorous conscientiousness." But he was "glad that, when the truth dawned, I had the grace to grin at myself and my pomposity and gratefully remember the incident as a first halting step into a new world." Despite his ethnic difference, he came from a similar social class, and he found The Hill's intellectual seriousness and moral earnestness congenial. Significantly, his sense of belonging was finally confirmed in a moment of triumph on the athletic field. Because of his health, there had been some question—raised by Father Hagedorn with the school's athletic director—over whether Hermann could continue in competitive sports. Coach Sweeney was confident that the discipline would do the boy good. At the end of May, in his last year at The Hill, he won an intensely competitive track event. For forty years thereafter he sent Mike Sweeney an annual remembrance of that day when "I gained my first firm foothold on the American shore . . . Within the limits of the community that was The Hill, I was part of the American social fabric." But it was more than the respect of the group that he had won; it was respect for his own body and a sense of self-worth. In his autobiography Hagedorn poignantly recalled that "none of my family witnessed my triumph, such as it was, or, three weeks later, my graduation. They were, as usual, in Germany."[22]

Despite the influence of The Hill and young Hermann's successful strivings for independence there, the peculiar character and constellation of his family relationships continued to dominate his emotional life. In that constellation, Father Hagedorn stood out most sharply. The senior Hagedorn's personality piled paradox on paradox: he was strong-minded with a deep streak of sentimentality; he was severe and yet tender; he had an extravagant sense of duty and a penchant for self-pity; one felt the force of his domination even while suffering from his repeated surrenders. Father Hagedorn, in fact, seems to have exemplified a pattern of personality and fatherhood common among German families in the nineteenth and twentieth centuries. The German father of this type is harsh and exacting, yet without real inner authority. He is the source of punishment, and all members of the family are subject to his wishes. Yet he is bound by a belief in hierarchy and behaves subserviently to those above him. He lays claim to omnipotence and omniscience but is often exposed as petty and sentimental. In these families a unity of affection frequently develops between the mother and children that is felt to be "secret" and against the father's wishes. According to Erik Erikson, "The little boy comes to feel that all the gratifying ties with his mother are a thorn in the father's side, and that her love and admiration—the model for so many later fulfillments and achievements—can be reached only without the father's knowledge, or against his explicit wishes."

In submitting to his father's authority, the young boy learns to devalue his own responses and feels weak and inferior. As a male child he identifies with his father, so that his impulses of hostility and opposition court guilt and self-punishment. In the course of adolescence, according to Erikson's model, he will fashion for himself some external ideal, "some mystic-romantic entity be it Nature, Fatherland or Art," which represents "a superimage of a pure mother." The chief requirements of this adolescent ideal are that it absorb the affect that attached to the mother, exclude the petty characteristics of the father, and invest the boy with a sense of spiritual power. To be meaningful it must, by definition, reject the base father. But the boy's earlier identification with his father has already implanted a set of patriarchal values, which may not be transgressed without punishment through guilt. Thus the adolescent is torn between rebellion and submission. Self-division, presumably the curse of the father, is inherited by the son.[23]

Erikson's model illuminates the experience and psychological development of Hermann Hagedorn, and points up interesting deviations attendant upon a partial shift of context to an American environment. As a young boy he feared and yet identified with Father Hagedorn's punitive authority. He learned obedience and consciousness of status, both of which heightened his sense of inadequacy. Experience taught him to distrust his father as well, for the man's strength was deceptive and his love capricious. Father Hagedorn came to represent the crassness and meanness of the material world. At the same time, Hermann allowed that his father indeed had a "heart"—a symbol in his writings of moral purity and enlightened authority—although the trouble was that it rarely governed his actions or relationships. He saw a fatal division in his father between spirit and pettiness, and it became his lifelong psychological goal to reconcile himself to the former while rejecting the latter.[24]

Whatever the truth of Hermann's portrait of his father, it reflected both his identification with and his deep ambivalence toward the man. One can observe the interplay of identification and rejection in a number of unconscious repetitions of his father's experience—with corrective revisions. Father Hagedorn was an active elder of the Lutheran church; Hermann abandoned Lutheranism but played an active role in the organizational activities of a new religious movement known in the 1930s as Moral Rearmament (and led by a Lutheran minister). Hermann "inherited" his father's dual national associations; but while the elder Hagedorn gave highest priority to his beloved Germany, the younger passionately chose America. Father Hagedorn behaved indulgently and with an elaborate sense of obligation to his German sisters. Hermann's solicitude for and devotion to his own sisters was no less marked—though he went out of his way to insist that they were utterly different from the *Tanten:* they were married and American.[25]

To a large extent, Hermann coped with his ambivalence toward his father by splitting off its components. The love side of his attachment found expression in his pursuit of ideal father-substitutes. He was to write several books about famous men whose lives were illuminated by spiritual strength. They were almost always idealized men for whom, as he saw it, the struggle for achievement was more important than the recognition that came with its attainment (*Die Tat ist alles, Nichts der Ruhm*).

His penchant for attaching himself to public figures who seemed to exemplify high moral purpose stemmed from the same need for an external authority to substitute for his father. Characteristically, he would oversimply his heroes in order to cancel out discordant realities. Fantasy contributed to the process of idealization. One of the recurrent themes implicit in his writings is the story of David, a youth whose enormous spiritual power rescues the world from Goliath. It was his deepest fantasy that God would give such power to him. On the morning of the day of his death, July 27, 1964, he lectured himself in his notebook: "Be open to God's direction for your part in building the new type of man who will build the new world. Beware of desire for personal approval. Expect the best. Live in the expectancy of miracles. You are not alone."[26]

The hate side of Hagedorn's ambivalence toward his father found direct expression in his autobiography. But more often it was displaced on other objects and ideas: Woodrow Wilson, the German government, German-Americans, paternalism, and unjust authority. Another way he coped with ambivalence besides splitting it into components was by projecting it wholly onto others—to exaggerate the "self-division" of his father, his father's family, and his father's land. At a climactic moment, in 1917, Hermann would turn the full force of his hostility, scorn, and anger on those "double-minded" German-Americans who were caught in a conflict of divided allegiance.

Through all the stages of Hermann's conflict-ridden relationship with his father, Annie Hagedorn provided the reality (or the image) of refuge. According to her son, she was unfailingly governed by her "heart." Her single flaw was a failure to make visible "the steel that was in her," a learned submissiveness of behavior that on occasion was false to her spiritual ideals and strengths. Hermann's deep affection for his mother became a model of that spiritualized love which he directed toward his moral ideals. It was this sublimated affect that disposed him to the ethical idealism of his mentors at The Hill, a career in poetry, an infatuation with "the ideal of America," a brief commitment to the Society of Friends, and a lengthy association with Moral Rearmament.

An idealized mother provided the basic model for Hermann Hagedorn's spiritual values. These values were shaped as well by his need to express the aggression elicited by his father. He found most congenial those religious beliefs which had a distinctly aggressive character. He was initially attracted to the Society of Friends by the figure of George Fox, its founder, who was a "fighting man." Despite the special appeal of Quaker fellowship and the reflected honor of being seated next to President Hoover at meetings in Washington, D.C., he withdrew from the group because he found its contemporary members and meetings "too pacific." His very interest in spiritual matters had a double function with respect to Father Hagedorn. It constituted a rejection of the petty man who rarely "listened" to his heart, wallowed in material concerns, and seemed to live only for his selfish interests. Yet it also enabled Hermann to find an ultimate authority to which he might freely submit, and to reconcile himself, finally, to the residual humanity even of his father.[27]

If early childhood experiences and relationships did much to fix the needs, force, and direction of Hermann Hagedorn's emotional life, The Hill School influenced the selection of forms through which it might be expressed. The Hill placed a high value on physical vigor, intellectual seriousness, and moral commitment, thus providing an environment in which Hermann could cope with fears of his own weakness, passivity, and sentimentality by compulsively asserting their opposites. It professed a deep belief in the possibility of individual self-improvement, and commended this as a worthy preoccupation. It promoted the peculiarly American idea of a democratic fellowship of youth. Marion Meigs was always advising Hermann on how to "get along" with the other boys and thus reinforcing his disposition to conform to American group norms. It took "proper" boys and taught them noblesse oblige as part of an ideal conception of democratic citizenship. In this microcosm, as Geoffrey Gorer has observed of the larger American society, "to reject authority became a praiseworthy and specifically American act, and the sanctions of society were added to the individual motives for rejecting the family authority personified in the father."[28]

As Hermann Hagedorn matured into young manhood, his appearance was that of a shy, sensitive youth with a slightly aloof but courteous manner. Tall, lean, and meticulously neat, he had a serious and intelligent face. His correspondence with "Mrs. John" Meigs, begun shortly after his graduation from The Hill, reveals an eagerness to please, a worldly innocence, and a certain air of prudishness. There was a gentle play of ingratiating humor, but the overall effect was one of anxious earnestness. His significant inner conflicts provided him with the life tasks of mastering the guilt-producing aggression and hostility evoked by his father and the equally painful self-doubt and self-division that issued from this relationship. His chief failure in adolescence had been an inadequate development of self-esteem. Every successful attempt he subsequently made to master conflict moved him in the direction of emotional wholeness and self-acceptance. Every failure renewed his self-destructive guilt and his childlike dependence on external authority.[29]

10 . . .

FINDING A VOCATION

By the time Hermann Hagedorn graduated from The Hill
School in 1901, his father had managed to amass a considerable
fortune on the cotton exchange and was habitually transporting
his entire household to Germany for half of each year. Adolph,
the oldest son, was working in the cotton goods business in
New York, and Father Hagedorn advised his youngest son to
do likewise. After a lengthy holiday in Göttingen, where he
found "everyone narrow-minded and small" in great "contrast
to The Hill and all my friends there," Hermann started work
as an office boy at Bliss Fabyan and Company. But he had no
calling for the work. His letters to Marion Meigs from 1901 to
1903 reveal this period in his life as one of fumbling uncertainty, ill-health, and self-absorption. The cards were hopelessly stacked against a business career, for he could find no
way to make it a moral undertaking. He was anxious to prove
himself in work, but felt that he was too dreamy and passive
for the business at hand. He worried about the impression of
"listlessness and lack of energy" that he gave to others, and he
determined to correct this image. A little over a year after he
started work his health broke and he quit the job. For about a
month he tried attending a business college in New York. In
May 1902 he wrote to Marion Meigs that "everything bad in
me seems to have 'bunched up' in one great effort to get the
better of me and I have been appalled at my own weakness."[1]

But for the first time he found the strength to resist family
demands that he spend the summer in Germany. In the fall he
began looking for a job in publishing, meanwhile teaching in a
YMCA Sunday school in New York: "So many things that I

have undertaken so far have failed that I have determined to make a success out of my Sunday School work, if I possibly can, just to make me feel that I'm not quite useless yet." In January 1903 he began writing for *The Reader,* an illustrated monthly magazine. Friends there recognized his talent and encouraged him to continue his education at Harvard. Shortly before his twenty-first birthday, Father Hagedorn supplied money for a three-month sojourn in Italy. Hermann's diary of the trip contained repeated references to his own "dreamy" nature: "I am not for the whirl and the war of things," he observed, "but rather for the quiet, the peace and the happy day-dreams." But there were ample references, too, to his gratitude for his father's financial support and his delight in meeting and mixing with "refined" (*vornehm*) elders. Despite his shift of career choice and his increasingly positive emphasis on his dreaminess in contrast to his father's bristling business style, there was no overt break with Father Hagedorn.[2]

Hermann entered Harvard in 1903. Initially preoccupied with his studies, he gradually began to "crawl" out of his shell and to become involved in extracurricular journalism, in the *Deutscher Verein,* and in work with a German theater group. For the first time since his days at The Hill he withdrew from his association with the YMCA, feeling that he could now put behind him his earlier "pharisaical interest in saving souls" and learn to do God's work in "unorthodox ways." At Harvard he began to come into a sense of his own powers and to feel "restive as a dependent son." He made inquiries about part-time work to support himself through college, but happily took Dean Le Baron Briggs's advice that he continue to accept his father's largesse in the light of "an obligation to go further than you might go, without it." He was dazzled by the life of the university and by the great men he met there—including Theodore Roosevelt on a visit to the *Harvard Advocate* office, where Hermann served as a member of the board. He became an ardent and devoted student of George Pierce Baker, and was elected to membership in several prestigious undergraduate clubs.[3]

In 1907 he graduated from Harvard with highest honors and

a confirmed sense of vocation as a poet and dramatist. His choice had been influenced, in part, by his self-image as a romantic dreamer. One of the chief models of that image was Alfred von Mauntz, a family friend in Göttingen, a Shakespearian scholar and translator whom he greatly admired. This career was especially congenial to Hermann because he conceived of the poet as a mediator of spiritual values, a man who —unlike Father Hagedorn—was sensitive to the human soul. In his view the primary function of poetry was to awaken men to their highest moral obligations. It was Grandmother Schwedler "and, to a lesser degree . . . Mother" who guided him in his conception of the poet as prophet, of "the responsibility of the poet to mankind." The class day poem he wrote for the 1907 Harvard commencement called upon his peers to seize the day with spiritual purpose:

> The portals are open, the white road leads
>> Through thicket and garden, o'er stone and sod.
> On, Up! Boot and saddle! Give spurs to your steeds!
>> There's a city beleaguered that cries for men's deeds.
>> For the faith that is strength and the love that
>>> is God!
>> On through the dawning! Humanity calls!
>>> Life's not a dream in the clover!
>> On to the walls, on to the walls,
>>> On to the walls, and over![4]

"A man has no right to give the world his negations," he wrote to Marion Meigs. "I shall keep those in my four walls and out of them build the sure, positive things for the world to see." This approach to poetry coincided exactly with the approach to life that Marion Meigs had urged upon him at The Hill. His class day poem, "A Troop of the Guard," with its rollicking cadence and moral uplift, received unexpected publicity and was widely reprinted in newspapers in Boston and New York. An editorial in the *Boston Traveler* on June 25, 1907, observed that "there is no one who will be watched more closely for the next few years than this young man." And critics continued to respond, in most of Hermann's early work, to the youthful vitality that he infused into the traditional forms and familiar moral concerns of "respectable" American poetry.[5]

By the time he left Harvard, Hermann Hagedorn had acquired more than a sense of vocation. He had experienced "three centuries of New England in four years—the aspirations, the discipline, the freedom; the respect for the individual, the urge to aspire and to venture; the challenge to think without any encouragement to believe that thinking was ever going to be anything but the 'tough' process that . . . [his teachers] declared it to be." Harvard was "wholly rooted in America," and it had become a part of him. The tradition he now "recognized as my own was not the German [one] I had been brought up on . . . but the tradition of Washington, Jefferson and Franklin, of Boone, Lincoln, Longfellow, Whitman and Emerson." There had been no overt rebellion against the German past, but rather a seemingly smooth shift of reference points and self-identity. The authority of traditionalism remained intact.[6]

In the same year that Hermann achieved a sense of legitimacy as an American son (symbolized by his Harvard degree), Father Hagedorn retired from business and moved permanently to Germany. While Hermann, Jr., had been busy extending his commitment to—and securing his status in—America, Father Hagedorn was embarking upon a "fantastic venture in sentimentalism," the building of a thirty-room mansion set in twenty acres of cultivated land near the small village of Niederwalluf on the Rhine. In 1907 he took his family to live there, in part to fulfill his promises to Charlotte and his obligations to his sisters, in part to be near his German son, but also to enact a grievously miscalculated vision of returning "home" in a blaze of glory.[7]

During his senior year at Harvard, while plans for the move to Germany progressed, Hermann began to work on a blank verse play entitled *The Silver Blade*. The play centers on the conflicting passions of Queen Guenevere of Scotland at the moment when she must decide whether or not to yield to Launcelot's entreaty that she go to England as King Arthur's betrothed. The immediate referent of the play, in Hagedorn's experience, would seem to have been his mother's "dismay" over leaving America for Father Hagedorn's castle-to-be in Niederwalluf. The play's hero is Edric, Guenevere's court clerk and confidant, a wise and gentle young man who idolizes the queen with a fervor beyond "common passion." Edric and Guenevere are "comrades." Although he occupies an inferior position as a clerk, Guenevere responds to him because "he hath kingdoms in his soul." To Edric, Guenevere is a goddess who would reduce herself to a mere woman by yielding to her "duty" to marry Arthur or to her physical passion for Launcelot. He urges her to be true to her soul only, to be "steeled and cold" to her foreign suitors.[8]

The basically Oedipal character of the story reflects the precipitating situation itself. Hagedorn represents his own feelings through the figure of Launcelot as well as through that of Edric. The knightly sentiments of the commencement day poem, which he also wrote in 1907, go well with Launcelot's bearing; and both embody the ideal of active service acquired at The Hill. Launcelot partakes of Hagedorn's father identification insofar as he is Arthur's agent, urging the queen to marry the king. But he is also a rival for Guenevere's love in his own right. When Launcelot speaks her name "very softly," Guenevere is unable to resist him.[9]

Despite Edric's arguments, Guenevere takes a worldly rather than a spiritual view of her duty, and her woman's weakness— so like Annie Hagedorn's—is successfully exploited by the king's agent. She accepts Arthur and Arthur's homeland as her "fate." After Launcelot leaves the scene, Guenevere suffers a moment of doubt and considers stabbing herself with a silver dagger, for she recognizes that "the soul's stolen from me." Edric restrains her only to confront her with her "women's guilt" and beg her to reconsider. When she confesses that she "cannot bear to let . . . [Launcelot] go," Edric decides that he must kill her in order to save her from Launcelot-Arthur. In despair, he grabs for the silver blade but is seized and killed with it himself by court retainers. The silver blade is presented explicitly as a symbol of "desire unfettered." " 'Tis a sharp blade," Edric observed earlier in the play: " 'Twill make a speedy ending for some sinner." His sin, it would seem, is the same as Launcelot's—physical desire. While Launcelot, free of moral compunction, carries off the queen, Edric must be punished for his own guilty love.[10]

Despite the fact that no one except Father Hagedorn had much heart for the family's return to Germany, his decision was beyond appeal. Plans were made also for Hermann to spend three years studying literature at German universities. He spent the first winter (1907–1908) at the University of Berlin, working on dramatic technique, but found his professors haughty and the university badly overcrowded. To Marion Meigs he confided that it was hard for him to remain away from America:

Europe gives so much . . . [but the] charm wears off quickly. There is so much sham about continental life. As soon as you rub off the gilt you find putty, instead of strength and sinew. America has no gilt . . . there strength is crude and often ugly and misapplied, but at least it is *strength*. When Americans are wicked they are so along the paths of strength, the Europeans along the lines of weakness. Our [sic] sins are the sins of the uncultured baby giant, not the sins of a degenerate.

At the end of the year he returned to America to begin graduate study at Columbia and to marry the American girl to whom he had been informally engaged for four years.[11]

Dorothy Oakley came "from a long line of Hudson River and Westchester County stalwarts," including, on her mother's side, the prominent inventor and industrialist Richard March Hoe and the well-known banker and art collector Cyrus J. Lawrence. To Hermann she was "American" in personality as well as in blood. She was intelligent, energetic, spirited, and "rich in faith that was . . . an instrument of . . . effective living." She conceived of marriage as a democratic partnership in the American tradition rather than as a state of servitude. Father Hagedorn had opposed a formal betrothal in 1904 on the ground that student engagements were neither fitting nor proper. But he posed no objection to the match with the well-born Dorothy in 1908—despite the fact that neither he nor Dorothy had been able to decide quite what to make of the other. Dorothy did not speak a word of German and found the Hagedorn family ways strange and alien. For his part, Father Hagedorn was shocked by her notions of marriage as a compact of equals. The young couple's honeymoon—six happy weeks exploring the wilds of Colorado and six strained weeks

at the Rhine villa—underscored for Hermann the wide gulf between his German and his American lives.[12]

Drawing upon the unsettling contrasts of his honeymoon
trip, Hermann began to work on a novel which took as its theme
the opposing ideals of marriage and family life in German and
American culture. The book is set in an isolated village in Germany, which is dominated by the cold, gloomy, and unhappy
manor house of Baron von Hallern. The heroine, Gudrun von
Hallern, is a beautiful and spirited German girl who has been
Americanized in the course of an extended visit to the United
States, particularly under the influence of her prospective
American husband, Jimmie Hammerdale, a Colorado rancher
and miner. Here Hagedorn represents himself and Dorothy
Oakley with sexes reversed. The story line of the novel develops around Gudrun-Hermann's relationships to the Baroness
von Hallern and to the village pastor, Adam Samuels. Both the
baroness and the pastor are modeled on Father Hagedorn. They
are self-centered, histrionic, domineering, sentimental, circum-
scribed by petty and mundane traditions, and given to frequent outbursts of ill-temper and hypochondria. The baroness
is locked in a struggle of will with her dutiful daughter, hoping
to prevent the marriage to Hammerdale. Gudrun-Hermann is
reluctant to cause an open break and delays the marriage.
Driven to extremity by her mother's intransigence, the heroine
determines to defy parental authority and assert her newly
learned "American" independence. Once she does so, the van-
quished baroness accedes to the wedding plans.[13]

But some larger spiritual mission, beyond rejection of her
past, is required to justify Gudrun-Hermann's rebellious act.
And there were other themes to be adapted from Hermann
Hagedorn's relationship to his father. Both of these purposes
are served by an elaborate subplot centering on Pastor Samuels's domestic affairs. Pastor Samuels is presented as an arche-
typal authoritarian German, obsequious to his betters and
tyrannical at home. But he is a feeling human being nonetheless. He is trapped by German cultural mores into a behavior
pattern that alternates between obsessive self-indulgence and
insensitive abuse of his gentle and submissive wife, Esperanza.

Gudrun-Hermann shames the pastor into mending his ways, into "opening his eyes to the failure of his soul." The heroine also effects a transformation of Esperanza's life, helping her to rise from her downtrodden estate. Sloughing off German tradition, the older couple determine to live together as comrades rather than as master and slave. Thus Gudrun-Hermann has rescued the mother figure (Esperanza) from the ogre father (unregenerate Adam). The "parents" are then reconciled, to be sure, but the pastor in his spiritual growth now resembles Hermann, Jr., more than Hermann, Sr. The spiritual victors of the novel are Gudrun and Jimmie Hammerdale. The young American rancher is presented as a faultless embodiment of the ideals of freedom and equality—like Dorothy Oakley. The German girl, ashamed of the German heritage she has accepted unquestioningly for so long, achieves her greatest moment when she rejects her past and takes the American tradition of human fellowship as her own.[14]

Besides adapting, in disguise, many of Hagedorn's emotional experiences, the story of this novel rectifies the real life outcome of the incident upon which it is based. When the junior Hagedorns left Niederwalluf to return to America, there had been no victories through personal defiance or through moral force. They had not convinced anyone of the superiority of their American life-style. But the story is "true" to Hagedorn's emotions and to his recurrent method of handling ambivalence toward his father. His feelings are split between the baroness and the pastor: the former is wholly rejected, the latter is converted into an object worthy of love, with whom the writer identifies himself.

Five months after his marriage to Dorothy Oakley, Hermann published a second volume of verse, a lengthy tale entitled *The Woman of Corinth*. This story develops some of the themes of *The Silver Blade*—themes of the pure and spiritually powerful woman, of idealized love that is more than passion ("love to godliness akin"), and of the worldly suitor who is unworthy of such love. Again, the figure of Annie Hagedorn clearly stands behind the heroine.[15]

Hagedorn's fourth volume of verse, *Poems and Ballads*, was

not published until 1912, but it derived its major inspiration from the emotional dislocation attendant upon his mother's sudden death in Germany in December 1908. There are a number of love songs in the collection; but the chief recurrent themes are death and the loss of loved ones. Love's presence is seen as a sanctuary, which is often contrasted with the bustling world. Love itself is a commingling of spirits that is capable of surviving physical separation. But the pain and anguish of that real separation emerge in the collection's most famous poem, "Doors":

> Like a young child who to his mother's door
> Runs eager for the welcoming embrace,
> And finds the door shut, and with troubled face
> Calls and through sobbing calls, and o'er and o'er
> Calling, storms at the panel—so before
> A door that will not open, sick and numb,
> I listen for a word that will not come,
> And know, at last, I may not enter more.
>
> Silence! And through the silence and the dark
> By that closed door, the distant sob of tears
> Beats on my spirit, as on fairy shores
> The spectral sea; and through the sobbing, hark!
> Down the fair-chambered corridor of years,
> The quiet shutting, one by one, of doors.[16]

For almost four years after the death of his mother, Hermann moved uncertainly in search of a congenial environment in which to practice his vocation. He left Columbia in 1909 to accept an instructorship in English at Harvard. But after a year or so in Cambridge he grew impatient with the academic "ivory tower" and yearned to establish contact with "men and men's things," with the arena of "real life" where "the fight is." There was a lengthy summer trip to Germany in 1911 and a short stay in California. New York, where he had grown up and watched his father rise to wealth and position, exerted strong attraction as a place to settle. But Hermann was determined to lead a "simple" life—a life as totally opposed to that villa on the Rhine as he could make it—and the young couple finally bought a farm in Fairfield, Connecticut. Despite the fact that Hermann was visibly struggling to establish himself as an independent writer, he remained very much a dependent son. On a brief Christmas visit to New York in 1910—a depressing experience for all parties—Father Hagedorn had agreed to finance his son's career. Hermann continued to look to his father for approval of the management of his own affairs.[17]

Hermann, Sr., and Annie Hagedorn remained dominant influences upon their son's imaginative life as well. The theme of painful separation from a loved one informs much of the vivid imagery in *The Great Maze*, a lengthy poem which Hagedorn published in 1915 and which he later regarded as his most important creative work. The poem retells the story of Agamemnon and Clytaemnestra, focusing on the ten-year period of loneliness and lifelessness that Clytaemnestra endured after Agamemnon's departure for Troy. The immediate referent of the situation, in Hagedorn's experience, appears to have been a time of trial in his parents' lives. Shortly after Father Hagedorn returned to Germany in 1908 he underwent a series of disappointments and disillusionments. First there was a monstrous bill for $180,000 in construction costs for the house at Niederwalluf. After that shock came the slow discovery that "he was no longer the distinguished foreigner; he was just another retired German merchant" in the eyes of the local gentry. Quarters had been provided in the new house for each of his children, but they began to marry and settle elsewhere. Finally, Grandmother Schwedler, who had followed the family to Germany, died in her unhappy exile. In the fall of 1908, Father Hagedorn's emotional distress erupted as a severe case of eczema. His overly solicitous sisters ensconced themselves in the household at Niederwalluf as his nurses. Their presence aggravated the normally high tensions within the family. Under the circumstances Father Hagedorn, always "susceptible to [their] adoration," permitted the aunts to arrange a stay for him in a Stuttgart sanitorium, where they alone would accompany him until he recovered. Annie Hagedorn apparently waited in vain for her husband to ask her to join him. When he failed to do so she "bit back the tears, and the anger, and watched them go with dry eyes and a lacerated heart."[18]

According to Hermann, Jr., she "hoped, from day to day, that

Father would send for her," but she received no direct word from him—only letters from the aunts. Annie Hagedorn's anguish clearly provided the model of Clytaemnestra's myriad nights of agony:

> . . . What those long nights were
> One heart and one heart only knows.
> . . . [for] ten years
> Day came in hope and died in misery.

But after several weeks of strain, Annie Hagedorn broke down in front of her daughters at Niederwalluf. Word was sent to Father Hagedorn, who got rid of the aunts immediately and summoned his wife to his side. Hermann and Annie Hagedorn had ten weeks together before her death. According to their son, Annie held no rancor against her husband: "It was not in her to nourish an abiding grievance." In their last days together they renewed "their youth, alone . . . as they had not been alone . . . since the first year of their marriage."[19]

In *The Great Maze*, Hagedorn tells the same story of anguished separation and autumnal reconciliation. The fictional version, however, rectifies real life in that the guilty father, not the innocent mother, dies at the end. But the plot is essentially a showcase for character studies of Agamemnon and Clytaemnestra. At the beginning of the poem, Agamemnon has just returned from the siege of Troy. He is unaware that he has wronged his wife by abandoning her and brought a curse upon his family by his willful sacrifice of the child Iphigenia. He is taken aback by Clytaemnestra's coldness and tells her that "I cannot fathom or pretend to pierce / With my man's inexperience of souls / That sea that is your spirit." Clytaemnestra scorns his approaches: "though you are a wise man in your world, / You are a very child in mine." Agamemnon's tragic flaw of character, like Father Hagedorn's, lies in his blindness to the world of spirit, in his vain, self-pitying pursuit of worldly things. He is accused of murdering his wife "in life." Though he is not "bad at heart," his weakness of character, issuing in the "murder" of his wife and the betrayal of his children (Electra and Orestes are also estranged from the family) inevitably brings retribution in suffering and death. As in Aeschylus' treatment of the story, the powerful king could have chosen alternative actions at the outset, but once he determined upon his course the consequences unfold with grim inevitability.[20]

But the figure of Clytaemnestra is vastly changed from Aeschylus' version. Far from being faithless, domineering and hypocritical, she is deeply honest, spiritually enlightened. Her coldness is the result of grief, which has not hardened into anger or hatred. To be sure, under the strain of her long and lonely trial she submitted to Aegisthus, and she bears the guilt of her woman's weakness. But that is in the past; in the course of the poem she gathers her spiritual strength and majestically rejects her lover:

> . . . I will not bow;
> I will not be raised up; I will not drink
> Mercy from any lips. My days are mine,
> And I will keep the government of them.

Agamemnon remains her only true lover, and her ties to him are so strong that she is able to overcome her sorrow and approach reconciliation with her husband: "There was a bond as firm as rapture shared. / And that was common misery." It is Aegisthus, unable to bear the sight of Clytaemnestra in Agamemnon's arms, who finally kills the king. In the climactic reconciliation scene of the poem, just before the king is killed, Agamemnon declares,

> Life is a great maze, Clytaemnestra. You
> And I were lost in it awhile. But look,
> Love is the thread of it, love is the key.
> We shall not walk in mazes anymore.

Suffering has brought wisdom to both of the protagonists: "they two who had seen love rise in glory and go down in shame" share a last moment of bittersweet happiness before they must submit to the inexorable forces of retribution.[21]

So completely did this poem gather up Hermann Hagedorn's profoundest emotional experiences that it would reverberate, forty-six years later, in the theme and structure of his autobiography, *The Hyphenated Family*. One can interpret his autobiography in terms that bring out parallels to the whole of the *Oresteia*, taking into account Hagedorn's earlier emendations.

It is the tale of a private blood feud. Father Hagedorn has placed the curse of hyphenation upon his family by his weak and sentimental betrayals. Hermann, in the role of Orestes, is determined to punish his father for the "life murder" of Annie Hagedorn and for the sinful "sacrifice" of the two sons sent to Germany. In effect, Father Hagedorn's children were betrayed by him because he failed to devote himself to their needs. Agamemnon confesses his guilt to Electra in *The Great Maze:*

> . . . You are betrayed,
> Not she [Clytaemnestra] nor I, save as one fault in both
> Betrayed us both. You with your loving heart . . .
> You are betrayed. All that asked light in you,
> All that asked love in you and wanted mirth
> And Quiet, growing days, all is betrayed.

In the poem, Hagedorn's own feelings are split. In part he is Aegisthus, nephew, love-rival, and slayer of the king; in part he is Electra-Orestes, wronged children of the guilty couple and accursed heirs of fate. At the end of his autobiography, written when Father Hagedorn had been dead for four decades, he would finally shift the emphasis away from Aegisthus' vengeance and Electra-Orestes' victimization to Orestes' role as reconciler and founder of a new order. Taken as a whole, his autobiography is an attempt to reconcile the past with the present; in its last pages he presents himself as the Father Hagedorn of a new generation.[22]

By the eve of World War I, Hermann Hagedorn had published six volumes of poetry, drama, and fiction. While occasional reviewers noted technical faults in his work, particularly a painful clumsiness in the rendering of American colloquial speech, most critics praised his seriousness, "dignity," and "firmness of feeling." It was widely agreed that the "unusual promise" of his early work was redeemed with the publication of *The Great Maze:* one popular reviewer asserted that there was "nothing finer in modern American poetry." Technically unsophisticated, his chief stock in trade as a writer was the passion stirred by his deep emotional conflicts.[23]

Meanwhile, Father Hagedorn was living alone at Niederwalluf. He was sick, lonely, and alienated both from the unexpectedly distasteful realities of German life and the happy

American past on which he had turned his back. According to Hermann, Jr., the whole disastrous venture of returning to Germany proved a perfect example of Father Hagedorn's poor judgment and self-will. Obviously he had never given thought to "the possibility that he might owe something to the country that had welcomed him . . . [and] given him an opportunity to make . . . a fortune, and thrown about him and his family the protection and the splendor of the institutions of free government." In Hermann's eyes, the move to Germany revealed Father Hagedorn to be a traitor to America—as he had earlier been a betrayer of his sons.[24]

Then came Nemesis—in the guise of the First World War:

I feel a chill in my spine as I regard, from a perspective of half a century, the unfolding of the process of retribution in Father's life. This Nemesis, hovering always in the shadows near him, whip in hand, is no spiteful goddess, jealous of his happiness and success. She is the child of law; she is herself law; cause and effect, sowing and reaping, the tree and its fruit. Without passion, inexorably, she moves through her inevitable sequences. Only one who has not felt her lash can withhold pity from this good man on whose anguished back the Shadow was about to rain her sharpest blows.

Beginning with the outbreak of war in 1914 and lasting until his death in 1919, Father Hagedorn would receive the cruel punishment that moral law demanded and that his son, despite a reluctant pity for the man, perceived as just. For Hermann Hagedorn, Jr., too, the years from 1914 to 1919 were a time of profound emotional turmoil. Events provided him with rich opportunities to fulfill his yearning to be "possessed" by America and to serve as her aggressive knight. But they also intensified cross-pressures that threatened his preciously small achievement of self-respect and self-control. Before the war was over, he would be driven to act out his inner conflicts and to take extraordinary measures to ward off attacks on his self-esteem.[25]

11 . . .
THE BATTLEFIELD:
PUBLIC AND PRIVATE

When war broke out in Europe in 1914, Hagedorn's initial reaction was horror. Letters from the aunts in Göttingen, from
Father Hagedorn, and from his beloved sister Irma exulted in
German victories and argued that the war, which made "one
. . . truly proud to be a German," had been launched in self-
defense. "Germany was the innocent lamb," they told him, "attacked by ravenous wolves who envied her her green pastures,
and anyone who intimated the contrary was inconceivably
mendacious." Father Hagedorn enjoined Hermann, "Do everything that you can to spread the truth about the war. We were
shamefully attacked. Everything has been prepared by our
foes, years in advance, everything settled, signed and sealed."
But Hermann could see no possibility of glory for anyone in
the war and looked elsewhere for the sources of it:

My horror [of the war] had a background of Germany's pride in her
military power, her glorification of war, and Father's pride in the easy
victories of the Franco-Prussian War, and the obvious itch of the naval
officers in Kiel to show what they could do. My background included the
dismay of the people we met in England in 1911 at the thought of war
. . . In the back of my mind, in 1914, was Father's hero-worship of Bismarck and Moltke and their military triumphs . . . war was something
glorious [to them].[1]

But his suspicion of the German cause was countered by the
bonds that tied him to his German past: "Soberly gratified
though I might be at every German setback, every German
victory set my Teutonic heart beating faster." For the moment
he stood apart from the controversy over who was to blame for
the war and, poised in indecision, condemned only the war it-

self. In the fall of 1914 he brought out a verse play that spoke
of

> . . . the ancient battle story!—
> Of stricken love and laughter slain
> And hearts beneath the loop of pain—
> But not a breath of human gain—
> And not a word of glory.

The play describes the pressures for war in two hypothetical,
well-intentioned countries. In one case a peace-loving monarch
succumbs to the wily machinations of his ministers; in the
other, a contractor, a manufacturer of guns, the owner of a
newspaper chain, legislative officials, and military personnel
conspire to lead their republican country into battle for their
personal gain. Exactly four years later Hagedorn would publish a lengthy poem, *Hymn of Free Peoples Triumphant,* which
celebrated the fighting and likened the war to a religious Armageddon in which all justice resided on the Allies' side.[2]

As family influence from Germany and countering peer pressure in America increased, he could no longer sustain his ambivalence toward his father's land or his indecision about the
combatants. When the first shock of the conflagration began
to wear off, Hagedorn found himself shifting his sense of outrage from the war itself to what appeared to be its chief, certainly its initiating, agent. Father Hagedorn reopened old
wounds when he renounced his American citizenship in February 1915, declaring that he was "grieved beyond reason . . .
that America has taken so hostile an attitude toward us." In
the same month Hagedorn vigorously supported the position
taken by Kuno Francke that German-Americans owed their
chief loyalty to the country whose citizenship they enjoyed, regardless of their emotional bonds to Germany. The sinking of
the *Lusitania* in May 1915 "crystallized for all clear thinking
men the cloudy issues of the war." Hagedorn projected his own
double-mindedness onto Germany in describing "the conception of military logic which the Prussian Junkers had imposed
on a people naturally humane and peace loving." Admitting
that there were rights and wrongs on both sides with respect

to strategic considerations and national interests, he fixed upon the indiscriminate use of force as the overriding moral issue. "Sensible people," he wrote to Irma, "recognized that Germany was quite justified in blowing up a ship . . . [which she believed to carry] such quantities of ammunition. What we cried out against was the fact that the passengers and crew were given no chance whatever to escape." He begged Irma to forgive him for his inability to agree with the German position, but argued that it was the Germans themselves who were responsible for his convictions. He had seen copies of the *Frankfurter Zeitung* and knew that the German people were being fed a one-sided version of the facts. He was outraged too by the "illogical and sophistical" statements that German professors gave to the receptive American press. Pro-German propagandists in America, he added, only poisoned the situation for "those of us who love Germany."[3]

His need to convince Irma of the moral basis of his position was overshadowed by the sharpening conflict between himself and his American brother Addie, "whose tender heart and gentle spirit—so like Mother's—"drew his affection. Addie seemed "to find all right and justice on the German side." He believed that American financial interests, inextricably bound to the Allies, exerted a pernicious influence on public opinion and government policy in America. The brothers were divided, in effect, between pro-German and pro-Allied positions "on almost every issue that arose." Forty-five years later, when Hermann Hagedorn still felt pangs of guilt for his harsh and punitive rejection of his German background, he would displace it onto his rejection of his brother:

As I look back to those dark days, I feel ashamed that I never gave my brother credit for his courage in maintaining, throughout the period of American neutrality, a point of view, shared indeed, by millions of Americans in the Middle West and Far West but sharply out of key with the opinions of most of his friends and associates in business and in social life in the East. It required no courage on my part to take the position I took. I was flowing with the tide. I was everybody's "fair-haired boy," who was linked by blood, tradition and kin to Germany, yet took the Allied side. But Addie stood almost alone, subject to malicious tongues and lifted eyebrows; and he stood fast.[4]

But at the time, Hagedorn's strong orientation toward America found fulfillment in his acceptance of majority opinion. His conformity was no mere drifting with the tide; it was active, involved—and exhilarating. It provided him with the "new faith" he had called upon his classmates to discover in his "Troop of the Guard." During the first year of the war, at the moment when his father renounced his American citizenship, he began to turn his own back "definitely, on Germany." It was both a condemnation of his father and a declaration of his own status as an American. He had certainly never been a full German or a German "diluted" by American birth, and it had already been decided by his mother that he was not to be "a man of two countries, who did not know in which he belonged, and really belonged to neither." It was Annie Hagedorn's idea "before it was my own" that he was to be an American.[5]

"A Keeper of the Light," a parable published in *Outlook* in 1918, told the story of a "Happy Eremite" who remembers visiting two German-American households in his childhood, one modeled on the Schwedler home and one on the Hagedorn home. To the daughter of the Schwedler-like family the world war "brought exaltation and the passionate longing to give," while the master of the other household found "only misery and resentment and bitterness." Addressing himself to the Schwedler-like daughter, the Happy Eremite murmurs, "of such as you, dear lady . . . the foundations of America are made. And the blood in the veins is neither here nor there. The vision is all." This imagined "exaltation" of his mother became the ideal model of Hagedorn's own behavior.

Now he had the opportunity to prove not only that he himself was undivided, but that there was no such entity as a German-American. Responding to George Sylvester Viereck's charges that he was a renegade from the German-American community, he wrote that "certain German-Americans, even those who are unquestionably loyal to the United States, seem to feel that Mr. Viereck has said something noteworthy. Those who knew my father [when he lived in America] even insist . . . that certain very limited endeavors of mine . . . constitute a disgrace to his name." But theirs was the false position, for German-Americanism "is . . . not a union of anything

. . . it is a wedge, with the sledge hammer in the hands of Germany." Theodore Roosevelt's "passionate devotion to his country" became Hagedorn's real model of behavior, as his mother was his ideal model.[6]

Hagedorn's affirmation of his American loyalty and his conversion to a pro-Allied, anti-German position brought him into line with the American subculture he most admired: the traditionalist literary establishment based in New England. It was this group that provided the immediate reference of his American identity and status aspirations. Later he would become a prominent official of the markedly Anglophilic National Institute of Arts and Letters, the most respected of literary associations. In the meantime, he shared with its members a keen admiration for Theodore Roosevelt, a distaste for Wilson's ambiguous neutrality, and an increasingly fervent commitment to the Allied cause. Besides the status and prestige that his affirmation brought him, there was a special sense of excitement and uplift in joining forces with American patriots. Not only did he belong to America; he was working "responsibly" to raise her to her greatest possibilities, to exhort upon her a unity of mind and effort in the cause of justice, to realize the idea of America that was Lincoln's dream, and Grandfather Schwedler's, and his own.[7]

Convinced of the inevitability of American participation in the war, of the justness of the cause, and of the imperative need for preparedness, Hagedorn contacted in the fall of 1916 several other writers who held similar views. Together they organized the Vigilantes, a committee of authors who agreed to donate their talents to the cause of educating Americans in their citizenship responsibilities. Initially they concerned themselves with encouraging mental, moral, and physical preparedness. Here were the elements of noblesse oblige that Hagedorn had learned at The Hill School. Their plan called for action to arouse "the spiritual forces of the country." America was "fat, flabby, and self-satisfied," as Europe had been before 1914. Europe had stripped down to hard muscle through the discipline of war. According to Hagedorn, the "vital question" the American people now faced was: *"Must we be thrashed into manhood or shall we wake up in time and substitute spiritual discipline for the discipline of the bayonet?"*

Hagedorn recommended "widespread [public] discussion of the meaning and scope of spiritual preparedness." He proposed a program of training youth for citizenship, with large-scale proselytizing campaigns conducted by young people during the summers. "Above all things," he wrote in a moment of self-deception, the spirit of the Vigilantes was to be "young, gay, hopeful, adventurous, the antithesis of all that is described by the word 'earnest.'" Early in 1917 he developed the thesis that it was the mission of American boys to save the world by dedicated service to their country's highest ideals. In *You Are the Hope of the World: An Appeal to the Girls and Boys of America,* he perceived the role of young people not as inheritors of a noble tradition but, significantly, as the sole conceivable agents of a radically new future.[8]

The operating program of the Vigilantes was considerably less ambitious—and more realistic—than the original plan. By the end of 1916 the committee had secured an impressive list of writers, artists, publicists, and patriots, and began placing their efforts with some 15,000 newspapers and syndicates. The organizers worked together with representatives of the National Security League and the American Defense Society in arranging distribution of patriotic publicity. After America's entry into the war, the Vigilantes shifted from preparedness to propaganda and combating "all the foes of our own household, open and covert; all the forces working against national unity." Its leaders conceived of the organization as an antidote to the pro-German propaganda machine and aimed their fire not so much at Germany as at pro-German militants and "the uncertain German-Americans." One of its members, echoing a theme of Wilson's 1916 presidential campaign, spoke explicitly of "our enemies the hyphenates."[9]

This was a curious way to define the enemy after April 1917. But the Vigilantes were far more concerned with internal threats than with external danger. Their focus was not so much on the justness of the nation's cause as on the need for national unity. German-American self-assertion stirred deep American anxieties that the nation would not hold together, that at a time of danger from without it would dissolve into its many parts. German-Americans quickly became the chief target of "one hundred percent Americanism," a slogan that embodied the social imperative to "total national loyalty" and active service to the state. In June 1917 Congress passed an Espionage Act that, in effect, suppressed "free speech for all opponents of . . . war." This was followed by state espionage laws and the federal Sedition Act of May 1918 imposing severe penalties on a wide range of unpatriotic language and behavior. Pro-America societies were organized among the German element in New York and elsewhere to boycott advertisers in the German-language press.[10]

Theodore Roosevelt, who in 1917 wrote to a friend recommending the "shooting . . . or hanging" of disloyal German-Americans, kept up a vigorous attack on hyphenates. In June 1917 he urged governmental censorship of the German-language press. In July he declared that it was not enough to favor America in the war; anyone who continued to prefer Germany over England was a traitor. A trustee of the American Defense Society, he lent support to the organization of vigilance committees to keep watch over streetcorner sedition.[11]

It was in the context of these developments that Hermann Hagedorn's wartime propaganda work took shape. Intensely personal considerations disposed him toward the antihyphen campaign: his own father was proof that divided loyalty had tragic consequences. As a Vigilante, Hermann could be the agent of his father's symbolic punishment and yet remain relatively free of guilt because the expression of hostility and aggression was shared by others.

Hagedorn's central role in the Vigilantes did not go unnoticed in the German-American community or in Germany itself. Many in both countries saw his action as a stab in the back. They were far more sensitive to Hagedorn's defection than to criticism from outsiders, who were not expected to share their values and loyalties. His repudiation seemed to announce to the world that the bonds that tied Germans to their cause and German-Americans to their community were fragile and unworthy. Hagedorn's assault on the impassioned pro-Germans was blunt and cruel. In November 1917 he drew public attention to Viereck, the editor of *The Fatherland*, in his "Portrait of a Rat":

> A little greasy, not quite clean,
> Conceited, snobbish, vain, obscene,
> Like flying poison are his smiles,
> And what he touches, he defiles.
> A poet, knowing Love and Art,
> He makes a brothel of his heart;
> A builder, gifted to build high,
> He dreams in filth and builds a sty
> To haggle in with foolish kings
> Over the price of wit and wings.
> And when his country calls her men
> With gun and sword, with brush and pen,
> He smirks and quotes the Crucified,
> And jabs his pen-knife in her side.

Viereck, accomplished in the art of wielding a penknife, responded with "Portrait of a Jackal":

> For love of ease he plays the knave;
> He spits upon his father's grave.
> Yea, for his master's sport his tongue
> Befouls the race from which he sprung—
> While eager, oily, smooth and kempt,
> He eats the crumbs of their contempt.
> A beggar, lacking love and art,
> He sells his malice on the mart.
> He casts a eunuch's jaundiced eyes
> Upon the Prophet's Paradise,
> And when his country calls for men,
> Gives all he can, a—fountain pen.
> His brave words hide a slacker's heart.
> Informer, sneak, he chose his part,
> A Jackal, ever on the run,
> Save when the odds are ten to one!

In Berlin, Fred Hagedorn came upon an article in the Cologne *Gazette* referring to Hermann's "unholy activities" and calling him a *Schweinehund*. He received "hints that there were thresholds that I should never cross again." More temperate voices within the New York "German crowd"—among whom Hermann had grown up and still numbered some friends—

urged restraint on him. It was one thing, they argued, to be loyal to America; they did not quarrel with that. "But voluntary, open and active espousal of the American cause, No; by all that was absolute, No. Any other course [but passive loyalty] was disloyal to my father and to the rest of the family now living in Germany and, in one way or another, fighting for Germany."[12]

But passive loyalty was inadmissible to Hermann Hagedorn, for it credited the claims of blood, soil, and tradition that German culture exalted and Father Hagedorn embodied. Those were the values most precisely opposed to his conception of his mother's ideals "of freedom for the individual to fashion his own life, and, in cooperation with others, a new society." Hostility toward his father bubbled to the surface in denunciations of potential traitors. Guilt was skillfully outflanked through a role reversal with his father: Father Hagedorn's blind faith in Germany marked him as naive and "childlike." Thus Hermann himself played the role of father, or wise elder, in administering deserved punishment to this "inferior" and guilty child. The compulsiveness of his fiercely uncompromising stand on the war issues was a measure of his inability to admit passivity, ambiguity, or weakness.[13]

Ironically, Hermann Hagedorn's behavior during the war resembled his father's in several ways. Both transformed their deep attachment to their mothers into passionate loyalty to their homelands; both were absolutely certain of the justness of their stands. Each was living in a situation in which his mixed national background attracted suspicion, and each responded with an extreme form of patriotism. They shared a deep hostility to the American President, Woodrow Wilson. While Father Hagedorn fumed over Wilson's alleged subservience to England and his failure to force a negotiated settlement of the war, Hermann castigated the "timid, hesitant and uncertain" President. Wilson's "weak-kneed helplessness in the face of the English Foreign Office" was matched only by his "flabby ineptitude . . . in his dealings with Germany." But Wilson's chief fault was his failure to provide the American people with vigorous leadership. In the wake of the *Lusitania* affair the President did not see that "nations are like children. . . . They must feel a controlling hand or they grow wild and break things." During the period of neutrality and afterward Wilson substituted rhetoric and evasion for effective actions and revealed himself fundamentally bereft of "soul."[14]

Hagedorn bitterly denounced the German-language press, conjured up a Pan-German conspiracy to consolidate the German element in the United States, found foreign influences in the National German-American Alliance, and lumped together the Exchange Professorships, Prince Henry's visit to the United States in 1902, the Alliance, the German-language press, the German embassy, and German government agents as instruments of a master plan to subvert the allegiance of German-Americans to their adopted country. His inner turmoil assumed mild paranoid dimensions: the inner pressures of his father-derived German conscience were seen by him as outer pressures exerted by German agents.[15]

Meanwhile surface relations between father and son began to alter. In August 1914 Hermann wrote to his father offering to give up his yearly income. Father Hagedorn insisted on standing by his compact, and although he transferred all of his assets to Germany in the fall of 1915 he left a $25,000 fund in the United States to secure Hermann's allowance. At the beginning of 1917 Father Hagedorn, suspecting need on the part of Hermann's growing family (two daughters, Mary and Dorothea, were born in 1909 and 1913 respectively; a son, David, followed in September 1918), directed his agents to double Hermann's payments. But when the family learned of Hermann's anti-German activities, his allowance was halved "as a first move to its complete finish." Retelling this story in 1941, Hagedorn recalled his despair: he was thirty-five years old and had never earned his own living; he had a family to support and no idea where to turn—except to place his fate in the hands of God. Many years later, in his autobiography, he recalled the matter in a context of moral self-justification: despite obligations to his art and his family's security, he grew restive under the moral burden of accepting his father's support while he engaged in activities directed against his father's beliefs. Following a crisis of conscience, he simply renounced his father's aid. Whether father or son was most responsible for the break,

Hermann found himself in the summer of 1917 in a state of deep estrangement.[16]

His ostensible declaration of independence only partially assuaged his conscience, for there remained the need to justify his actions in terms of his moral idealism. In a sense he had to justify himself to Annie Hagedorn. To this end he spent part of that same summer writing a disguised apologia. "A Family Letter from a German-American to His Brother" was published pseudonymously in December 1917 and addressed to "Dear Felix." The fictitious Felix was obviously a stand-in for Adolph Hagedorn, who was, in turn, "so like Mother." The two brothers, Hermann and Adolph, had disagreed over the war issues for three years. Hermann now summed up his case with three major propositions. First, he argued, the retention of loyalty to Germany—to the past—was based on "clannishness and sentimentality," perverse and evil-engendering characteristics of German culture, which had warped the Hagedorn family's life. These corrupting traits were stimulated by German-language teachers, pastors, editors, and fathers, all of whom were henchmen of the German government. Second, the notion that it was possible to serve two masters through passive loyalty to America was erroneous. "We dare not be passive," Hagedorn warned his brother, for divided feeling among German-Americans would mean that "this country would be split into fragments as our family is now split, the members torn from each other and each member torn within himself." Loyalty, in other words, must be no less than "one hundred percent." Third, American unity was more than a political need; it was a spiritual necessity. The future of America, the realization of the American ideal, depended on the melting away of ethnic differences and their transformation into a new, spiritually unique way of life.

Here Hagedorn's personal referent was his own and not his family's experience, for he wrote obliquely of the way in which his German background handicapped his assimilation into American society. His conception of Americanism turned out to be the same exclusive one that had made him an outsider. Unconsciously revealing his earlier sense of inferiority, he now denounced as un-American those traits which he deemed most characteristic of his own youth. He called upon his brother to

join in "shaming" those German-Americans who continued to
hold back from the Allied cause out of sentimentality.[17]

On one level, Hagedorn's "Family Letter" is an indirect indictment of Father Hagedorn. But when he wrote that "there
seem to be times when a man must renounce father and mother,
brother and sister, in order to be loyal to something higher than
blood relatives," he alluded both to his father's failure and to
his own success. Having placed himself in a conflict situation
analogous to that of his father at an earlier time, he took a
totally different course and felt himself morally "cleansed" by
his own break with Germany. The "Family Letter" reveals Hermann's attempt to arrest guilt by invoking national loyalty as a
moral imperative: "we cannot afford to let the lesser loyalty of
the family or the tribe interfere with the larger loyalty due the
country that has protected us and given us happiness and the
opportunity to achieve success; or the loyalty, even wider yet,
which is due to the principles of justice and liberty on which
this country rests." There were no grounds for compromise or
reconciliation in Hermann Hagedorn's ultimatum to his brother.
One may infer from his behavior the existence of a prudential
motive: a desire to obviate suspicions that would otherwise
attach to him because of his family's activities in Germany.[18]

In 1918 Hagedorn published an overt attack on the leadership of the German-American community in the form of an
appeal to "Americans of German Origin" to shake off their
double-mindedness and take a firm stand on the war. During
the period of American neutrality, he argued, many German-
Americans understandably had nursed an instinctive sympathy
for the German cause. This sympathy was fed by resentment
over the pro-Allied policies of the government, press, and business community. It encouraged them to remain silent and passive when America finally entered the war, misbelieving that
it was their right as citizens to do so. Hagedorn sought to convince them that American entry created a radically new situation, which demanded an absolute choice, on their part, between
loyalty and disloyalty. In the absence of effective leadership,
German-Americans failed to perceive the imperative need for
choice because they were blinded by sentiment: "It is natural-
born sentimentality which has tied the German-American to a

Fatherland which he left for excellent reasons . . . Like all sentimentalists, he wants to have his cake and eat it, too . . . America is his wife, but he keeps Germany as his soul-mate, and is puzzled and offended when his wife boxes his ears, and hales him into court and asks, 'Heinrich, where do you stand?' "[19]

Assuming the role of friendly prosecutor, Hagedorn presented a list of American grievances against the German-American community. Americans believed that German-Americans accepted German propaganda uncritically and were insufficiently aware of the differences between German and American ideals. Americans looked upon German-American leadership as "undisguisedly and above all . . . [pro-] German." They saw venal editors, politicians, businessmen, and teachers playing on the prejudices of German-Americans for their private gain. And they observed that some of the more influential leaders were either agents of the German government or "wined and dined by the Kaiser." Hagedorn placed specific blame for this failure of leadership on the snobbish and exclusive German-American upper classes, the "upper crust" among whom his father had moved in earlier days, who would have provided a natural leadership for the community had they not considered themselves a caste apart: "they did not care to speak. Not one of them raised his voice against the pompous drivel of the German-American Alliance orators." Nor would these men of education, social position, and influence deign to champion America; they were parlor citizens. They knew the Alliance for what it was but retreated before it in "snobbish or sullen indifference."

When its natural leaders abdicated their responsibility, Hagedorn argued, the German-American community fell under the sway of lesser guides. Old men with old illusions, these petty politicians—editors and Alliancemen—adopted an automatically defensive position on behalf of Germany and ended up by becoming mere tools of the German government. They allowed themselves to place German rights above American rights, praised the martial spirit in Germany and supported pacifism in America, criticized American capitalists and ignored German Junkers, and refused to credit hard evidence of sabotage and spying. They regarded "all things American as censurable and all things German as perfect."

If these "hyphenates" earned Hagedorn's greatest scorn, he
clearly distinguished between them and "Americans of German
Origin." The latter group he hoped to save by his exhortation
to eschew passivity, to see that "there . . . [can be] no neutrals
in this war" and to understand that after April 6, 1917, the issue
was fairly drawn by Americans in the following terms: "He who
is not [wholly] for us is against us." In 1914 it had been possible
to view the war as an economic conflict. But the course of
events had revealed that the real character of the conflict was
ideological: between autocracy on the one hand and democracy
on the other. "No American of German blood can in this crisis
cleave with his heart to Germany and be anything but disloyal
to the United States." If they persisted in their divided allegiance then their repression would be justified, for there was a
real danger that they might fatally weaken America. As an
agent of the American spirit, Hermann felt compelled to rescue
the motherland by isolating her enemies.[20]

Despite the bitter excess of Hagedorn's condemnation of their
leadership, many German-Americans responded to his appeal.
There was no denying the fact that America's entry into the
war altered their situation. Adolph Hagedorn "thoroughly approved" of the book; expressions of support also came from
"many editors of German language newspapers and periodicals"
and from members of Hagedorn's old "German crowd" in New
York. On the recommendation of Frances Kellor, Hagedorn was
"invited . . . to serve as a dollar-a-year racial adviser on Americans of German origin" to the office of the federal Commis-
sioner of Education. In this capacity he called together a group
of "reformed" German-American editors, publishers, and dele-
gates from German social clubs in New York City, whom he
hoped to weld into a new organization in the spring of 1918.
His plan was that the National Patriotic Council of Loyal
Americans of German Origin would "testify to . . . [the]
single-minded loyalty" of responsible elements in the German-
American community.[21]

But Hagedorn's efforts "crossed wires" with the government-
sponsored Friends of German Democracy, and proved unsuccessful. He had barely launched his organization when he was
humiliated by the denial of a government appointment, alleg-

edly as the result of pressure from George Creel, Wilson's propaganda chief. At the same time Franz Sigel, head of the Friends
of German Democracy, charged that the National Patriotic
Council was a racist organization: unlike the Friends, its membership was open only to Germans. The charge put Hagedorn
in an awkward position. He tried to dismiss his rivals on the
ground that "any effort to develop among German-Americans
an interest in German democracy was beside the point"; such
efforts tended to exploit the double-mindedness of the hyphenate community rather than direct it on an exclusively American path. "Our aim was simply to make German-Americans
into straight Americans, looking forward, not back." But his
rejoinder did not come to grips with the charge of German-
American separatism, and the National Council died aborning.[22]

Hagedorn's humiliation fed his growing hostility toward
government-sponsored propaganda activities. Creel's usual approach to the German-American issue, he believed, was "to
paint in blacks and whites, and to . . . [deal] in terms of the
bludgeon." His own approach to saving the misguided souls of
German-Americans was to use "caring and tact," to show "compassion, reason and faith." According to Hagedorn, he and
Creel differed fundamentally over whether private citizens
should "educate" the members of the hyphenate community or
the federal government, using coercion, should force conformity upon them. This description was palpably unfair to Creel.
And Hagedorn's own style, while it aimed at persuasion, was
scarcely forgiving.

The difference between the two men lay on another level. By
this time Hagedorn was identified as one of Theodore Roosevelt's lieutenants. Creel, an official in Wilson's government, was
not anxious to hand over to him the organization of the German-
American community. When Hagedorn proffered the assistance
of the Vigilantes to the Committee on Public Information in the
early months of 1917, Creel is alleged to have replied: "We
don't want you! You're all Roosevelt men."[23]

Hagedorn saw Theodore Roosevelt at Sagamore Hill for the
first time in May 1916. About a year and a half later, he accepted Roosevelt's invitation to write *The Boy's Life of Theodore Roosevelt* and became a regular visitor. His decision to

undertake the biography was the consequence of a "miracle" in the summer of 1917. After his financial break with Father Hagedorn, he waited passively for God to take a hand in his affairs. Theodore Roosevelt became the agent of "My Forty-five Year Miracle" when he suddenly brought forward his invitation to write the *Boy's Life*—a book that sold well and paid modest royalties until Hagedorn's death in 1964. The book also led, in 1919, to his appointment to the staff of the Theodore Roosevelt Memorial Association. It was a turning point in Hermann Hagedorn's life, not least because at the very moment when relations deteriorated with his inadequate "blood" father he was able to give himself in spirit wholly to a new and more acceptable master.[24]

Roosevelt was as awesome a figure to Hagedorn as Bismarck had been to his father. TR seemed to be the quintessential American, whose vigor and sound judgment never wavered. Roosevelt's love of his country was informed by a commitment to the American ideal of a united society undiminished by class or ethnic cleavage. His compound of physical vigor, moral strength, and patrician style embodied Hagedorn's deepest yearnings. In the course of writing TR's biography he "came to know him as he lived and breathed. Face to face with him, in laughter, in anger and sorrow, I saw how great a man he was, how lovable and how magnificent a human being." And it was as a human being that Roosevelt came, first and last, to dominate Hagedorn's imagination. His aggressive manner and self-confidence became for Hagedorn a form of spiritual power. He seemed to represent the kind of enlightened authority to which a man might happily submit, and consider himself strengthened thereby. Significantly, it was as the author of a book on the Roosevelt family—on Roosevelt as husband, father, and master of the house at Sagamore Hill—that Hagedorn was to make his most substantial contribution to the legend of the ex-President. At Sagamore Hill, the antithesis of Haus Hagedorn at Niederwalluf, Hagedorn found Roosevelt to be a "tender, true and gay . . . father . . . and playmate to [his] children . . . yet always helping them to grow in strength, compassion and courage; expecting the best of them, yet never too hard on them when they [fell] short." Hagedorn chose to believe that this was the role Roosevelt cherished as the most important one in his life.[25]

Just as he made Roosevelt into an ideal father, Hagedorn drew a picture of Edith Carew Roosevelt, TR's second wife, that was compounded of Annie Hagedorn and Marion Meigs. He saw the ex-President's wife as a woman who had been brought up with high moral standards, who "as a mother . . . was . . . sympathetic, firm, courageous, imaginative, untiring, full of understanding and humor." The Roosevelts had an ideal marriage: in Theodore's words, his wife was "always loving, yet when necessary, [she] pointed out where I was thoughtless, instead of submitting."

Hagedorn's identification with Roosevelt grew steadily after 1917. At the end of his researches for a book on *Roosevelt in the Bad Lands* (1921) he wrote that "I have myself come to know . . . the life that Roosevelt knew thirty-five years ago . . . I have felt in all its potency the spell which the 'short grass country' cast over . . . [him]; and I cannot hear the word Dakota without feeling a stirring in my blood." To no small degree the Roosevelt family at Sagamore Hill represented his reshaping of his own past and an imaginative resolution of the smoldering conflicts of his emotional life.[26]

If Roosevelt exemplified Hagedorn's moral ideals as man and father, he also—not surprisingly—represented them in the arena of politics. Both men were partisans of the preparedness movement and were critical of Wilson's "weak" leadership and "hypocritical" rhetoric. For them the distinguishing character of moral rectitude was a willingness to use force, not a skill with words. Hagedorn resisted Wilson's idealistic formulations of American policy out of a deep suspicion of the President's passivity; the notion that one might be "too proud to fight" smacked to him—as to Roosevelt—of cowardice. Both men also believed that the "philosophy of sweet reasonableness" put forth by pacifists was a delusion. But Hagedorn was not fundamentally concerned with strategic considerations—neither with Roosevelt's conviction that American security depended upon an Allied victory nor with Wilson's conception that the larger American interest might be served by strategic retreats. Wilson's policy evoked his indignation because submission—even to a lesser of evils—could not be countenanced.

Roosevelt's great virtue was that he "seemed to know . . . where he was going, to be afraid of nothing and nobody, and to be willing to risk, if necessary, whatever political future he might have." What impressed Hagedorn was the commanding style of the man (his "genius for action") and his single-minded Americanism. This air of authority had appealed to many German-Americans before the war. Despite Roosevelt's wartime attacks on the hyphenate community, Hugo Münsterberg continued to view him sympathetically. Much of the German-language press, however, chastised Roosevelt for his patriotic excesses. Hagedorn defended him ritualistically, countercharging that German-American newspapers carped at Roosevelt because they feared the consequences of his single-minded prosecution of American interests. If Roosevelt's "passionate idealism" reached a point of frenzy during 1918 in his insistence on an all-powerful war machine, a fight to the finish, and one hundred percent Americanism, Hagedorn was in a special position to understand that he was "fighting with a kind of berserker rage that would not forget, would not forgive, the past." Roosevelt's seeming rage to settle scores out of America's past provided a public parallel—and a full and noble disguise—for Hagedorn's own private rage to settle scores out of his familial past.[27]

During the brief period of American belligerency, Hagedorn was so intensely caught up in the passions of war that he later recalled with shame the "heartlessness" of his ecstasy over the Allied victory. His father, brother, and sisters were living through the nightmare of those "desperate days following the German collapse." Out of his own anguish, Father Hagedorn wrote: "How frightful, what has befallen us! I cannot grasp it. What we here are going through and suffering daily! My heart breaks and I can scarcely breathe for fear and anxiety." This ardent patriot of the fatherland closely identified with his country in its hour of humiliation. In July, 1919, he wrote,

we have been weighed in the balance and found wanting. We must have erred greatly, sinned greatly, and we can only hope and pray that God will help us . . . I think, I stew, I castigate myself, asking myself over and over, why did it have to be that the whole world should hate us? Was the intelligence of our Kaiser the cause of our downfall? He wanted to do something himself, suffering no opposition. Was this the nemesis?

Years later Hermann, Jr., like his father, settled on a scapegoat, although his perception of the Kaiser differed significantly. The German tragedy of 1914, he would write, "was due to a large extent to the emotional instability of the Kaiser." He had been "a basically good man, a patriot and a dedicated ruler," whose major fault was that he yielded to stronger personalities. It was a portrait, similar in its ambivalence, to the one he drew of Father Hagedorn in his autobiography. In his final hours of "self-questioning," Hermann wrote, the elder Hagedorn "grew at last to his full stature" as a "greathearted human being who loved his Fatherland 'not wisely but too well.'" Ironically, a measure of forgiveness flowed from Hermann to his father when he recognized himself in the elder Hagedorn's anguished self-doubt.[28]

Yet Father Hagedorn's last-minute redemption through suffering was not sufficient to justify Hermann's extremist behavior during the war. Residual guilt was projected onto his father, whose original sins were responsible for the "tragic" division and failures of his progeny. Fred Hagedorn was a case in point. As food administrator for Greater Berlin in the postwar years, Fred had important responsibilities. In Hermann's admiring eyes his older brother was capable of "moving in on the wavering leaders of his country and using . . . [his] determination and courage . . . to pull the German people" out of the moral collapse that military defeat had engendered. But Fred failed to rise to the crisis. Years later, Hermann wondered why: "Was it some deep-seated self-distrust, planted in his boyhood by Father's conviction that the thoughts of youth are irrelevant, and cultivated by Grandmother Hagedorn's conviction—ruthlessly expressed to Mother, and no doubt to him—that he would never amount to anything?" Father Hagedorn, according to Hermann, bore fundamental responsibility for the weaknesses and failures of his children, and such a man deserved to be punished! The fortune he had made in America was wiped out by his investment in German war bonds. The legacy he left when he died in November 1919 was the fruit of misguided sentiment: a son, Fred, retired from public life on an estate in Schleswig-Holstein, two daughters chained by marriage to the sick and bewildered world of postwar Germany, and two American sons haunted throughout their lives by the history of their hyphenated family. If Hermann Hagedorn was moved to pity for his father at the last, this emotion could not erase the contempt in which he held the weak and vacillating man who had ruled the lives of his wife and children with such insensitive authority.[29]

12 . . .
THE DÉNOUEMENT

After the exultation of victory over Germany and the ultimate punishment of Father Hagedorn, Hermann returned to his quieter career as a writer. He traveled to Germany in 1922 and was deeply affected by what he saw there. He found the people tired and depressed, unable to think beyond the class interests that had scarred and polarized their prewar society, wracked by wild inflation, and hopelessly deficient in self-reliance. This, he concluded, was the logical consequence of the German prewar system of "paternal government by experts, with the inequality and the concentration of power in a few possibly efficient but irresponsible hands, that . . . go with such a form of government." Though Germany's defeat was deserved, he was pained by its issue in human suffering. His own sense of familial guilt persisted, and his defenses against it multiplied. He was certain that Father Hagedorn would not have been distressed by full knowledge of his "unholy activities." He was apologetic to Irma when he learned that his "Family Letter" had upset the German branch of the family, explaining that he "never thought anyone would trace the authorship and therefore embarrass the family." His association with the Roosevelt Memorial Association was proving financially rewarding and he expressed the "wish that *Vatting* might have lived to see me something beside a financial burden." He began to send small gifts of money to help with relief work in Göttingen.[1]

As a defense against remorse, Hagedorn began to project his past guilt-producing behavior onto others. He bitterly attacked the Versailles settlement as "brutal, demagogic and economic idiocy," scoring its emphasis on punishment and its absence of

Christian forgiveness. In a private letter he charged the editors of TR's old magazine *Outlook* with arrogance and vengefulness in their view of postwar Germany. America, too, had behaved badly. It had failed to live up to its "contract" to build a peace settlement on the Fourteen Points. It stood by, uncaring, in the face of chaotic conditions in Germany. In subsequent books Hagedorn developed the theme that Woodrow Wilson bore the major portion of blame for Germany's postwar demoralization. The President's oratorical style and grandiose promises had raised expectations and established obligations, which he had reprehensibly failed to meet.[2]

Through the 1920s Hagedorn looked for a way to justify his past beliefs and for new moral commitments. His Lutheranism had become "an attenuated and tepid faith" by 1922, and the "blazing religion of service to which I had been exposed at the Hill School" gave no answers to the "greed of statesmen . . . or the bitterness of a people, defeated, starving." He was disillusioned with the Republican party and its yearning "for the good old times . . . I am so mortal sick of the conservative mind which imagines that God ordained that the few should exploit the many and that the Republican Party is God's chosen and anointed instrument." He was unable to choose between Coolidge conservatives and LaFollette radicals, and felt out of place in postwar America. Just before leaving for Germany in 1922, he wrote to Irma's husband, "We don't any of us have to recede from our essential positions to recognize and admit that we all of us on both sides of the Atlantic believed a lot of things that were not so and said a lot of things, in sharper tones than was necessary, that were not altogether justifiable."

After the exhilaration of total commitment during the war, there was a profound letdown:

> This is the time of year to remember vows
>   Broken; shrill words; and torches that went out;
> And dreams that set their faces toward high mountains,
>   And went a little way and turned about.

New York City suddenly seemed to him "terribly crowded and every woman's face is painted and a spirit of haste and sordidness and greed and materialism is on everything." If the world was to become "normal" again, he wrote to Irma, people in all countries must learn to forgive and forget the past. A new faith was needed by all; not least by Hermann Hagedorn.[3]

In part he found it by devoting himself, like a loving son, to the memory of Theodore Roosevelt (who had died in the same year as Father Hagedorn). He published numerous articles and several books about Roosevelt, including a best-selling novel, *Rough Rider,* and prepared a memorial edition of Roosevelt's works from 1923 to 1926. He served at various times between 1920 and 1959 as a trustee, director, and secretary of the Roosevelt Memorial Association, and he headed the Theodore Roosevelt Centennial Commission from 1955 to 1959. His hero worship of TR extended to the ex-President's intimate friend, General Leonard Wood. A campaign biography, published in 1920, eulogized Wood as a presidential aspirant. In 1931 Hagedorn published a two-volume biography of Wood which showed him to be an exemplar of those virtues so prized in Roosevelt: moral integrity, strenuous activism, and a belligerent aggressiveness. Wood became a leading figure in Hagedorn's pantheon of heroes because he convinced himself that Wood—like Roosevelt—was a dreamer at heart: "for all his hard, practical sense, given to dreaming; occasionally for his own future; more often of a worthy cause."[4]

If the Roosevelt books and devotional exercises gave Hagedorn an opportunity to celebrate his ideals of Americanism, the Wood biography offered specific occasion to justify many of his wartime beliefs and activities. Wood, after all, had been the chief architect of preparedness ("a call to national service"), and he had often crossed swords with Wilson. Denouncing Wilson at every turn, Hagedorn depicted the former President as an "egocentric solitary, interested in men only as they fed his personality or his ambition." Moving "amid shadows," Wilson had been not only "wobbly" but positively "devious" as a leader. As far as Hagedorn was concerned, Roosevelt and Wood saw preparedness exclusively as a moral issue; only Wilson played politics with it. Wood was virtue incarnate, and only the blindness and corruption of the world prevented his triumph.

Hagedorn's account is filled with autobiographical projections. He did not identify with the general as he was, making selections here and adding emotional charges there. Rather, he wrote his own story into Wood's. His account of Wilson's refusal to send Wood to the fighting front in 1917 is prefaced by the tale of George Creel's rejection of his own services through the Vigilantes committee. Wood's greatest achievement, in Hagedorn's eyes, was the self-mastery with which he accepted his defeats at the hands of politicians jealous of his "popular strength."[5]

Despite a prodigious outpouring of writings in the 1920s, Hagedorn could not find lasting relief from internal conflict either in self-justification or by sitting at the feet of idols. During and immediately after the war he had handled his ambivalence toward his father by separating its components: but this was an emergency defense to forestall disorder, and offered only temporary surcease. Self-doubt continued to plague him despite his assertions to the contrary, and the force of conscience was such that with every expression of hostility guilt grew more painful and the need to moralize aggression became more insistent.

After the Wood manuscript was completed, Hagedorn looked to the Society of Friends for emotional refuge—briefly and without success. He grew restless and decided to spend some time abroad with his family. In 1932, while in Germany, he considered enrolling in the Pelman Institute [of London] for the Scientific Development of Mind, Memory and Personality. When asked to state on the application form what were the causes of his mental inefficiency, he wrote that "mental and intellectual laziness" often plagued him: "A German upbringing distinctly cramped my mental development, making me distrust my own ideas." He complained that he could not remember the names or faces of people and sometimes forgot the characters in his own books. His education had been defective and he was never able to develop self-discipline. In his personal notebook he chided himself for a "devastating lack of concentration" which manifested itself in his inability to stay in one place. During the past twenty-five years, he complained, he had lived in Germany three times, in California twice, and, on occasion, in five other states; he had written plays, lyrics, narrative and dramatic verse, novels, biographies, essays, and propaganda; he had pub-

lished with seven different houses. He was disturbed by a sense
of having spent his energies diffusely. Later he would recall
this period around his fiftieth birthday as a time when he was
dispirited and depressed. He felt that he was second-rate, that
his life gave "evidence . . . of rocket-dreams and falling-stick
achievement," that there was "shallowness and bluff behind
[my] intellectual front." Dramatizing his condition, he claimed
that occasionally he "thought . . . hopefully, of a not impossible truck turning a corner suddenly and catching me un-
awares."[6]

There is no record of aid received from the advocates of self-
development at the Pelman Institute. But Hagedorn did find,
in 1933, a new religious belief which offered absolution and
regeneration. The Oxford Movement began to gather strength
in England in the early 1920s as a nonsectarian faith. It promoted public confession as a way to forgiveness from sin and
proffered the fellowship of men who "listen to God's direction."
In the beginning, it attracted young college students addicted
to introspection. By the time Hagedorn caught up with the
movement in the thirties, it had developed a broader geographical and generational appeal. Nevertheless, it retained its early
emphasis on youth and on confession and fellowship. From the
outset, the movement was dominated by the charismatic Lutheran minister Frank Buchman. Its religious practices evolved
from the basic assumptions that all men are sinners, that they
can purify themselves through confession, that "changed souls"
have direct access to the power of God, and that absolute moral
virtue is the condition of spiritual life. Disclosing one's sins to
others was an essential procedure, as was "submitting" to God
in the sense of obeying His moral imperatives. God was omni-
scient and omnipotent, a power before whom material differences, economic and political forces, faded into insignificance.

During the Depression years a growing number of the social
and economic elite of Europe found refuge in the movement.
In recognition of the mounting social crisis everywhere, its name
was changed to Moral Rearmament. It championed spiritual
strength as the sole "solution" to the rising tide of problems
created by political and economic upheaval.[7]

The movement was tailor-made for Hermann Hagedorn. Its

aggressive emphasis on saving souls and casting out one's sins, together with its exhortation to submit oneself to an external, enlightened authority, offered avenues of expression for both his active and his passive needs. The ethical absolutes of the faith—purity, honesty, love, and unselfishness—conformed exactly to Annie Hagedorn's moral ideals. His first contact with the movement came in 1933 when his daughters were invited to attend a "session" at Oxford University:

What struck us instantly about these girls, and about all the women, in fact, was that none of them wore rouge or lipstick, and none of them smoked . . . the release of the guests was obvious and their high spirits were astonishing to anyone accustomed to regard cocktails as essential ice-breakers in any gathering. Meals taken together . . . encouraged an unstrained fellowship . . . There was a vitality and enterprise [among young and old] that I . . . had not dreamed [possible].

If the moral earnestness of the participants first caught his eye, he later came to see the movement as a "religion of democracy." While it expected individual self-rule, it emphasized the rewards of fellowship based on shared values. In arguing for the essentially collective character of the spiritual life, Moral Rearmament gave Hagedorn a ready means of reconciling the stern dictates of a demanding conscience with his need for affiliation. The "believers" who later assembled at Buchman's "house-parties"—the principal organizational medium of the faithful—were a congenial group of serious-minded, relatively upper-class people assimilated to an affluent international lifestyle. Some of Buchman's followers were extremely wealthy; many were well born or highly placed. Buchman often stressed the importance of converting "key" people who could, in turn, mediate God's direction to the masses. In the late thirties, a number of people were attracted to the movement as a counter-revolutionary force, one that could halt the spread of Communism and preserve the social position of the morally virtuous.[8]

Moral Rearmament, in short, offered a view of the world in which complex social and economic problems were reduced to moral terms. If one made oneself pure, one might "live in the expectancy of miracles." Miracles, of course, are wish-fulfillments. Hagedorn's belief in them undoubtedly contained a fantasy element of returning to the protected world of infancy, in which the maternal figure cares for all needs. In the cosmology of MRA, everything hinged on God's authority; and God, for Hermann Hagedorn, was a voice speaking his mother's words with his father's force. Here at last was a fusion of Father Hagedorn's strength and Annie's ideals; an authority he could love wholly, without ambivalence. Through the concept of moral rearmament he could share in God's authority at the very moment he submitted to it. The procedural imperatives of the group enjoined this compulsive man to be ever vigilant (as his father had been in pursuing even minor lapses from "proper behavior"); its moral emphasis absorbed his moral obsessiveness and justified aggression on God's behalf. He was oppressed by a sense of sin and by feelings of inadequacy; MRA promised him that it was still possible to become worthy. Moreover, to overcome greed and selfishness in oneself—and one's family— was to become part of a new world community which transcended existing political divisions. "I had, all my adult life, suffered as a consequence of conflicting national loyalties," Hagedorn wrote. MRA revealed to him a "new dimension of living" in which neither national antagonisms nor ethnic cleavages played a part.[9]

Reflecting his new sense of purpose, Hagedorn wrote "Manifest Destiny," a poem that makes an extraordinary companion piece to the sonnet "Doors" written after his mother's death:

> You and I—and America. There is no more dread.
> We are strong who were feeble, alive who were dead.
> We are stars who were storm, we are day who were night.
> We, who crawled with the adder, we are wings, we are flight.
>
> You and I—and America. We are flesh who were stone.
> We plough who were ploughed, we sow who were sown.
> We are rock who were sand, we are cups who were sieves.
> We are conquerors who, last night, were fugitives.
>
> You and I—and America. Dawn is in our eyes.
> We who crouched in a cave are astride of the skies.
> We, the wind, are the mountain; we, the wave, are the shore.
> For God knocked and we opened. We opened the door.

The spiritual sanctuary that Hagedorn sought throughout his life had evolved from the basic image of his mother's purity to the "idea" of America. But this spiritualized nationalism could

not offer relief from guilt, for it was intimately tied to his opposition to his father. Moral Rearmament provided him with
a notion of God that subsumed mother and father, for it held
as a fundamental principle the unity of all human beings, the
residual "heart" even of Father Hagedorn. Through confession
and repentence one might outmaneuver guilt over the past.
MRA, in fact, was as unconcerned with the past as with the
present; its orientation was wholly toward the future.[10]

Much as Hagedorn sought a new reconciliation with his father, the old ambivalence was difficult to repress. Late in 1939,
he joined a small group of disaffected men who "have quietly
severed our connections with the Moral Rearmament Movement and Dr. Buchman, while holding very definitely to the
philosophy and the aims he originally set forth." Buchman, it
seems, had "gone back on a lot of what he has preached" about
purity, honesty, love, and unselfishness, and the sterner moral-
ists among his followers "just couldn't stick it." Whatever the
specific incident (Hagedorn alludes to an involvement with a
girl), Buchman had betrayed his "family." Hagedorn, critical
and "nursing grievances," tried not to sit in judgment but
parted company all the same.[11]

For the next two years Hagedorn endured difficult times. His
two older brothers died, and he himself was ill for the better
part of a year. He was unemployed, living off the few hundred
dollars that his wife drew monthly from trust funds, and unable to find a market for his free-lance writing. Two volumes of
verse that appeared in 1940 (*Combat at Midnight* and *The
Bugle That Woke America*) had miserably small sales. Rescued
once again by a part-time staff appointment to the Theodore
Roosevelt Memorial Association, he moved to Washington,
D.C., in the fall of 1941.

Despite his continuing celebration of American ideals and
American heroes (Leonard Wood, William Boyce Thompson,
Robert Brookings) through the 1930s, Hagedorn was distinctly
out of sympathy with Franklin D. Roosevelt and the New
Deal. A lifelong Republican in the image of Grandfather
Schwedler, he could remember parading in his nursery at the
age of two under the banner of James G. Blaine. Father Hage-
dorn had been a Cleveland Democrat and had fought bitterly

with Hermann's father-in-law over the campaign. Franklin Roosevelt's social policies and pragmatic style offended Hagedorn's patrician values and moralistic concerns. He saw FDR as a dictator who had seized absolute power and turned America toward materialistic socialism.[12]

But the developing international crisis inevitably rekindled Hagedorn's political activism. He was anti-Hitler and internationalist in principle, but he did not take up the cudgels specifically against pro-German publicists or sympathizers in the late thirties. Instead, he served as the director of National Rededication, a coalition of seventeen organizations attempting to restore a sense of self-confident purpose to the uncertain American Democracy.

Equally characteristic of Hagedorn's response to the disintegration of world order was a poem lamenting American guilt, entitled "America to Europe, 1939":

> We have reproached and reproved you, denounced you,
>   condemned:
> Explained we are holier than you, thanked God for our
>   noble souls.
> Now in your agony, in the kindling of the pyre,
> The rush of the flame through the tinder . . .
> You, who are doomed to the burning, forgive, if you can!
>
> . . . .
>
> [We] made peace as the fox or the lion make peace,
>   stretched the rack,
> Yoked, and suffered the yoke, pursued the pariah.
> Evaded, betrayed; blew fierce the fires of division.
> All these, we, too, the free, we, the enlightened!
>
> . . . .
>
> God give us shame, God give us tears, God bow our heads!
> We have not tended the beacon that once cut
> A road of glorious fire across the dark waters.
> Forgive, where you plunge in the storm, forgive, if
>   you can![13]

Even after America's entry into the war, Hagedorn held himself aloof from anti-German propaganda activity. Writing to an old friend in 1942, he asked,

How is this new war hitting you? It is like the old mess, yet so different . . . I wish I felt like plunging into work this time as I did then, writing, organizing, making poems, making speeches. I feel no "call," as the preachers say . . . So I do meaningless little things like serving on the boards of the Loyal Americans of German Descent and of the Volunteer Land Corps (which seeks to get boys and girls on farms not only to work the soil but to learn something about America) . . . I hunger and thirst for a job that can really enlist whatever enthusiasm and energy I have left . . . it is . . . the ancient hunger of the infinitesimal human creature to feel important, at least to himself.[14]

Nevertheless, Hagedorn's view of the Second World War bore a significant resemblance to his view of the First. Both represented moments of personal truth finding for him, moments when he chose, in different ways, to "cleanse" himself by turning his back "definitely" on the past. His vision of World War II is summed up in a lengthy poem, *The Bomb That Fell on America,* published in 1946. It poses the issue explicitly in terms of a contrast between the evil past and the hopeful future. The atomic explosion at Hiroshima had enmeshed the most idealistic of nations in sin and guilt. The bomb was a symbol of both the extraordinary achievements of the "brain of man" and the limitation of intelligence uncontrolled by "heart and soul." The bomb burst on America in the sense that it forced a choice between a radically new spiritual beginning and the death of the planet. It dramatized the need for men of spiritual perception to act together in "solitary dedication and self-forgetfulness," to bring a new fellowship to men and to harness the tremendous power of the human soul.[15]

If the religious doctrine underlying the poem was undiluted Moral Rearmament (Hagedorn rejoined the movement in 1945), it was at the same time carefully adapted to express his specific perceptions of himself and the world. In it one finds his characteristic rejection of the material world and his emphasis on spirit as an aggressive and powerful force. Pervading the poem is a sense of sin and guilt ("our bodies have grown fat and our souls thin"). The "voice of conscience" lacerates the American people for their complicity in dropping the bomb. In a colloquy between God and the poet, the latter admits that he has "fed on lies" and is "unclean." God holds out hope of salvation in a new and active dedication to spiritual values. Thus nations as well as individuals are guilty and must strive for moral rebirth and reconciliation. Hagedorn's passionate identification with America remained intact, for he saw America's chief problem as one of self-division, conflict between weak (materialistic, self-interested) and strong (idealistic, spiritually oriented) principles. This was yet another projection of his own inner struggle between the "weak boy" and the "strong man." His poem enjoined America—as he had often told himself—to "grow up."

It was entirely characteristic of each man that while George Sylvester Viereck saw in the Hiroshima bomb a symbol of the ultimate bankruptcy of civilization, Hagedorn saw in it both the visible manifestation of sin and the possibility of a new life based on a break with the past. Indeed, after the two men accidentally met on the street in New York City in 1956, Viereck casually reported that "I met Hermann Hagedorn, and we buried the hatchet—after forty years." It was as if nothing that had happened had really mattered. Hagedorn, on the other hand, earlier confessed to Viereck's biographer Elmer Gertz: "I am sorry for the kind of hate-fest in which I indulged myself . . . (it) does . . . harm to the person who indulges himself in it and . . . social damage in addition . . . I have come to see that my neighbors' are less my responsibility than my own sins."[16]

During the post–World War II years, while Viereck languished in bitterness and defeat, Hagedorn viewed the world with compulsive optimism. He was impressed by the "moral and economic recovery" of the German people and the transformation of their government into "the protagonist in the struggle for a united European family of nations." His return to the fold of Moral Rearmament was keyed to a new hope for the prospects of international fellowship, brotherhood, and unity. At the prompting of his daughter Dorothea (an active participant in international MRA teamwork), Hagedorn came to believe that his own history and that of his hyphenated family were about to take a radically new turn, to become a "more inspiring story of a human family losing and finding itself in a world family; of nationalism transcended . . . in the individual's identification, in action, with the peoples of all nations—their problems, their sins, and their hunger to achieve the inner unity, the freedom and the power of the God-centered life."[17]

Despite his determination to look to the future only, Hagedorn worked for at least a dozen years putting together his recollections of the past in *The Hyphenated Family: An American Saga*. If the ultimate purpose of the book was to assuage guilt over past actions and feelings, it yet revealed how little he had succeeded in mastering hostility. As one reviewer perceived, the book was intended to show "how completely he got rid of the hyphen." In Hagedorn's background notes for the book, he drew as its major theme his father's looking to the past, to kings, tradition, and position, as opposed to his own orientation to the future, to democracy and free government. He contrasted his father's childish dependence on authority with his own determination to be a responsible citizen, his father's insistence on living in two countries with his own full identification with America. Father Hagedorn's course set the stage for tragedy and had been the source of anguish and unhappiness for everyone connected with him.[18]

The far-flung members of the Hagedorn family who lived to read the story (which Hermann sent to all of them) objected to the extreme emphasis on Father Hagedorn's faults. Adolph's widow may have protested out of the sentimentality of old age, but Fred's widow had good reason not to look back on Father Hagedorn through rose-colored glasses. There were objections, too, to the unrelievedly hostile portraits of Charlotte Hagedorn and the maiden aunts. But whatever the book lost in historical truth, it gained in its recording of a man's obsession with sin and the mechanisms of his self-defense.[19]

Hermann Hagedorn's response to the First World War, like that of every other intensely involved partisan, was the result of psychological, intellectual, social, and political forces that conditioned and limited his range of choices. In his case the war presented an opportunity to link himself to the literary establishment of New England, to affirm the "Americanism" derived from his mother and attributed to the majority culture, and to repudiate the German father he hated. There is paradox in his parental images: his mother was the spiritually dominant of the two personalities, and yet she submitted in most things to the authority of her husband. To the extent that she was passive, German, and in league with the father, she had imperfections that disappointed Hagedorn and would later be reflected in his sense that America, too, fell short of her greatest possibilities. But Annie Hagedorn was the object of considerable affect, which Hagedorn displaced on to moral values, the idea of America, and God. The underlying psychological motive of his identification with his mother's ideals was to make himself worthy of love, to enhance self-love, to find God in himself.

The central conflict of his emotional life came from his relationship to Father Hagedorn. His father held absolute physical authority over the family, but exercised it in a spiritually submissive, weak, vacillating, and "sentimental" manner. From childhood onward, Father Hagedorn elicited an ambivalent response from his son. As a child Hermann felt betrayed and rejected by his father, but to a considerable extent he identified with him. Thus arose the curious psychological situation that in venting aggression against his father he exposed himself to moral anxiety and self-destruction. Burdened with a sense of sin, which represented guilt and self-distrust, Hagedorn struggled against it throughout his life. To avoid guilt he displaced or projected hostility onto father substitutes—hating Woodrow Wilson, for example, or feeling persecuted by Wilson's men. Similarly, he coped with self-division by projection and reaction-formation—the valuation of qualities opposite to those he detested in himself. Despite these mechanisms of self-defense and adaptation, the pressure put upon him by the controversy over World War I released a flood of scarcely cloaked aggression against his father.

If the original threat to his self-esteem came from his German-American father and issued in his own painful self-division, it is easy to see why he should have fixed upon the hyphenate community as the chief enemy of America during the war years. Hagedorn saw his father's sentimentality—the visible aspect of his divided allegiance—as the cause of the "fall of the house of Hagedorn. "His father had unforgivably denied his obligations to his family and to the country in which he had prospered. He had handicapped his son by binding him to foreign—and thus by definition inferior—ways. Hagedorn's vitriolic attack on the "double-minded" German-Americans and their leaders was out of all proportion to the reality of the threat they posed to American morale or to the war effort. Characteristically, he perceived all of the issues raised by the war in moral rather than strategic terms. The uncompromising nature of his positions, the passionate quality of his one hundred percent Americanism, betrayed his fundamental fear of showing weakness. Systematically developing the differences between himself and his German father, he was curiously like the older man in clinging dogmatically to his own conception of social relationships.

Hagedorn was in a sense "saved" by his attachment to his mother. To be sure, he reached a reconciliation of sorts with his father, but there was something forced about it: the crumbs of redemption held out to Father Hagedorn at the end of *The Hyphenated Family* strike one not as symbols of forgiveness but as the grudging penance required to allay guilt. His need for Annie Hagedorn's approval enabled him to control overt aggression and resulted in a public "personality" that was shy and aloof. Equally significant, his attachment to his mother enforced an orientation toward his American future rather than his German past. In this he stood as an exemplar of a whole generation of "Americans of German Descent" who chose rapid assimilation over a continued affiliation with a widely deprecated ethnic heritage. During the First World War he was able to speak, out of his own private needs, for numbers of other German-Americans caught up in a cultural crisis that came to a head in the form of an injunction to slay the European father.

EPILOGUE

Three men; a social crisis: three states of belonging.

Multiple loyalties were at the very center of Hugo Münster-berg's emotional life. Intensely German in education, outlook, and manner, he took pride in "belonging" to the German nation. Germany embodied for him the qualities that he associated with his father: authority, manliness, moral rectitude. His inability to entertain doubts as to Germany's pristine innocence blinded this apostle of "objective" psychology to his own biases and led others falsely to interpret his behavior as that of a German agent.

While Münsterberg's commitment to Germany was an essential part of his self-image, so were his roles at Harvard and in the United States and his ambition to serve as an international ambassador interpreting Germany and America to each other. But he could not reconcile—could not choose among—the various parts of his life (and of himself). Disposed by character to make adjustments to outside pressure so as to maintain self-esteem, he retreated from controversy when pro-German militancy and the antihyphenate response threatened his place in American life. His was the classic ambivalence—and the classic fate—of the man in the middle.

George Sylvester Viereck's defense of the German cause was more aggressive than Münsterberg's, though it rested less on a sense of "belonging" to Germany. Nor did Viereck truly speak for German-Americans as an ethnic group. More fully assimilated than Münsterberg or Hagedorn, he believed himself to be so much an insider in America that he could afford—more, was obliged—to assert his independence. He sought as a minority spokesman to excoriate the majority culture. His militancy enabled him to play the congenial role of rebel. Well after the controversies of the First World War died down, his insistent need to set himself apart from other Americans convinced many that his was the moral obtuseness of a traitor.

Viereck's excessive contrariety was no less psychologically grounded than Münsterberg's compulsive need to intermediate. The cornerstone of Viereck's emotional life was an intense and ambivalent attachment to his mother, which expressed itself through the exploration of various forms of infidelity. These led, in turn, to endless self-justifications: atonements to his father; rationalizations of his sexual behavior, social life, and political activities. Viereck's narcissistic self-absorption controlled his actions: his infidelities and extremism reflected complex emotional responses more than intellectual belief. The fragility of his ties to the outside world was the very characteristic that made him, ultimately, a social outcast.

One might reasonably expect that the most assimilated of these German-Americans would be the prowar patriot. But Herman Hagedorn was the only one of the three men to have grown up in an encapsulated German-American environment. The American culture that Viereck and Münsterberg viewed ambivalently was for Hagedorn a beckoning oasis. Precisely because the bonds of hyphenation were so tightly drawn within his own family, this morally fastidious man found it necessary to couple his yearning identification with American values to a ferocious rejection of his German background. In later years, the continuing anguish of a sense of separation— and of guilt—drove him to a series of religious affirmations.

The personal experiences recorded here resonate in a variety of directions. These men of letters may be taken to stand for important elements in turn-of-the-century American literary and cultural life. Münsterberg was the very embodiment of an assured, arrogant positivism. Viereck was a prime example of the subjectivism and egoism that characterized the artistic liberation of the early 1900s. Hagedorn exemplified the thin idealism of the genteel tradition.

One might reach out for equivalence to a very different time, a very different set of experiences. In more recent years American Jews and blacks have had their own problems of loyalty and identification. Jews have had to face the imputation that they seek to advance the interests of Israel without regard for American national interest. Blacks, too, have been charged with promoting discord by pressing for group advantages no matter what the consequence for others. Neither group has had to face the flash point of divided loyalty—the necessity for choice—that confronted German-Americans in 1917. But the possibility remains that some day they might have to do so.

There are other contemporary echoes of the states of belonging explored here. The persistence of fellow travelers—true believers in the Marxian "socialist" dream, whatever the reality —suggests that they too are a characterological type, rebels who use a foreign ideology to express their alienation from their native culture. Nationalism is an equally recurrent and compelling mode of identification because it amply fulfills the quest for identity that is so central to modern life.

But when all is said and done, the states of belonging attained by Münsterberg, Viereck, and Hagedorn have their strongest social meaning in the context of the German-American experience.

The First World War intruded on the lives of German-Americans in successive phases. At first, public condemnation of the German military attack on Belgium caused many of their leaders to call for a fair hearing of the German side on the issues of the war. In part this was a response to the anti-German rhetoric of Allied supporters, in part the work of pro-German spokesmen seeking to consolidate what was in fact a notably loose-knit ethnic group. The intensification of pressure for ethnic identity gave many German-Americans a context for organizing their initial wartime experiences of spontaneous sympathy for the fatherland and of loss of status in their adopted land.

During the next phase, American opinion increasingly saw the war in terms of threats to the national interest posed by German submarine activity and sabotage by German agents. The rising group consciousness of German-Americans came to be seen not as a defensive but as an offensive act. The "hyphen" was condemned not merely as a sign of foreign allegiance, but as a cause of divisive—un-American—domestic consequence.

German-Americans tried to argue that sympathy for the father-land did not conflict with loyalty to America. But their efforts at group solidarity only induced growing hostility outside the community and dissent within.

Finally, American entry into the war forced German-Americans to decide whether they were Germans *or* Americans. The declaration of war foreclosed the option of their remaining German-Americans who placed American interests first.

When war-born passions turned against German culture as well as German policy, German-Americans bristled at the imputation that theirs was an inferior group, a second-class citizenship. It heightened their wartime sense of community. For many spokesmen this took the psychological form of aggressive defensiveness. After America's entry into the war in April 1917, however, the great majority of German-Americans resolved their problem by suppressing their Germanism and denying that they had ever had a choice to make.

This crisis of identity inevitably took an intensely personal, individualized form. Many German-Americans expressed their quandary in terms of rival familial attachments: Cannot a man love both his mother and his wife? The resolution of conflicting loyalties drew upon private, affective relationships and self-images as well as more public, policy choices. Indeed, politics provided an external forum for the working out of psychological strains.

The German-American leaders I have discussed here underwent in an intense and public way this trial of inner conflict and resolution. Their responses were intimately related to their personalities, their private lives, their public careers. While each man's experience was in one sense unique, what they said and did carried a larger authority because it echoed the trauma of others who underwent the same experience.

Describing the dominant ethnic groups in New York City during the early 1960s, Nathan Glazer and Daniel P. Moynihan commented on a notable absence, a dog that did not bark:

in terms of size and the achievement of its members, the Germans ought certainly to be included among the principal ethnic groups of the city. If never quite as numerous as the Irish, they were indisputably the second largest group in the late nineteenth century, accounting for perhaps a third of the population and enjoying the highest reputation. But to-day, while German influence is to be seen in virtually every aspect of the city's life, the Germans *as a group* are vanished.[1]

This disappearance was the product of many forces. German immigration declined steadily after 1890. The German-language press, schools, and churches were unable to hold supporters without ultimately self-destructive adaptations to American life. Intermarriage and suburbanization reinforced the already substantial diversity and looseness of German-American culture.

Given the long-term trend toward assimilation, why was the 1914–1919 experience so traumatic? By the same token, one might have expected that after the passions of the war period died down there would be a rebirth of German-American consciousness, as has been the case with some ethnic groups in recent years. Why has their denial of their group identity been so complete?[2]

At least part of the reason lies in the special character of the challenge posed by the war. The crucial question was not the German-Americans' ties to Germany, but the seeming incompatibility of their group identity with the requirements of American citizenship. However much the issue for German-Americans was one of individual self-identification, for the society at large it became a matter of public identification. German-Americans' states of belonging ultimately involved the question of belonging to the State.

Insofar as they set themselves apart as a political bloc, German-Americans raised a social issue more profound than the passing wartime demand for conformity. American involvement in the war posed the question of whether their ethnic allegiance was congruent with national loyalty. Ultimately, they could preserve their place in American life only at the cost of their group identity. This was the tragedy of German-America; and it was the tragedy of Hugo Münsterberg, George Sylvester Viereck, and Hermann Hagedorn.

MANUSCRIPT SOURCES

PART ONE: HUGO MÜNSTERBERG

Charles W. Eliot Papers (EP), Harvard University Archives.

Kuno Francke Manuscripts, Harvard University Archives.

William Ernest Hocking Papers (HP), Hocking Library, Madison, New Hampshire.

William James Papers (JP), Houghton Library, Harvard University.

A. Lawrence Lowell Papers (LP), Harvard University Archives.

Hugo Münsterberg Manuscripts (MM), Boston Public Library.

Hugo Munsterberg II Papers (MP), in the possession of Hugo Munsterberg II.

Ella Münsterberg Papers (EMP), were in the possession of the late Ella Münsterberg.

C. Alphonso Smith Papers (SP), University of Virginia Library.

Oswald Garrison Villard Papers (VP), Houghton Library, Harvard University.

PART TWO: GEORGE SYLVESTER VIERECK

Sigmund Freud Letters, Manuscripts Division, Library of Congress.

Elmer Gertz Manuscripts, Manuscripts Division, Library of Congress.

Edward M. House Manuscripts, Yale University Library.

George S. Viereck Papers, Special Collections Department, University of Iowa Library.

George S. Viereck Scrapbooks (SBS), Hoover Institution on War, Revolution and Peace, Stanford University.

PART THREE: HERMANN HAGEDORN

Hagedorn Correspondence, Beinecke Library, Yale University.

Hagedorn File, Archives of the Library of Congress.

Hagedorn Letters, Houghton Library, Harvard University.
Hagedorn Manuscripts, Sterling Library, Yale University.
Hagedorn Papers, in the possession of Dorothea Hagedorn Parfit.
Pulsifer Letters, Colby College Library.

NOTES

INTRODUCTION

1. John Higham, *Strangers in the Land* (New Brunswick, N.J.: Rutgers University Press, 1955), 196. The 1910 census lists a total of eight million persons of German extraction (8.7 percent of the total U.S. population), 2.3 million of them born in Germany and the other 5.7 million native-born of foreign or mixed parentage. Regionally, the German-born and German stock clustered in the Middle Atlantic and East North Central states, with about a third distributed between Boston and Pittsburgh and slightly more than half between Pittsburgh and Denver. Occupational diversity reflected differences in time of migration and place of settlement. About a third of German immigrants were Roman Catholic; well over half came with Lutheran, Reformed, or Evangelical Protestant church affiliations.

2. *Mitteilungen* (Bulletin of the National German-American Alliance), December 1915, 3.

PART ONE: HUGO MÜNSTERBERG

Introduction

1. Clipping dated June 1, 1915, MM.

2. Münsterberg to W. H. Taft, June 24, 1909; to C. W. Eliot, November 11, 1908; Hugo Münsterberg, "Twenty-five Years in America," typescript. MM.

1. Childhood and Youth

1. Diary of Moritz Münsterberg, 2/27/55, 2/6/56, MP.

2. Ibid., 1/21/55, 2/4/55, 2/27/55, 2/6/56, 2/7/56, 2/10/61, 2/9/62, 2/4/66, 2/24/66, 2/7/69, 2/7/70; Margaret Münsterberg,

Hugo Münsterberg: His Life and Work (New York: D. Appleton Co., 1922), 16–17.

3. Danzig State Archives, Registry no. 36, 247–249, and Registry no. 24, 151, 161; Diary of Moritz, 1/31/61, 2/9/62.

4. Diary of Moritz, 2/23/62, 1/23/76, 1/28/77, 2/2/79; Hugo to Moritz, 1869, EMP. According to Danzig historian Samuel Echt there were five small congregations of Jews in the city; Moritz Münsterberg became president of one of them in 1876. Religious education was limited and most Danzig Jews actively engaged in the city's cultural life. Personal communication, May 29, 1971.

5. Diary of Moritz, 2/7/69, 2/7/70, 1/23/76. Otto to Moritz, 1/24/68; Hugo to Anna, 2/25/73, 9/4/73, 6/29/74, 7/7/75; Hugo to Moritz, 1/15/77; Moritz to Fanny Bernhardi, 6/25/67, 8/15/67; Albert Münsterberg to Moritz, 9/4/73. EMP.

6. Hugo to Anna, 2/22/73, 2/27/74, EMP.

7. Ibid., 9/4/73, 2/25/73, 6/26/74, 6/29/74; Hugo to Moritz, 1869, 2/17/71, 2/19/71, 1/22/76, 2/5/76, EMP.

8. Hugo to parents, 9/11/73, EMP; Hugo Münsterberg, *American Traits* (Boston: Houghton Mifflin, 1902), 49; Margaret Münsterberg, *Hugo*, 4–8.

9. Hugo to Moritz, 5/29/75, 7/2/75, 7/5/75; "Meditations on the 3rd of June, 1876." EMP.

10. Hugo to Anna, 2/25/73; to parents, 9/4/73, 9/21/73; to Moritz, 6/27/75, 7/7/75, 7/17/75, 1/10/76, 1/17/77, 1/26/77, 1/31/77, 2/3/77, 2/14/77, 1/20/79, 1/25/79, 2/6/79, 7/9/79, 1880 (undated). EMP.

11. Diary of Moritz, 2/2/79.

12. Hugo to Otto, 4/20/82, 4/27/82, 5/9/82, 5/27/82, 6/6/82, 8/3/82, EMP.

13. Ibid., 4/9/82, 4/27/82, 5/9/82, 5/11/82, 5/23/82, 6/6/82, 6/11/82.

14. Ibid., 4/20/82, 5/23/82, 7/5/82.

15. Ibid., 6/6/82, 6/20/82, 7/5/82.

16. Ibid., 4/27/82, 5/23/82, 7/12/82; Margaret Münsterberg, *Hugo*, 20. For Hugo's later recollection of the affair with Mina as a platonic friendship see "Crossroads" in Hugo Terberg [pseud.], *Verse* (Groszenhain: Baumert and Ronge, 1897), 42.

17. Hugo to Otto, 5/9/82, 7/5/82, 8/3/82, 9/15/82, 9/21/82, EMP.

18. Ibid., 8/3/82. In a later poem, "Epistle to a Friend," Hugo offers the advice that one must not succumb to flattery *or* criticism, but stick to one's goals and "float" free of others who might drag

one down. One should not become involved with any group but keep control of one's life in one's own hands. *Verse*, 33.

19. Ismar Elbogen, *A Century of Jewish Life* (Philadelphia: Jewish Publication Society, 1946), 81–97; Samuel Echt, personal communication, May 29, 1971. All four of Moritz Münsterberg's sons (and seven of his eight grandchildren) married gentiles: Otto's wife was the sister of a "professional" anti-Semite; Emil married into the aristocratic von Spangenberg family; Oskar married an Anglo-American. Hugo's wife came from a Jewish line but her father had converted before she was born. Among the sons, only Otto remained a Jew—probably for business reasons—until he died. When his daughter, Anna, married a Jew the alliance was considered unfortunate. Emil's daughter, Else, moved to England to marry William Dawson, a Germanophile and a Nazi sympathizer. Interview with Hugo Munsterberg, son of Oskar, March 5, 1971.

20. A. A. Roback, "Hugo Münsterberg—The Dramatic Figure in Psychology," *B'nai B'rith Magazine* (1926), vol. xli, no. 3, p. 120.

21. "Wedding Toast, June 30, 1913," MM; "Dann," p. 8, and "Sleighriding," p. 30, in *Verse*.

22. See "Epistle to a Friend," p. 33, and "The Valley of Knowledge," p. 38, in *Verse*; Hugo to Oskar, 7/22/81, EMP.

23. See "Homeward," p. 36, and "The Future," p. 38, in *Verse*.

2. Choosing a Vocation

1. Fritz Ringer, *The Decline of the German Mandarins* (Cambridge: Harvard University Press, 1969), 40–41, 136; Margaret Münsterberg, *Hugo*, 14–15, 23; Hugo to Otto, 7/5/82, 8/3/82, EMP.

2. Joseph Ben David and Randall Collins, "Social Factors in the Origins of a New Science: The Case of Psychology," *American Sociological Review* 31, no. 4 (August 1966): 463. See also Dorothy Ross, "On the Origins of Psychology," ibid. 32, no. 3 (June 1967): 466–469, for a dissenting view of the significance of status considerations in the founding of scientific psychology.

3. R. S. Peters, ed., *Brett's History of Psychology* (Cambridge: M.I.T. Press, 1965), 504–513.

4. A. A. Roback, *A History of American Psychology* (New York: Collier Books, 1964), 213.

5. Fritz Ringer points out (*German Mandarins*, 136) that "the position of the instructor offered a perfect opportunity to the young Jewish intellectual . . . because it lay outside the framework of official careers." Although instructors were certified by academic

officials they were in fact self-employed. Only associate and full professors enjoyed official appointments (and government salaries) at German universities.

6. Hugo Münsterberg, *Willenshandlung* (Freiburg: J. C. B. Mohr, 1888); William James, *Principles of Psychology* (New York: H. Holt Co., 1890), II, 505; James, *Psychology: A Briefer Course* (New York: H. Holt Co., 1892), 379. James first published his view in 1884.

7. Margaret Münsterberg, *Hugo,* 307; Hugo Münsterberg, *Ursprung der Sittlichkeit* [Origin of Morality] (Freiburg: J. C. B. Mohr, 1889); idem, *Psychotherapy* (New York: Moffat, Yard and Co., 1909), ix. James R. Angell, Howard C. Warren, and Mary W. Calkins, later outstanding psychologists, planned to go to Freiburg to study with Münsterberg. Carl Murchison, ed., *A History of Psychology in Autobiography* (Worcester: Clark University Press, 1930–1967, 5 vols.), III, 7; I, 33; I, 453.

8. James to Münsterberg, 8/27/90, 7/8/91, 4/13/93, JP; Murchison, *Psychology,* I, 401; II, 215–216.

9. James to Münsterberg, 2/21/92; James to Royce, 6/22/92, JP.

10. Royce to Münsterberg, 7/14/92, MM; Samuel Eliot Morison, ed., *The Development of Harvard University, 1868–1929* (Cambridge: Harvard University Press, 1930), 18; Margaret Münsterberg, *Hugo,* 48; Münsterberg, "Twenty-five Years"; James to Carl Stumpf, 1/24/94, JP.

11. Selma Münsterberg, "Old Memories," EMP; Münsterberg, "Twenty-five Years." Mary Calkins, who had been a student of William James and who opened a psychological laboratory at Wellesley College in 1893, worked on and off in Münsterberg's Harvard laboratory from 1892 to 1895. Expressing her intellectual debt to him, she later wrote that he was "a man of deep learning, high originality and astounding versatility, interested alike in systematic psychology [and] in the setting and solution of experimental problems . . . Dr. Münsterberg . . . swung the Laboratory doors open to me" at a time when access for women was "unprecedented." Murchison, *Psychology,* I, 33–34.

12. Münsterberg to C. W. Eliot, 9/14/94, EP; Münsterberg to William James, 9/14/94, JP.

13. Münsterberg, "Twenty-five Years"; Hall to Münsterberg, 5/4/95, MM; Selma Münsterberg, "Old Memories." Hall was convinced that his own laboratory at Clark held preeminence.

14. Royce to Eliot, 2/19/97, EP; Eliot to Münsterberg, 3/3/97, MM.

15. Mark Baldwin to Münsterberg, 3/30/97, and Eliot to Münsterberg, 3/3/97, MM; Roback, *History*, 214; Selma Münsterberg, "Old Memories." While opportunities were available to both Jews and Jewish converts at the *Privatdocent* level (about 12 percent of the former and 7 percent of the latter served as instructors in 1909–1910), movement into the upper ranks of the professoriat was difficult. In 1909–1910 "less than 3% of full professors at German universities were of the Jewish religion, and another 4% were converts." Ringer, *German Mandarins*, 136. Münsterberg's religious background would have made it easy for Wundt or Müller to blackball him.

16. Münsterberg to James, 3/19/97, JP; Münsterberg, "Twenty-five Years."

17. George H. Palmer to Münsterberg, 4/14/97, MM; Morison, *Development of Harvard*, 17–18. The book, *Psychology and Life* (Boston: Houghton Mifflin, 1899) included several essays previously published in the *Psychological Review* and in the *Atlantic Monthly*. Münsterberg eventually developed a strong and clear English prose style, but he never lost his German accent. Howard Warren recalls his appearance before the American Psychological Association in 1894 as an occasion when Münsterberg "brought down the house. Caldwell had been entertaining us during the evening with comic songs. There followed loud calls for Münsterberg: 'Gentlemen, Mr. Caldwell has been singing the funny songs: now you want to hear the man with the funny English.'" Murchison, *Psychology*, I, 456–457.

3. An American Career

1. Murchison, *Psychology*, II, 42.

2. Ibid., II, 41; IV, 4, 80, 326; V, 316 (comments are by K. Dunlap, E. C. Tolman, R. M. Elliott, and S. L. Pressey); Roback, *History*, 224.

3. Roback, *History*, 222; Murchison, *Psychology*, I, 35; II, 376, 389; IV, 40, 326; V, 6, 290, 316 (comments are by R. S. Woodworth, E. C. Tollman, G. Allport, H. A. Murray, S. L. Pressey, M. Calkins, R. Yerkes, and R. M. Elliott); Edwin G. Boring, *A History of Experimental Psychology* (New York: Appleton Century Crofts, 1957), 428.

4. Hugo Münsterberg, *Psychology: General and Applied* (New York: D. Appleton Co., 1914), 139–144; idem, *Grundzüge der Psychologie* (Leipzig: J. A. Barth, 1900), 402–562; Peters, *Brett's Psy-*

chology, 657–659. According to Gardner Murphy, Münsterberg's theory does not account for (1) reflex action, i.e., times when paths are open yet discharge is not accompanied by clear consciousness, and (2) the development of habit, i.e., learned regular responses of which the organism is less and less conscious with repetition. His theory demands the opposite of this. Gardner Murphy, *Historical Introduction to Modern Psychology* (rev. ed., New York: Harcourt Brace, 1950), 220.

5. Peters, *Brett's Psychology,* 687.

6. Münsterberg, *Psychology and Life,* 1–34, 179–228; idem, *Psychology: General and Applied,* 285–296; idem, *Science and Idealism* (Boston: Houghton Mifflin, 1906); Münsterberg, ed., *Harvard Psychological Studies* (New York: MacMillan Co., 1906), I, 643. Münsterberg's view of the position of scientific psychology in the "system of knowledge" placed him squarely in the philosophic tradition of the Baden School of neoidealists, in which his friend Heinrich Rickert was a leading figure. For a useful analysis of Münsterberg's idealistic metaphysics see Bruce Kuklick, *The Rise of American Philosophy* (New Haven: Yale University Press, 1977), 203–208.

7. Murchison, *Psychology,* IV, 79; V, 6, 423 (comments are by G. Allport, R. M. Elliott, and M. S. Viteles.

8. Ibid., IV, 79; V, 423 (Elliott and Viteles).

9. *Verse,* 126.

10. *American Traits,* 155–156, 219.

11. Münsterberg, *The Americans* (New York: McClure, Phillips Co., 1904), 234, 254.

12. Ibid., viii–x.

13. William James to Münsterberg, 7/8/91, MM; George F. Palmer to Alice Freeman Palmer, June 18, 1901, Palmer Papers, Houghton Library, Harvard University; Margaret Münsterberg, *Hugo,* 88.

14. Münsterberg to Evelyn M. Albright, May 18, 1916, MM; William James to J. I. Ward, July 31, 1904, cited in Ralph Barton Perry, *The Thought and Character of William James* (Boston: Little, Brown Co., 1935), II, 151, 700; Münsterberg, "The Scientific Plan of the Congress," in Howard J. Rogers, ed., *Congress of Arts and Science* (Boston: Houghton Mifflin, 1905), I, 85–134.

15. Margaret Münsterberg, *Hugo,* 125; Münsterberg, "Twenty-five Years"; Notes of William Ernest Hocking, October 1916, HP. Münsterberg believed that Emerson Hall would be a monument to

the unity of all branches of philosophy, happily placed in the center of Harvard Yard. *Science and Idealism,* 3–5.

16. *American Traits* 97, 114–119.

17. Münsterberg to A. L. Lowell, October 21, 1909, MM; Ringer, *German Mandarins,* 136. Münsterberg also claimed to have refused a lectureship at Oxford in 1897 because it was deficient in status and laboratory provision. But the offer itself appears to have been quite indefinite. W. T. Gill to Münsterberg, 8/22/98, 9/17/98, MM. Despite his financial independence, Münsterberg never missed an opportunity to press Eliot or Lowell for a salary increase. He was among the highest-paid professors at Harvard around 1900.

18. Perry, *James,* II, 147.

19. James to Münsterberg, April 11, 1901, JP; Margaret Münsterberg, *Hugo,* 72; James to C. W. Eliot, December 28, 1905, EP; Münsterberg to Eliot, December 28, 29, 1905, and Eliot to Münsterberg, December 29, 1905, MM.

20. James to Münsterberg, June 18, 1900, JP; James to Eliot, June 20, 1904, EP; F. O. Matthiessen and K. Murdock, eds., *The Notebooks of Henry James* (New York: Oxford University Press, 1961), 317.

21. Münsterberg to Eliot, December 28, 1905, and November 11, 1908, MM.

22. Münsterberg to C. H. Judd, March 13, 1909, JP; James to Münsterberg, March 16, 1909, and Münsterberg to James, March 17, 1909, MM.

23. Münsterberg to C. L. Dana, November 19, 1909, MM; Münsterberg, "My Friends, The Spiritualists," reprinted in *American Problems* (New York: Moffat, Yard and Co., 1910), 122, 142–143.

24. James to Münsterberg, October 22, 1909; Joseph Jastrow to Münsterberg, June 8, 1914, and June 12, 1914. MM.

25. Münsterberg to Jastrow, June 10, 1914, and to James Mc-Keen Cattell, January 29, 1913, MM; Nathan G. Hale, Jr., *Freud and the Americans* (New York: Oxford University Press, 1971), 275.

26. Margaret Münsterberg, *Hugo,* 143–147, 374–375; Münsterberg, "Experiments with Harry Orchard," typescript, MM; Clarence Darrow to Münsterberg, August 16, 1907, MM. Münsterberg almost certainly knew of Carl Jung's work on word association. In response to charges levied by the psychiatrist S. I. Jelliffe that he was "a plagiarist" who knew nothing about the "practical side of criminology," Münsterberg argued that men of his position

were often liable to misquotation and attack. He claimed that he freely acknowledged his debts to other scientists. Although it is true that he never claimed to have invented the word association tests, his writings imply that the techniques he used were his own. See "Dr. Jelliffe's Attack on Dr. Münsterberg Absurd and Utterly Untrue," typescript, 1910, MM.

27. McClure to Münsterberg, July 24, 1907, MM. Münsterberg sold three articles on courtroom psychology to the *New York Times* (for $1000) and three to McClure (for an undisclosed sum) in 1907.

28. William James to C. W. Eliot, June 20, 1904, EP; Edwin B. Holt, *The Freudian Wish* (New York: H. Holt Co., 1915), 37–39.

29. Münsterberg to Holt, March 24, 1916, MM. Ironically, Münsterberg's collected articles on truth detection in legal proceedings (*On the Witness Stand*) were dedicated to Holt.

30. Münsterberg, *Psychotherapy* (New York: Moffat, Yard and Co., 1909), ix, 1, 44–45. The book was quite popular, selling 3,000 copies within two months of publication. Münsterberg's general definition of the psychotherapist's task accorded with the opinion of most American and French neurologists, who largely ignored the "deeper" therapies. Hale, *Freud*, 170.

31. Münsterberg, *Psychotherapy*, 86, 97, 106, and passim. Münsterberg was acquainted with Janet's work before he left Germany, but Janet also lectured at the Lowell Institute in Boston in 1904 and at Harvard in 1906. Münsterberg's own "suggestion therapy" closely follows that of Professor Hippolyte Bernheim, with this difference: Bernheim believed that his therapy worked through the acting out of an idea planted with rapport in a field of limited attention. Münsterberg's conception of suggestion therapy involved the forced imposition on the patient's mind of a proposition for action—forced in such a way that the impulse to the opposite is inhibited: i.e., therapy as a method that forces the mind to yield. See *Psychology and Social Sanity* (New York: Doubleday, Page, 1914), 259. Most other neurologists characterized the physician's role as exercising a far more passive moral influence. Hale, *Freud*, 170.

32. Münsterberg, *Psychotherapy*, 25, 27–71, 125, 152, 265, 296, 349, and passim. See also Münsterberg et al., *Subconscious Phenomena* (Boston: R. G. Badger, 1910), 16–32.

33. Münsterberg to Titchener, August 10, 1909, Titchener Papers, Cornell University; Münsterberg, *Psychotherapy*, ix–x; Hale, *Freud*, 274–275. Münsterberg served as an associate editor of

Prince's *Journal of Abnormal Psychology* along with James Putnam, Boris Sidis, and Adolph Meyer.

34. Margaret Brennan and Merton Gill, *Hypnotherapy* (New York: International Universities Press, 1964), 11; Margaret Münsterberg, *Hugo*, 173.

35. Münsterberg, *Psychotherapy*, 382.

36. E. G. Boring, "Wilhelm Wundt," in *International Encyclopedia of the Social Sciences* (New York: MacMillan Co., 1968), 16:584; A. A. Roback, *Aspects of Applied Psychology and Crime* (Cambridge: Sci-Art, 1964), 21, 28. *Psychology and the Teacher* (New York: D. Appleton Co., 1910), capitalized on contemporary interest in pedagogical reform by outlining psychological knowledge useful to educators. But it urged restraint in both amateurish application and the "enthusiastic belief that psychology and pedagogy can be a substitute for true scholarship" on the part of the teacher. *Teacher*, 87. The book enjoyed a popularity second only to *Psychotherapy*.

37. Münsterberg, *Psychology and Industrial Efficiency* (Boston: Houghton Mifflin, 1913), 56, 63–82; "Report to the American Association of Labor Legislation, Atlantic City, N.J., June 5, 1912," typescript, EMP. *Psychology and Industrial Efficiency*, an English version of *Psychologie und Wirtschaftsleben* (Leipzig: J. A. Barth, 1912), ran to several printings. Encouraged by the interest in his work, Münsterberg proposed to the Secretary of Commerce that a national institute of research in industrial psychology be set up along the lines of the agricultural stations. Münsterberg to Secretary of Commerce William C. Redfield, May 24, 1913, MM.

38. Margaret Münsterberg, *Hugo*, 209; *Industrial Efficiency*, 32–33 and passim; Loren Baritz, *The Servants of Power* (Middletown: Wesleyan University Press, 1960), 37.

39. Willy Hellpach, "Hugo Münsterberg, *Psychologie und Wirtschaftsleben*," in *Zeitschrift fur angewandte Psychologie* 8 (1913–1914), 567–583; Ringer, *German Mandarins*, 85, 314.

40. Münsterberg, *The Eternal Values* (Boston: Houghton Mifflin, 1909), vii. *Psychologie der Werte* (Leipzig: J. A. Barth, 1908), *Psychologie und Wirtschaftsleben* (Leipzig: J. A. Barth, 1912), and *Die Amerikaner* (Berlin: E. S. Mittler und Sohn, 1903), all preceded their English language equivalents. *Grundzüge der Psychotechnik* (Leipzig: J. A. Barth, 1914) was not translated. In the preface to his major philosophical treatise Münsterberg explained, "the author in me has presented a case of double personality. For

many years the one person has written in English, but published only light books and essays; all that time the other person has written in German, but has insisted on writing scholarly papers and systematic works. The one tried to address a wider public; the other sought only the ear of the scholar . . . When the philosophical striving of my whole life had led me to a new idealistic standpoint from which I saw the ultimate problem of the world in a new light, it seemed only natural that the German in me should say it in his mother tongue and with the seriousness of scholarly formulation. The product was my *Philosophie der Werte.*" Cf. Viereck's statement about his bilingual heritage in chapter 6.

41. Münsterberg, *Vocation and Learning* (St. Louis: People's University, 1912), preface.

42. Münsterberg, *Psychology and Social Sanity* (New York: Doubleday, Page, 1914), viii, ix, 3–68, 276.

43. Münsterberg, *Problems,* 21, 27, 52, 63–65, 71, 104–113.

44. Ibid., 71, 99; Münsterberg to Editors of the *New Republic,* February 6, 1913, MM.

45. Münsterberg to Lowell, June 23, 1909, MM; to J. Walter Thompson, February 25, 1909, in Houghton Library, Harvard University. Busch promised $50,000 to the Germanic Museum a few weeks prior to the appearance of Münsterberg's article in 1908. The coincidence of timing aroused suspicion.

46. Münsterberg, *American Patriotism* (New York: Moffat, Yard and Co., 1913), 16–17, 86–87, 91. Before leaving for Europe in 1910, Münsterberg signed a $2000 contract with McClure for a series of four to five articles to be entitled "When I Came Home." When they were written, McClure found the essays too impersonal and highbrow, and rejected them. The two men quarreled bitterly about their obligations under the contract, Münsterberg taking the position that he was a writer of such public standing that to make a contract with him was to agree to publish whatever he wrote. He refused to revise his material. McClure published one short piece and settled the contract for $1000. Münsterberg published the other pieces elsewhere and collected them in *American Patriotism.* Willa Cather to Münsterberg, May 6, 1910; Münsterberg to McClure, April 27, 1911; McClure to Münsterberg, October 16, 1911. MM.

47. Münsterberg, *Patriotism,* 6, 19.

48. In *American Problems* (p. 2) he described "the overflow of useless movements from the chewing of gum to the ceaseless motion of the rocking chair . . . the hustling and pushing of the pub-

lic life, the hasty passing from one interest to another" as characteristic of the "nervous condition" of American society.

49. C. W. Eliot to Münsterberg, March 22, 1904; October 11, 1898; February 14, 1902; to William James, December 29, 1905. EP. Münsterberg wanted Harvard to require Latin, Greek, and advanced mathematics for admission. Eliot argued that such requirements would cripple the influence of Harvard by cutting off whole classes of the population attending public schools that did not offer Greek. Eliot to Münsterberg, January 26, 1899, EP. In 1899 the Harvard Corporation rejected Münsterberg's proposal that an honorary degree be awarded to German Ambassador Holleben. Even though Eliot himself supported the proposal, Münsterberg took its rejection as a personal rebuke. Again, in 1901, he was insulted when Harvard presented him with an honorary Master's degree—the traditional way in which Harvard honored its own faculty members. George H. Palmer to Münsterberg, May 29, 1901. When Prince Henry visited Harvard to present an art collection to the Germanic Museum in 1902, Eliot committed several social gaffes by failing to take "proper" notice of the decoration presented to him by the Prince. Henry James, *Charles W. Eliot* (Boston: Houghton Mifflin, 1930), II, 141–142.

50. Eliot to Münsterberg, April 8, 1908, MM.

51. Münsterberg to Eliot, November 29, 1902; February 26, 1906; October 29, 1908. MM. Münsterberg proposed sharp limitations on the program, including short visits instead of year-long terms and its application to professors of literature and language only.

52. Eliot to Münsterberg, November 6, 1908; Münsterberg to Eliot, November 11, 1908. MM.

53. Eliot to Münsterberg, November 16, 1908, MM.

54. Münsterberg to Eliot, November 17, 1908; December 7, 1908; Eliot to Münsterberg, December 5, 1908. MM.

55. Eliot to Münsterberg, December 10, 1908; Münsterberg to Eliot, November 11, 1908; December 10, 1908. MM.

56. Münsterberg to Eliot, February 4, 1908, MM.

57. Münsterberg to Eliot, April 29, 1909, and Eliot to Münsterberg, April 30, 1909, MM.

58. Münsterberg to Lowell, October 21, 1909; Lowell to Friedrich Schmidt, October 22, 1909. LP. Jacob Schiff to Münsterberg, May 14, 1910; Münsterberg to Arthur von Briesen, November 22, 1910; to Lowell, December 12, 1910; to Alice Hofer, January 12,

1911. MM. Lowell told Schmidt that he would not suggest Münsterberg unless requested to do so because he understood the plan
of the exchange to call for the appointment of an American from
Harvard. The usual procedure was for the Ministry of Culture to
make a selection from a list provided by Harvard.

59. Münsterberg, *Patriotism,* 11; Münsterberg to Lowell, December 15, 1910, and Lowell to Münsterberg, February 23, 1911, LP.

60. Münsterberg, "Twenty-five Years."

61. Butler to Münsterberg, May 25, 1904, Butler Manuscripts,
Columbia University; Boston *Evening Transcript,* April 16, 1907;
Münsterberg to Butler, March 6, 1911, MM. Münsterberg initiated
the exchange with Butler in 1904 by relaying the information that
the German scholar was insulted by Butler's offer. Münsterberg to
Butler, May 19, 1904, Butler MSS. In 1911 he reminded Butler of
this incident and claimed that he could have ruined Butler's reputation in Germany at the time by showing his damaging remarks to
a number of German professors. Münsterberg to Butler, March 6,
1911, MM.

62. Münsterberg to Lowell, November 15, 1910, and December 15, 1910, MM.

63. Münsterberg to Ralph Barton Perry, December 14, 1910,
EMP; Lowell to Münsterberg, March 9, 1911, MM; Münsterberg,
Patriotism, 74. In his letter to Perry, Münsterberg also noted with
great pride that "for two months every evening has found me at a
party"—implying that he was lionized by his German hosts. According to Margaret Münsterberg (*Hugo,* 206), however, some of these
parties were in his own home and confined "mostly [to his] American friends." The Smith-Münsterberg story was enjoyed at the
University of Virginia, where Smith held a professorship. Southern
papers told it as the triumph of an American over a German and a
Virginian over a Harvard man. Clipping, SP.

64. Smith to D. J. Hill, February 3, 1911, SP; Münsterberg to
Butler, March 6, 1911, MM; to Smith, September 22, 1910, SP; to
Lowell, February 3, 1911, LP.

65. Münsterberg to Butler, March 6, 1911; Smith to Butler,
February 4, 1911. SP.

66. F. W. Wile to Münsterberg, March 2, 1911, MM; *New
York Times,* March 18, 1911, 1:5; New York *Evening Post,* March
24, 1911; Frank McLean to Smith, July 31, 1911, SP.

67. Münsterberg to W. H. Taft, September 11, 1911, MM; Hill
to Lowell, April 27, 1911, and Lowell to Münsterberg, April 12,
1911, LP.

68. Smith to Hill, February 3, 1911, and to Excellency von Trott zu Solz, January 31, 1911, SP; Schmidt to Lowell, May 4, 1913, LP. Ironically, Francke was a key figure in the establishment of the Berlin-Harvard Exchange in 1905. The plan developed from his initiative in bringing German scholars to Harvard to lecture at the Germanic Museum. See C. W. Eliot, "On the Origin of the Germanic Museum and the Harvard-Berlin Exchange Professorships," LP.

69. Münsterberg to W. H. Taft, September 11, 1911, MM.

70. Membership in the foundation was extended to include all of the descendants of Meyer Münsterberg (1791-1858) after Moritz's brother Albert donated 10,000 marks. In 1917 the foundation was officially registered with the city of Danzig. It held assets of 20,000 marks. It was started with gifts of 40 marks from each of Moritz's sons. Recordbook in the possession of Hugo Munsterberg.

71. Otto and Oskar sailed for the United States with Hugo at the end of the latter's summer visit in 1912. Aboard ship, Oskar met an American girl, Helen Rice, whom he subsequently married. Their son, named after Hugo, fled Germany in the 1930s and became an American citizen and a professor of art history.

72. Münsterberg to Jacob G. Schurman, August 29, 1895; to Andrew Carnegie, 1909; Jacob Schiff to Münsterberg, May 8, 1905; J. D. Rockefeller to Münsterberg, June 24, 1910; Gustav Pabst to Münsterberg, March 19, 1912. MM. Münsterberg to O. G. Villard, February 21, 1905, VP.

73. See *Aus Deutsch-Amerika* (Berlin: E. S. Mittler, 1909) for a collection of Münsterberg's speeches and essays. Münsterberg to W. H. Taft, February 28, 1912; Hon. Richard E. Bartholdt to Münsterberg, March 7, 1912; Münsterberg to Bartholdt, March 12, 1912. MM. Boston contained fewer Germans in 1910 than any other large American city. There had been relatively few German settlers in New England, and with the exception of a handful of intellectuals and scholars they never gained more than a patronizing recognition. See Barbara M. Solomon, *Ancestors and Immigrants* (Cambridge: Harvard University Press, 1956), 156–159, for an account of Yankee attitudes toward Boston Germans.

74. Münsterberg to R. W. Drechsler, September 21, 1911; to Editor, *Boston Herald*, September 22, 1913. MM.

75. Morison, *Development of Harvard*, 19.

4. The War

1. Solomon, *Ancestors*, 156–158; Margaret Münsterberg, *Hugo*, 263–264; Morison, *Three Centuries of Harvard* (Cambridge: Harvard University Press, 1965), 450–451.

2. Münsterberg to Gerald Stanley Lee, April 5, 1916; Rutger B. Jewett (for D. Appleton) to Münsterberg, September 6, 1914. MM. Lee had published a book in which he charged that Münsterberg fastened on the German side with unseemly haste and in general led German-Americans in a display of arrogant self-assertion. Gerald S. Lee, *We* (New York: Doubleday Page Co., 1916), 608–612.

3. *The War and America* (New York: D. Appleton Co., 1914), preface, 4, 11–14, 37, and passim.

4. Ibid., 43, 78, 82, 185, 190, 200–201, and passim. For variants on the theme of Germany's defensive aggression, see John L. Stoddard, *Letter Dated October 1914* (Bremen, 1914); Edmund von Mach, *Germany's Point of View* (Chicago: A. C. McClurg Co., 1915), Kuno Francke, "Germany's Defensive Aggression," *The Fatherland*, August 10, 1914; John W. Burgess, *The European War of 1914: Its Causes, Purposes and Notable Results* (Chicago: A. C. McClurg Co., 1915); Eugen Kuehnemann, *Germany, America and the War* (New York, Issues and Events Booklet, 1915); Kuno Francke, *Germany's Fateful Hour* (Chicago: Germanistic Society of Chicago, 1915); E. Stauffen, *Europe Bled White* (pamphlet, November 1914); Bernard Dernburg, *Searchlights on the War* (New York, 1915). Von Mach's and Dernburg's books reprint articles originally published in newspapers and magazines from October 1914 to May 1915.

5. *The War and America*, 28, 75–76, 96–97.

6. The theme of Germany's encirclement had considerable significance in German history and continued to exert great power over the German imagination after 1914. Erik Erikson, *Childhood and Society* (2nd ed., New York: Norton Co., 1963), 354. See also Frederick Hertz, *Nationality in History and Politics* (New York: Oxford University Press, 1944), 45–48. The theme was developed for American consumption in (among others) Kuehnemann, *Germany, America and the War*.

7. *The War and America*, 17, 19, 23–24, 33. Münsterberg's conviction of press bias survived an offer from the *New York Times* on September 3 of an assignment as Berlin correspondent. Telegram to Münsterberg, September 3, 1914. MM. For the views of putative

"Anglophobes" see *England: A Private Nation* (war pamphlet); F. F. Schrader, *The German-American Handbook* (New York, 1916); George von Skal, *The German-American and the European War* (New York, 1915); Rudolph Cronau, *Do We Need a Third War for Independence?* (New York: G. J. Speyer Co., 1914); Shaemas O'Sheel, *A Trip thru Headline Land* (New York: The Fatherland Corp., 1915); *New York Times,* August 31, 1914, 4;5; September 13, 1914, VI, 1:1; William M. Sloane, *Fair Play and Neutrality* (New York: German-American Literary Defense Committee); Thomas C. Hall, *The English Yellow Press* (New York, 1915).

8. Franz Boas to Eliot, March 15, 1916, Boas Manuscripts, Columbia University; Charles S. Todd (a physician in St. Louis) to Münsterberg, June 20, 1915, MM; *The War and America,* 30–31, 33–40, 46–47.

9. Münsterberg to N. Peterson, Principal of McGill University, October 26, 1914; to James F. Thierry, February 1, 1915. MM.

10. *The Nation,* 99:470, October 15, 1915; John Cowper Powys, *The War and Culture: A Reply to Professor Münsterberg* (New York: G. A. Shaw, 1914), 11, 15, 85; W. W. Seymour to Münsterberg, October 15, 1914, and Anon. to Münsterberg, September 21, 1914, MM; Münsterberg to O. G. Villard, November 23, 1914, VP.

11. Letter from "A Bavarian" to Münsterberg, October 16, 1914, MM; Eliot to the *New York Times,* September 4, 1914; October 2, 1914. Eliot believed that an English victory was inevitable. While he did not advocate intervention, he saw no reason to be neutral in feeling. He thought Münsterberg gave false hope to Germany by underestimating the hostile sentiment in America toward its policies and actions. Ibid., October 16, 1914.

12. Münsterberg to Eliot, October 10, 1914, and October 16, 1914; Eliot to Münsterberg, October 15, 1914, and November 16, 1914. MM.

13. Münsterberg to Eliot, November 18, 1914, and November 20, 1914; Eliot to Münsterberg, November 19, 1914, and November 21, 1914. MM. Later Münsterberg claimed McCombs had asked him to raise $100,000. Münsterberg to Lowell, October 18, 1916, LP. McCombs was a politically conservative lawyer who had been a pupil of Wilson's at Princeton and his campaign manager in 1912. He was "a weak southern born Wall Streeter who mistakenly fancied himself as Thurlow Weed." A nervous and unstable personality, he quarreled with Wilson over the distribution of patronage by the Democratic National Committee and lost control of it to Joe Tu-

multy, resigning in 1915. John Blum, *Joe Tumulty and the Wilson Era* (Boston: Houghton Mifflin, 1951), 43, 72, 110.

14. Bernstorff to Münsterberg, December 31, 1914, MM.

15. A. L. Lowell to Münsterberg, September 25, 1914, MM. Clarence Wiener to the Dean of Harvard College, September 26, 1916; Wiener to Lowell, September 30, 1914, and January 20, 1915. LP.

16. A. H. Propper (a Boston lawyer) to Lowell, October 10, 1914, MM; Lowell to E. Bell, February 3, 1915, and Münsterberg to the President and Fellows of Harvard College, October 15, 1914, LP; R. B. Perry to Münsterberg, October 13, 1914, MM; *New York Times*, October 11, 1914, II, 3:7; copy of remarks sent as a letter to the President and Fellows of Harvard, October 13, 1914, MM; Henry A. Yeomans, *Abbott Lawrence Lowell* (Cambridge, 1948), 314; Lowell to Münsterberg, October 19, 1914, MM.

Wiener originally came from Philadelphia. He served as a staff member under General Frederick D. Grant in Cuba in 1898, as a war correspondent in South Africa, and later as a major in command of the Prince of Wales' Light Horse, a Welsh regiment. *New York Times*, October 11, 1914, II, 3:7. His relatives and associates allegedly reported that he inherited a modest financial independence from his father, a noted music teacher, but was unlikely to have resources worth ten million dollars. Ibid., October 16, 1914, 10:7. Wiener was expelled from Harvard for disorderly behavior in 1898. Edmund von Mach, then a proctor at Dunster House, brought the charges against him that resulted in his dismissal. Von Mach recalled that at the time Wiener threatened to get even with him and now suggested to Lowell that perhaps Wiener had mixed him up with Münsterberg. Von Mach to Lowell, October 11, 1914, LP. Münsterberg speculated that Wiener was stirred up by an article in the *London Times* on September 26, 1914, naming Münsterberg as one of "The Kaiser's Agents in America."

Officially the corporation requested that Münsterberg withdraw his resignation, for "the University cannot tolerate any suggestion that it would be willing to accept money to abridge free free speech, to remove a professor, or to accept his resignation." Lowell to Professor J. Squair, November 9, 1914, LP.

17. Lowell to Edmund von Mach, October 13, 1914, MM.

18. *New York Times*, October 16, 1914, 10:7; Lowell to F. P. Sheldon, June 18, 1915, LP; William Roscoe Thayer to O. G. Villard, October 21, 1914, and Villard to Thayer, October 22, 1914, VP. Lowell's landmark statement on academic freedom was made in

1917. It contrasted sharply with the views of the American Association of University Professors—which suggested that professors might legitimately be removed from their posts for certain attitudes or conduct, whether public or private, in relation to the war. Charles W. Eliot supported Lowell's position on Münsterberg. Responding to a letter from one of the prominent Boston alumni who had been particularly critical of Harvard's providing a shelter for Münsterberg's propaganda work, he wrote, "I suppose . . . everybody connected with Harvard would be relieved if Professor Münsterberg should voluntarily resign, but the tenure of a professorship at Harvard is a life tenure; and that fact is an important asset of the University in securing the services of competent men; so that I doubt if the governing boards . . . would ask Professor Münsterberg to resign." Eliot to William C. Hunneman, October 20, 1914, EP. Other Harvard professors under attack were Kuno Francke and the sharply outspoken John A. Walz.

Thayer initially wrote to Villard to congratulate him on his vitriolic review of *The War and America*. Born to a wealthy and prominent family of German descent, Villard was a lifelong admirer of German culture. He now argued that militarism was imposed on the German people by an alien and corrupt leadership. An ardent (and belligerent) pacifist, he condemned German aggression as a political act that violated the sentiment of the German people. Villard, "The Real Crime against Germany," *New York Post*, August 8, 1914; idem, *Germany Embattled* (New York: C. Scribner's Sons, 1915), 30–44. See also Michael Wreszin, *Oswald Garrison Villard: Pacifist at War* (Bloomington: Indiana University Press, 1965).

19. Morison, *Three Centuries*, 453; Münsterberg to John T. Jeffries, May 1, 1915, MM.

20. Emil Witte to Eliot, October 15, 1901, EP; Münsterberg to Editor, *Boston Herald,* February 8, 1915, and to Herman Schonfeld, February 4, 1915, MM. According to Münsterberg, Witte tried to blackmail him before denouncing him to the State Department. An investigation allegedly exonerated him. Münsterberg to Lowell, February 5, 1915, LP. Münsterberg "admitted" writing speeches for ambassadors Holleben and Sternburg. Münsterberg to Woodrow Wilson, February 24, 1915, MM.

21. Frederic William Wile, *The German-American Plot* (London; C. A. Pearson, 1915), 50, 91–98. Wile was the chief correspondent of the *London Daily Mail* in Germany for seven years, and served as a Berlin correspondent for the *New York Times*. Mün-

sterberg believed that Wile was trying to get even with him for his sharp criticism of the foreign press corps in Berlin in 1910. Münsterberg to Adolph Ochs, October 16, 1914, MM.

22. George Sylvester Viereck, *Spreading Germs of Hate* (New York: H. Liveright, 1930), 52; Margaret Münsterberg, *Hugo,* 296; Alfred Rau to Münsterberg, October 1, 1914, and Münsterberg to Messrs. Hugo and John Jaburg of New York, November 12, 1914, MM. In San Francisco, Edward F. Delgar, president of the German-American Auxiliary, headed a similar propaganda bureau supported by "prominent Germans and German-Americans." Its existence and financial backing were also kept secret. Delgar to Münsterberg, January 23, 1915, MM.

23. Münsterberg to Messrs. Jaburg, November 12, 1914; Gustav Pabst to Münsterberg, October 2, 1914; Rau to Münsterberg, October 12, 1914, and October 21, 1914. MM. Pamphlets such as *The Truth about the War as Viewed by Eminent American Writers and Thinkers* were printed and distributed in numbers over 100,000. Rau to Münsterberg, October 12, 1914, MM.

24. Münsterberg to Theodore Roosevelt, December 5, 1914, MM.

25. Münsterberg to James Speyer, December 30, 1914, MM. Speyer refused to contribute.

26. Münsterberg to Dr. H. Schweitzer, December 24, 1914; to C. J. Hexamer, December 19, 1914; to A. A. Busch, December 30, 1914. MM.

27. Münsterberg to Woodrow Wilson, August 5, 1914, and November 7, 1914, MM.

28. Wilson to Münsterberg, November 10, 1914; Münsterberg to Viereck, November 12, 1914; to Wilson, November 19, 1914. MM. Münsterberg's letter to Wilson provided the basis for a planted query from the chairman of the Senate Foreign Relations Committee to the Secretary of State on January 8, 1915. The plan was hatched by a State Department lawyer as a device to enable Secretary Bryan to respond to critics with a public explication of the government's legal position and a refutation of factual errors in the argument mounted by German sympathizers. John C. Crighton, *Missouri and the World War, 1914–1917* (Columbia: University of Missouri Press, 1947), 92.

29. Münsterberg to Wilson, February 24, 1915, MM.

30. Roosevelt to Münsterberg, August 8, 1914; October 3, 1914; November 2, 1914; January 4, 1915. MM.

31. Münsterberg, *The Peace and America* (New York: D. Appleton Co., 1915), 21, 26–56.

32. Ibid., 173–175.

33. Ibid., 36, 43, 87–118, 151, 215, 244.

34. Ibid., 3, 6–7, 9–11, 13–14, 17–20, 85, 234, 256, 262–268.

35. Ibid., 16, 265–270, 275.

36. Charles W. Squiers, *Münsterberg and Militarism Checked* (Toronto, pamphlet, 1915), 5; *New York Times*, April 3, 1915, 2:7; *American Political Science Review* 9 (August 1915):581.

37. Salmon O. Levinson to C. W. Eliot, February 2, 1915; Eliot to John Haynes Holmes, April 8, 1915; Levinson to Eliot, April 21, 1915; Eliot to Editor, *New York Times*, April 24, 1915; Eliot to Levinson, April 24, 1915. EP.

38. Münsterberg to Wilson, April 13, 1915, MM; Eliot to Levinson, February 2, 1915, EP.

39. Levinson to Eliot, June 14, 1915, EP; Augustus J. Cadwalader, Secretary, National Provisional Committee of the League of Peace, to Münsterberg, June 9, 1915, and Executive Secretary of the German University League to Münsterberg, June 14, 1915, MM.

40. Interview with Ella Münsterberg, July 1967. Münsterberg coveted Francke's position as founder and director of the Germanic Museum and interfered in its affairs at every opportunity. Münsterberg to Lowell, February 2, 1910, MM. He unconvincingly told Lowell that he deliberately steered clear of the museum because of Francke's jealous possessiveness of his job. Münsterberg to Lowell, June 23, 1909, MM. In 1967, Ella Münsterberg wistfully recalled the "democratic equality" of Francke's household. Francke, apparently, was not the patriarch that Münsterberg was.

41. Münsterberg to Francke, February 6, 1915, MM; Francke to Lowell, December 25, 1914, LP; *New York Times*, February 3, 1915, 10:6. In addition to the Washington Conference, Francke also criticized Alliance efforts to foster political self-consciousness among German-Americans. Kuno Francke, *Die Deutschamerikaner die Harvard Universitat und der Krieg* (Cambridge, pamphlet, 1915), Francke MSS.

42. Münsterberg to Francke, undated, MM.

43. Ibid.

44. Francke to Münsterberg, February 5, 1915, and April 18, 1915, MM. Born in Kiel in 1855, Francke took his doctorate at Munich and came to the United States in 1880. He married an American woman and authored several books on German literature

and culture. In 1914 he began a long and painful period of wrestling with his "intellectual bigamy." Francke, *Deutsche Arbeit in Amerika* (Leipzig: F. Meiner, 1930), 29. He lectured and wrote widely on "the German point of view" on the war until May 1915. After the *Lusitania* affair he gave up public lectures and confined his writing to explications of the German spirit, without specific reference to the war issues. Although the German agent Heinrich Albert was his nephew, he appears to have had no direct connection with the New York propaganda bureau. When the American government broke relations with Germany, he decided that his position as a German scholar at an American university was untenable and resigned from Harvard. Lowell accepted his resignation reluctantly, for both he and Eliot respected Francke's judiciousness; earlier, Eliot had written of him that he aided "the cause of his Fatherland in this community with great good feeling and good judgment, both by speech and by writing. He make the best of the German cause; whereas Professor Münsterberg makes the worst of it." Lowell to Francke, February 13, 1917, Francke MSS; Eliot to Dr. F. Schmidt, September 25, 1914, EP. In 1917 Francke's only son enlisted in the American Sanitary Service. He and his wife retired from Cambridge to a summer home. Still, he was not spared the harassment and petty persecutions that German-Americans suffered after 1917. A sensitive and temperate man, Francke endured great agony in thinking through the obligations and responsibilities imposed by cleaving to seemingly irreconcilable attachments. His final resolve did not eradicate the German involvements of his emotional and intellectual life. What it did was establish an order of priority and a clarification of self-identity. Before the war he viewed himself as a German and as an American. Through bitter experience he came to see that his German attachment was subject to the strictest obligations of his American commitment. The Germanic Museum, largely developed through Francke's efforts, closed down because of a "coal shortage" in November 1917, and remained closed to the public until April 1921 when fears for its safety finally lapsed. Lowell to Ferdinand Hartz, November 8, 1917; to Francke, October 31, 1917, and October 16, 1919; Ellery Sedgwick to Lowell, December 14, 1921. LP. Hunnewell to Francke, October 29, 1919, Francke MSS. See also Phyllis Keller, "German America and the First World War" (Ph.D. diss., University of Pennsylvania, 1969), 181–186.

45. Münsterberg to F. W. Taussig, April 8, 1915, MM; F. W. Taussig, "The Spirit of Harvard," *Harvard Alumni Bulletin*, May 1,

1915. One effusive supporter of Francke was the patriotic Hermann Hagedorn. Hagedorn to Francke, May 28, 1915, Francke MSS.

46. Royce to Münsterberg, May 10, 1915, MM. Several weeks earlier, in a lighter vein, George Santayana wrote a playful "squib" to German-Americans, which he considered publishing anonymously. The squib was a six-page "address" purportedly "delivered in the Great Grand Hotel Auditorium of Chicago by Real Privy Councillor Professor Moritz Rosenbaum, Dr. Phil. et Jur., Chief of the German American World Press Bureau." Its parody of Münsterberg's manner and rhetoric bordered on the vicious. Santayana to A. J. Onderdonk, February 23, 1915 (from Cambridge, England), Houghton Library, Harvard University. Münsterberg had been one of Santayana's principal protectors in the Philosophy Department at Harvard, vigorously supporting his tenure despite Eliot's doubts and reservations. Eliot to Münsterberg, January 25, 1898, and January 27, 1898, EMP.

47. Münsterberg to Royce, May 11, 1915, and Royce to Münsterberg, May 12, 1915, MM.

48. Münsterberg to Royce, May 13, 1915, MM.

49. Ibid.; Royce to Münsterberg, May 14, 1915, MM.

50. Margaret Münsterberg, Hugo, 274; Münsterberg to Lowell, May 3, 1916, LP.

51. Münsterberg, The Film: A Psychological Study (New York: Dover Publications, 1970), 64–65, 74, 95. The book was originally published as The Photoplay (New York, 1916).

52. "The Impeachment of the German-Americans," New York Times, September 19, 1915, V, 1:1. Münsterberg to Editor, Boston Transcript, September 22, 1915; to Editor, Boston Herald, undated. MM.

53. Bernard Ridder to Münsterberg, November 10, 1915, MM; "Münsterberg's Plea for German-Americans," Literary Digest 51, no. 2 (October 2, 1915): 710–711; New York Times, September 20, 1915, 8:4; A. B. Hart, "German-Americans and the United States," Boston Sunday Herald, September 26, 1915, Hart MSS, Harvard Archives; U.S. 65th Congress, 2nd Session, Senate, Hearings before the Subcommittee of the Committee of the Judiciary. Brewing and Liquor Interests and German Propaganda (hereinafter cited as Brewers Investigation) (Washington, 1919), II, 1627. An outspoken opponent of American intervention, Hart was later accused of pro-German sympathy when his name was found on a list taken from Karl Fuehr's files. The list named prominent men who might

be approached for propaganda work. Hart was on it because he held a doctorate from a German university. *Brewers Investigation,* II, 1399.

54. Reinhold Niebuhr, "The Failure of German-Americanism," *Atlantic Monthly,* July 1916; Niebuhr to Münsterberg, September 4, 1916, MM. F. F. Schrader, writing in *The Fatherland* (August 9, 1916), was far more critical than Münsterberg of Niebuhr's "realities." His article is a flat denial of the charges.

55. *The Fatherland,* December 22, 1915; "Colonel Roosevelt as the German-Americans' Candidate," *Literary Digest* 52, no. 1 (January 1, 1916):3–4. Münsterberg to Alphonse G. Koelble, March 16, 1916; Koelble to Münsterberg, May 3, 1916; Bernstorff to Münsterberg, February 25, 1916. MM. Most German-American leaders were united in their fury over Roosevelt's antihyphenism. Whether they supported Wilson or looked for a sympathetic Republican candidate, Roosevelt's name was anathema. Alphonse Koelble, a New York lawyer, founded the German-American Citizens League of New York, was president of the United German Societies there, and served as president of the New York State Alliance. A native-born Catholic, he was active in Democratic party politics in the city but dropped his associations to support Hughes.

56. Roosevelt to Münsterberg, January 19, 1915, and Münsterberg to Roosevelt, January 26, 1916, MM. After the nominations, Münsterberg shifted his party preference and supported Wilson. He shared Bernstorff's belief that Wilson would try to avoid American intervention.

57. Karl Fuehr to Münsterberg, October 23, 1915, and October 31, 1915; Münsterberg to Fuehr, October 27, 1915; Albert to Münsterberg, June 5, 1916. MM. Diary of Ella Münsterberg, 1916, EMP. James Speyer, in rejecting Münsterberg's request for $1000, wrote, "only a few people in this country will read now things written by Germans . . . If any missionary work is to be done . . . it must be done through American, not German, writers." Speyer to Münsterberg, October 27, 1915, MM. The milk-provision strategy turned into a propaganda boomerang. The idea was to mail dried milk for "starving German babies," which would doubtless be intercepted by the British. Then anti-British sentiment could be stirred. Instead, the German government protested the insinuation by German-Americans that German babies were starving.

58. *New York Times,* January 2, 1916, IV, 6:1; Münsterberg to Mrs. White, February 14, 1916, and to William Phillips, Assistant Secretary of State, April 22, 1916, MM.

59. "The Allies of the Future," *New York Times,* July 30, 1916, V, 1:1.

60. *New York Times,* August 13, 1916, VII, 2:7; August 18, 1916, 9:2; "The Harvard Peace Kite," *The Living Age* 291 (October 14, 1916):119. Viereck to Münsterberg, undated; Fuehr to Münsterberg, August 23, 1916; Walter Jaeger to Münsterberg, August 23, 1916. MM.

61. Münsterberg to F. W. Meyer, October 25, 1916, MM.

62. Münsterberg to Wilson, October 24, 1916, MM.

63. Münsterberg to Mrs. White, February 14, 1916, MM. In March, Münsterberg resigned from the American Academy of Arts and Sciences. The following September he jumped to the (erroneous) conclusion that he was being dropped from a program of church lectures when he did not hear from the organizer for four weeks. Münsterberg to J. Gardner Smith, September 2, 1916, and Smith to Münsterberg, undated, MM. Again, in November, he withdrew from the program of the twenty-fifth Annual Meeting of the American Psychological Association—at which all past presidents were invited to speak. Robert S. Woodworth personally offered his regrets that Münsterberg felt it necessary to do so. Woodworth to Münsterberg, November 6, 1916, MM.

64. Herbert C. Sanborn (Professor of Philosophy at Vanderbilt University and President of the Tennessee branch of the German-American Alliance) to Münsterberg, March 16, 1916; Münsterberg to Holt, March 24, 1916; March 30, 1916; April 12, 1916; Holt to Münsterberg, March 27, 1916; April 4, 1916. MM. Note that Münsterberg's encounter with Lowell took place four days after he wrote to a State Department official (n. 58) pleading for special privileges on the ground of his university work.

Although Holt had started out as an assistant to Münsterberg in the Psychological Laboratory, he had long since gone his own philosophical way, joining with Ralph Barton Perry in the formation of a school of "neo-realists." This school was profoundly opposed to Münsterberg's idealism and subjectivism. Personally, Holt was known to be a difficult man, very much under the sway of his mother. He never married. In January 1918 he resigned his position at Harvard in a letter that glancingly referred to Münsterberg (two years after his death) as "the late Hun." The reasons he gave for his resignation were that he had been passed over for promotion too often and was disgusted with academic politics. Holt to Lowell, January 25, 1918, LP.

65. Münsterberg to Lowell, May 3, 1916, MM; Lowell to

Münsterberg, March 31, 1916, EMP; Münsterberg to Lowell, April 3, 1916, LP; Ringer, *German Mandarins,* 55–56. On Holt, see also Münsterberg to Lowell, February 17, 1910, LP; Lowell to Münsterberg, December 19, 1910, MM. On Yerkes, see Yerkes to Münsterberg, January 18, 1911, and Münsterberg to Yerkes, January 30, 1911, EMP; to Lowell, January, 1911, MM; Yerkes to Münsterberg, December 18, 1911, and Münsterberg to Yerkes, December 19, 1911. On Herbert Langfeld, see Münsterberg to Langfeld, January 1, 1912, MM; Lowell to Münsterberg, December 27, 1911, EMP.

66. Münsterberg to Lowell, May 3, 1916, MM.

67. Ibid.

68. Arthur Upham Pope, "The Real Münsterberg," *New Republic* 27 (August 17, 1921):327. Although Lowell thought that Münsterberg often acted irresponsibly, he held fast to his belief in academic freedom and protected Münsterberg. Later Lowell resisted wartime pressure to drop the German language requirement for a Harvard College degree. But the requirement was dropped in 1920 on the recommendation of the Committee on Prescribed Courses. Lowell to Daniel Kelleher, October 4, 1919; C. W. Greenough to R. A. de Turenne, February 21, 1920. LP.

69. Münsterberg to Reginald C. Robbins, November 21, 1916, MM.

70. Robbins to Münsterberg, November 22, 1916, MM. The same Reginald Robbins had promised his "lasting gratitude" for Münsterberg's (unsuccessful) attempts to secure him an honorary degree from Harvard. Now he believed that Münsterberg was a German agent and that his "concern for a speedy peace [was] a sentiment shared with every bandit who finds himself caught and cornered at last." Robbins to Munsterberg, May 31, 1912, EMP; November 28, 1916, MM.

71. *New York Times,* October 11, 1916, 10:2. The letter was originally published in the *Times* on August 8, 1916 (10:1) as the work of "a well known German scholar." At the time, Münsterberg denied any connection with it. W. E. Hocking, "Notes" dated October 18, 1916, HP. Its release to the press was one in a series of brilliant moves by Allied agents. German agents in the United States were plagued by their habit of keeping records. The sensational and timely exposure of these documents gave Allied propagandists an enormous edge. Bethmann-Hollweg was an obvious contact for Münsterberg to make. He vigorously resisted German war policies that risked American intervention.

72. William E. Hocking to Münsterberg, October 13, 1916, MM; to Lowell, October 21, 1916, LP.

73. Münsterberg to Hocking, undated, and October 16, 1916, MM. The letter was printed in the *New York Times* and several Boston papers on October 16 and 17, 1916.

74. Ibid.; *New York Evening Globe,* October 17, 1916; *New York Evening Post,* October 19, 1916; *Nation* 103 (October 26, 1916):387; *New York Tribune,* October 29, 1916; *Brooklyn Citizen,* October 18, 1916; *New York Times,* October 23, 1916, 8:6; October 24, 1916, 24:5; *Boston Globe,* December 16, 1916. MM. Hocking to Lowell, October 21, 1916, HP. Hocking described Münsterberg as a "personage apart, preoccupied with Weltpolitik, faithful to all his academic engagements in body . . . but not in heart and soul. He wanted to be the center of everything. I am afraid he will never be able to make academic work his main interest, or to lay aside the conceptions of monarchy and divine right in the management of a department. But I think most of us really like Münsterberg personally, and would be sorry to see any cataclysm from above add to the anxieties of himself and his family at the present time." Ibid.

75. Münsterberg to Lowell, September 5, 1916; to Barrett Wendell, September 21, 1916; to F. W. Taussig, October 25, 1916. MM. On Royce's funeral, Münsterberg was quoted in a Boston paper as saying that "our political opinions were so different, to say nothing of our standards of courtesy, that I think it better to absent myself." He subsequently denied the quotation and Lowell moved to dismiss the young assistant professor of English who had maliciously reported it to the press. Lowell to Wendell, September 21, 1916, LP.

76. Münsterberg, *Tomorrow* (New York: D. Appleton Co., 1916), 270–271, 123, and passim.

77. Ibid., 81–82, 107, 112.

78. Ibid., 41, 76–77, 92.

79. Margaret Münsterberg, *Hugo,* 297; Münsterberg to George Sarton, November 28, 1916, and December 8, 1916, MM.

80. *Boston American,* December 16, 1916, MM; "Twenty-five Years"; Selma Münsterberg, "Old Memories."

81. Selma Münsterberg, "Old Memories." Yerkes immediately led an unsuccessful effort to obtain financial support from Harvard for the widow. Yerkes to Lowell, December 22, 1916, LP. Viereck and Curt Reisinger were more effective, raising a memorial fund of $11,000, which was used to purchase Hugo's private library from

his wife. The ten-thousand-item collection was subsequently presented to Harvard. Münsterberg's wealth, invested for him by his brothers in Germany, was substantially wiped out by the war.

82. A. A. Berle, quoted in the *Boston Post,* December 17, 1916; *Boston Globe,* December 18, 1916; *Rochester Herald,* December 18, 1916; *The Fatherland,* December 27, 1916. MM.

83. Interview with May Binion, December 1967; Viereck, *Roosevelt: A Study in Ambivalence* (New York: Jackson Press, 1919), 42–43; Verfassungsgebende Deutsche Nationalversammlung, 15. Ausschuss, Stenographischer Bericht über die öffentlichen Verhandlugen des Untersuchungsausschusses. 6. Sitzung des 2. Unterausschusses. Mittwoch den 5. November 1919. PP. 259–260. It is no small irony that Bernstorff's efficacy in the propaganda contest was closely questioned while Münsterberg received unequivocal posthumous praise.

84. *Business Psychology* (Chicago: La Salle Extension University, 1915), 230.

85. The plan of Münsterberg's autobiography included fourteen chapters, beginning with "The Pilgrimage" and ending with "The Cataclysm." The final chapter was to take a broad view of the various positions in the war controversy, stress the battle "against corruption," and indicate his future hope for "politics, scholarship, social culture, philosophy and internationalism" in America.

PART TWO: GEORGE SYLVESTER VIERECK

5. Family and Childhood

1. Erna Schmidt Viereck to Elmer Gertz, undated, Gertz MSS; *New York Times,* June 29, 1907, Viereck SBS; George Sylvester Viereck, *My Flesh and Blood: A Lyric Autobiography with Indiscreet Annotations* (New York: H. Liveright, 1931), 238–239, 261. Erna Schmidt Viereck was the daughter of Louis's mother's youngest brother. Viereck suggested that some people believed that Prillwitz assumed the paternity of young Louis in order to protect William I. Ibid., 237.

2. Erna Schmidt Viereck to Elmer Gertz, undated, Gertz MSS; biographical records in Gertz MSS; Viereck, *My Flesh,* 240–241. Louis was expelled on the grounds that he was "too moderate and dangerously opportunistic." Elmer Gertz, "Stormy Petrel," unpublished biography of George Sylvester Viereck, ch. 3, p. 12, Gertz MSS.

3. Louis Viereck died in Wildungen, Germany, in 1922. Frank Viereck was born on December 6, 1876, and died in Columbus, Ohio, on December 6, 1933.

4. Diary of Laura Viereck, in Gertz MSS, entries dated January 1, 1918, and January 29, 1918; Viereck, *My Flesh,* 236, 242–243; Erna Schmidt Viereck to Elmer Gertz, undated, Gertz MSS. The wedding of Laura and Louis, for some indiscernible reason, was held in London in 1881. Friedrich Engels acted as a witness.

5. Frances Viereck Schmidt to Elmer Gertz, undated, Gertz MSS. Frau Schmidt reports several other incidents of conflict between the parents centering on the boy's welfare.

6. George Sylvester Viereck, "In Memoriam—Pictures from Little Eddy's Life," Gertz MSS, dated January 29, 1900; Frances Viereck Schmidt to Gertz, undated, Gertz MSS. From Baltimore Frank later moved to Columbus, Ohio. Sylvester kept in touch with Frank and Frank's family throughout his lifetime. Frank's son was a legatee of his will.

7. "Notebook of Viereck's Mother," in Viereck Papers. There is considerable confusion of chronology, beginning with the birth of Little Eddy, in Gertz's manuscript biography of Sylvester Viereck. He has followed the dates set down in Sylvester's memorial to his brother. I have followed the dates set down, in her own hand, in Laura Viereck's "Notebook."

8. Gertz, "Stormy Petrel," ch. 4, p. 6.

9. Viereck, *My Flesh,* 287; Gertz, "Stormy Petrel," ch. 4, pp. 16, 18–19; Elmer Gertz, "A Bizarre Fellowship," *The Chicago Jewish Forum* 3 (1944–1945): 98.

10. Viereck, "In Memoriam."

11. For a general discussion of developmental processes in adolescence, see Peter Blos, *On Adolescence* (New York: Free Press of Glencoe, 1962), esp. 87–128.

12. Viereck, *My Flesh,* 202, 239–240, 243; Alexander Harvey to Gertz, April 13, 1935, Gertz MSS. Margaret ("Gretchen") Edith Hein, whom Viereck married in September 1915, was the daughter of one of his father's most intimate friends. In 1911, when the elder Vierecks returned to Germany, Sylvester lived briefly in the Hein household and referred to the Heins as his "adopted" family.

Other evidence of Viereck's primary identification with his father may be gleaned from his description of his nineteen-year-old wife as "a Peter Pan type," who was "curiously" like him in physical appearance: "We are both slight of stature, our eyes are blue and we are both blond. [She] . . . has a glint of red in her hair that pleases me. It may be that it stirs memories of Helene von Doenniges [his father's mistress]." Viereck, *My Flesh*, 328; "Memorandum of a Psychiatric Consultation at the Johns Hopkins Hospital," December 27, 1940, Viereck Papers. By means of this marriage, Sylvester seemed to be taking his father's role in wished-for relations between his father and himself-as-a-child, Margaret figuring as a child-bride, as the child of a father-figure (Louis's friend), and as a physical double for Sylvester himself. The association with Helene von Doenniges perhaps carries the connotation of Gretchen as an illicit sex object. But these primary identifications were evidently insecure, and Sylvester's secondary identifications through reliving his father's life predominated from adolescence on.

13. George Sylvester Viereck, *Glimpses of the Great* (London: Duckworth, 1930), 34; Viereck to Gertz, December 7, 1934, Gertz MSS.

14. Viereck, *My Flesh*, 242; Viereck to Gertz, July 20, 1935, Gertz MSS. A letter from Viereck to his parents in 1910 begins, "Dearest Mouse and well-beloved Pentarch." Gertz, "Stormy Petrel," ch. 17, p. 4.

15. Viereck, *My Flesh*, 242.

16. "Psychiatric Consultation," in Viereck Papers. Several friends commented on Viereck's active "homosexualism" in his early twenties. See also Leonard Abbott to Gertz, September 3, 1935; Shaemas O'Sheel to Gertz, May 12, 1935; Harry Benjamin to Gertz, October 3, 1935. Gertz MSS. The Steinach operation, a simple surgical procedure involving the ligature of a testicle, was supposed to increase the secretion of sperm and thus cure "pre-senile exhaustion." Eugen Steinach, *Sex and Life* (New York: The Viking Press, 1940), 166–171. Viereck was greatly impressed with Steinach's work and published a popular book about it. See George Four Corners (pseud.), *Rejuvenation: How Steinach Makes People Young* (New York: T. Seltzer, 1923).

6. Flirtation with the Muse of Poetry

1. Viereck, *My Flesh*, 202; diary entry dated November 1901, Gertz MSS; Gertz, "Stormy Petrel," ch. 5, p. 2. About this time Viereck also wrote a short unpublished novel (in German) entitled "Elinor, the Autobiography of a Degenerate" (Bloomington, University of Indiana Library, Kinsey Archives). The manuscript reveals his juvenile fascination with the lore of sexology as derived

from his readings in Kraft-Ebbing, Havelock Ellis, and the Marquis de Sade.

2. Gertz, "A Bizarre Fellowship."

3. Ibid.; Ludwig Lewisohn, "German-American Poetry," *Sewanee Review* 12 (1904):225; Viereck, *My Flesh*, 348. According to Viereck, Lewisohn had a "fatherly, or older-brother attitude towards me" and occasionally addressed him in letters as "Dear Little Boy." It was, he later recalled, a "lyric, impetuous, youthful" friendship. Viereck to Gertz, June 24, 1935, Gertz MSS. The book of German verse was *Gedichte* (New York: Progressive Printing Co., 1904). Lewisohn was hardly affluent at the time.

4. Viereck to Gertz, December 7, 1934, and September 6, 1935, Gertz MSS; *Gedichte; Nineveh and Other Poems* (New York: Moffat, Yard and Co., 1907); *A Game at Love and Other Plays* (New York: Brentano, 1906); Lewisohn, "German-American Poetry," 223–224; Percival Pollard, "Town Topics," quoted in Viereck, *My Flesh*, 390; Ludwig Lewisohn, *Expression in America* (New York: Harper and Bros., 1932), 365; clipping in Viereck SBS.

5. Viereck, *My Flesh*, 5, 26, 142–143, 181, 199; Lewisohn, "German-American Poetry," 224–225.

6. Viereck, *Nineveh*, 65–66.

7. Viereck, *My Flesh*, 14, 185–186; Viereck, *Candle and Flame*, 42. The plays collected in *A Game at Love* also dwell on the themes of sexual passion and of love as a struggle between the sexes. The male is depicted as a generally superior being; the female, usually an older woman, is skilled in the ways of love.

8. "George Sylvester Viereck," clipping from *Brentano's Book Chat* (October 1907), Gertz MSS.

9. Viereck, *My Flesh*, 27. On the "Innocent Rebellion" see Henry May, *The End of American Innocence* (New York: Knopf, 1959), esp. 193–216.

10. George Sylvester Viereck, *Confessions of a Barbarian* (New York: Moffat, Yard and Co., 1910), vii, 51, 206–207.

11. Ibid., 196, 203–206.

12. Alfred Rau to Gertz, undated; Leonard Abbott to Gertz, September 3, 1935. Gertz MSS. Alexander Harvey to Gertz, quoted in "Stormy Petrel," ch. 9; Elsa Barker to Gertz, quoted in "Stormy Petrel," ch. 11, pp. 17–18. In 1908 Upton Sinclair put "the young poet of Diabolism" into his novel, *The Metropolis*. He described Viereck (Strathcona) as lively, witty, and talented, the focus of a depraved cult: "He took the sum-total of the moral experience of the human race, and turned it upside down and jumbled it about,

and used it as bits of glass in a kaleidoscope. And the hearers would gasp, and whisper 'Diabolical!' " Upton Sinclair, *The Metropolis* (New York: Moffat, Yard and Co., 1908), 283–285. On fellow staff writers, Viereck told Abbott's son (March 23, 1953, Gertz MSS) that "we were the three musketeers of journalism." The image recalls his earlier relationship with Leonard and Lewisohn.

13. Harvey to Gertz, quoted in "Stormy Petrel," ch. 9; Viereck to Gertz, December 7, 1934, and September 4, 1935, Gertz MSS. The title of the new monthly journal was *Rundschau Zweier Welten.*

14. Viereck, *Candle and Flame*, xiii–xiv; idem, *My Flesh*, 186, 203.

15. Viereck to Münsterberg, January 19, 1914, and October 1911, MM. Louis Viereck, an avid admirer of Theodore Roosevelt, had written an article for *Success Magazine*, "Roosevelt's German Days," in October 1905. Under the previous editorship of Walter Lippmann and Russell Herts, *The International* had been devoted exclusively to literary affairs.

7. *Domestic Crisis and World War*

1. Viereck, *My Flesh*, 276.

2. For a theoretical discussion of the genesis of ambivalence and its adaptations to social objects, see Talcott Parsons, *The Social System* (New York: Free Press of Glencoe, 1964), 249–267. For a discussion of the relationship between deviant behavior and social structure, see Robert Merton, *Social Theory and Social Structure* (Glencoe, Ill.: The Free Press, 1957; rev. ed.), 131–160.

3. For accounts of the founding of *The Fatherland*, see "The Story of The Fatherland," *The Fatherland*, August 11, 1915; Alfred Rau to Gertz, undated, and Viereck to Gertz, December 4, 1935, Gertz MSS; Viereck to Münsterberg, August 3, 1914, MM; George Sylvester Viereck, *Spreading Germs of Hate* (New York: H. Liveright, 1930), 50. The circulation of *The Fatherland* later stabilized at 75,000; in contrast, *The International* merely doubled in circulation and remained stable at 4,000 after 1914. Viereck contrasted his own role with those of Münsterberg, whom he believed to speak only as a German citizen, and of the Ridder family, who were limited by their German-language newspaper outlets to the relatively unassimilated group of German-Americans.

4. U.S., 65th Congress, 2nd Session, Senate, Hearings before the Subcommittee of the Committee on the Judiciary. *National*

German-American Alliance (Washington, 1918), 609 (hereinafter cited as *Alliance Hearings*); *New York Times,* July 26, 1918, 20:1; July 28, 1918, 10:1; *Brewers Investigation,* II, 1425–1429, 1432, Viereck SBS, July 1918. Free copies of *The Fatherland* were sent to 2350 American dailies, 90 foreign-language papers, 103 magazines, all members of Congress, and 209 other individuals. *The Fatherland,* March 17, 1915.

5. Albert to Viereck, July 1, 1915, in *New York Times,* August 16, 1915, 3:4; *New York World,* August 17, 1915, Viereck SBS; *New York Times,* July 28, 1918, 10:1; Viereck, *Germs of Hate,* 75–76; *New York Times,* December 8, 1918, 1:1.

6. *New York Times,* July 28, 1918, 10:1; Viereck to Münsterberg, September 26, 1914, and Rau to Münsterberg, October 5, 1914, MM; *Brewers Investigation,* II, 1541, 1686, 1698; George Sylvester Viereck, *Roosevelt: A Study in Ambivalence* (New York: Jackson Press, 1919), 15. Dernburg, a forceful and intelligent man, came to the United States as the ostensible representative of the German Red Cross. But his mission was to raise funds for German government purchases in America. Balked in this endeavor, he turned full time to the administration of the New York propaganda headquarters. Disliked by German Embassy officials in Washington, he worked independently of them. The German Information Bureau initially was run by Matthew S. von Claussen, an agent for the Hamburg-Amerika Line. It distributed pro-German news and feature stories to several hundred American newspapers and sent weekly news reports on American opinion to Berlin. It was later taken over by Karl Fuehr, on leave of absence from Embassy duties in Japan. The American journalist William Bayard Hale worked for the Bureau on a retainer of $15,000 per year. The German government invested almost $800,000 in the bureau during its first year of operations. Viereck, *Germs of Hate,* 52, 55–57; *Brewers Investigation,* II, 1393, 1910. Both Dernburg and Fuehr were installed in the same building as Viereck's editorial offices.

7. The quick success of *The Fatherland* led Viereck to place *The International* in the background of his concerns. But he continued as editor of the older journal until August 1917. Both papers occupied offices at 1123 Broadway, and Viereck controlled the stock of both parent corporations. He tried to interest Albert in aiding *The International,* but its circulation was too small and it was too literary in tone and international in purview. Nevertheless, the issues raised by pro-German partisans increasingly crept onto its pages after 1914, although the tone adopted by its writers—and

Viereck's editorials—was considerably more moderate than that taken on by *The Fatherland's* staff. After America's entry into the war, the magazine stopped carrying editorials by Viereck and eschewed war comment except for a continued anti-British bias. This bias was the special province of the flamboyant and eccentric English poet Aleister Crowley, whom Viereck hired to replace himself as editor in 1917. Viereck was undoubtedly attracted by the poet's personal manner, for Crowley billed himself as a satyr, a devil worshipper, and the wickedest man in the world. Yet he was also a vigorous writer and a passionate—if indiscriminate—hater, whose energies Viereck enthusiastically enlisted in the propaganda campaign. After the war Crowley claimed that he had been acting as a double agent whose mission was "to wreck the German propaganda on the roof of Reductio Ad Absurdum." He had, in fact, neither undermined nor aided it materially, for the magazine ran essentially true to its prewar character with its wartime propaganda line firmly under Viereck's control. John Symonds, *The Great Beast: The Life of Aleister Crowley* (London: Rider, 1951), 129 and passim. *The International* folded in 1918.

8. *The Fatherland,* August 10, 1914; August 17, 1914; September 23, 1914.

9. Ibid., October 15, 1914; December 30, 1914.

10. Ibid., November 18, 1915; February 10, 1915; November 18, 1914; February 17, 1915.

11. Ibid., March 31, 1915; April 28, 1915; August 11, 1915.

12. Ibid., June 16, 1915; February 10, 1915.

13. Ibid., March 17, 1915; *Alliance Hearings,* 476. Profits from advertised souvenirs—iron-cross jewelry and special calendars—were to go to aid wounded German soldiers. Similar enterprises were widely conducted in the German-language press.

14. See eight installments of "Why the Money Trust Backs the Allies" in the fall issues of *The Fatherland,* commencing August 25, 1915; *New York Tribune,* July 4, 1915, Viereck SBS; *The Fatherland,* July 14, 1915.

15. *The Fatherland,* February 24, 1915; March 31, 1915; November 17, 1915; April 21, 1915; June 23, 1915.

16. Ibid., February 10, 1915; March 3, 1915. Viereck to Francke, February 6, 1915, Francke MSS.

17. Viereck, *Germs of Hate,* 59; *The Fatherland,* May 12, 1915; May 19, 1915; May 26, 1915; June 16, 1915. The *Gulflight* was torpedoed on May 1, 1915.

18. Clifton J. Child, *The German-Americans in Politics, 1914–1917* (Madison: University of Wisconsin Press, 1939), 62–63.

19. Münsterberg to Viereck, July 27, 1915, in *The Fatherland,* August 11, 1915; *The Fatherland,* September 1, 1915; August 25, 1915.

20. *The Fatherland,* September 15, 1915; September 22, 1915; *The International,* October 1915.

21. *The Fatherland,* December 8, 1915; *Brewers Investigation,* II, 1699, 2615–2618, 2626. The correspondent, J. J. Dickinson, later gave information to a congressional committee that led to a raid on Viereck's offices in 1917. Ibid., II, 2616–2617, 2640.

22. Walter Millis, *Road to War* (Boston: Houghton Mifflin, 1935), 316; *Minnesota Sentinel,* October 17, 1915, Viereck SBS; *The Fatherland,* June 7, 1915; November 22, 1916; *The International,* October 1916; Viereck SBS, September 1916; George Sylvester Viereck, *The Strangest Friendship in History* (New York: H. Liveright, 1932), 60, 160. By the fall of 1916 Albert, too, grew irritated with Viereck. In a fit of pique he wrote to the Foreign Office in Berlin that "I should . . . be glad to be free from *The Fatherland,* which has shown itself to be of little value." *Brewers Investigation,* II, 1481.

23. *The Fatherland,* November 8, 1916; *Milwaukee Journal,* September 2, 1919, Viereck SBS. German-American voters, who were expected to count beyond their number because of their location in pivotal states, failed to control any electoral votes—with the possible exception of Maryland, which went Democratic. Despite vigorous endorsements of Hughes by many Alliance leaders and German-language newspaper editors, German-American voters themselves were clearly divided about the candidates and the relative importance of the issues in the campaign. In Saint Louis, for example, anti-Prohibition sentiment dwarfed the hyphen issue and worked in favor of the Democrats. In Milwaukee, where over half of the population was of German stock, pro-German extremists provoked a reaction even among German-Americans, and the city gave Wilson a plurality of 6,000 votes. Both parties played a double game with the German-Americans throughout the campaign: on the Republican side, TR whipped them in his own free-wheeling style while Hughes scrupulously avoided giving offense. On the Democratic side, "hyphenism" was made an issue and the nation was asked to crush the movement to oust Wilson for "insulting" Germany at the same time that German-Americans were told that

Wilson had, after all, kept the United States from going to war against the fatherland. Thus there was no clear "German interest" to determine party preference. In any event, no nationally consistent German-American voting pattern materialized. *New York Times,* November 13, 1916, 6:6; Arthur Link, *Woodrow Wilson and the Progressive Era* (New York: Harper, 1954), 24; *New York Evening Sun,* November 9, 1916, Viereck SBS; Carl Wittke, *German-Americans and the World War* (Columbus: The Ohio State Archeological and Historical Society, 1936), 99–100; *The Nation* 103 (October 26, 1916):389.

24. *Brewers Investigation,* II, 1697–1698.

25. *The American Weekly,* February 21, 1917; March 14, 1917; Viereck to W. R. Hearst in *Brewers Investigation,* II, 1611.

26. *The American Weekly,* April 11, 1917. The New York State Alliance, with a membership of 150,000, similarly pledged support of the war declaration but rejected, at the same time, a resolution blaming the war on Germany. *New York Times,* April 9, 1917, 8:5. Initially opposing American entry into the war, the German-language press worked itself around to vigorous displays of patriotism by the summer of 1917. Wittke, *German-Americans,* 119, 123, 128–129.

27. Viereck to "Mama and Papa," May 2, 1917, in *Brewers Investigation,* II, 2029. The advisory board of the Agricultural Bureau consisted of Professor Kuno Francke, Max Hein (Viereck's father-in-law), William Ellery Leonard, Mrs. Philip Lewisohn, Abraham Grill (Viereck's lawyer), and others. Grill, Congressman Henry Vollmer, and Harry Rubens, a Chicago lawyer and a prominent German-American activist, served on the Legal Information Bureau.

28. *The American Weekly,* May 18, 1917; June 17, 1917; July 18, 1917; July 4, 1917; T. Everett Harre in *Fort Wayne Journal Gazette,* February 6, 1918; *Milwaukee Journal,* July 12, 1917; *Richmond Journal,* May 15, 1917. Viereck SBS. Viereck supported universal military service, conscription, and a selective draft; his exclusive concern was for German-American exemption. Later he campaigned vigorously against limiting German instruction in the public schools. *New York Times,* August 19, 1917, I, 11:3.

29. Viereck to "Mama and Papa," May 2, 1917, in *Brewers Investigation,* II, 2029.

30. *New York Times,* March 12, 1918, 9:4; July 26, 1918, 20:1; August 16, 1918, 12:4; Viereck SBS, April 1918 and August 1918. Viereck attempted to resign from both the Authors League and the

Athletic Club, but his resignations were refused so that he could be expelled. He was not especially perturbed by these expulsions except for the fact that Theodore Roosevelt took a hand in his repudiation by the Authors League. Viereck, *My Flesh*, 300. Roosevelt wrote of Viereck in 1917 that "if I were in power I would put Viereck . . . instantly in jail . . . for Viereck is conducting a campaign of treason against this country." Roosevelt to Ralph M. Easley, July 5, 1917, in Elting E. Morison and John M. Blum, eds., *The Letters of Theodore Roosevelt* (Cambridge: Harvard University Press, 1954), VIII, 1207. The Attorney General's interrogation of Viereck came in connection with an investigation into the ownership of the *New York Daily Mail* (which had been purchased with German funds).

31. *New York Times*, July 28, 1918, 10:1; *New York Sun*, July 28, 1918, Viereck SBS; *The American Weekly*, August 7, 1918. According to Becker, Viereck had $100,000 in personal bank accounts in 1918; he had started out with nothing in 1914. *New York Times*, July 28, 1918, 10:1.

32. *Brewers Investigation*, II, 1699, 2029; Viereck, *Roosevelt*, 27–28; *New York Sun, New York Evening Mail, New York Journal*, and *New York Telegram*, November 25, 1918, Viereck SBS.

33. Viereck, *Roosevelt*, 26–29; *New York Times*, August 8, 1918, 11:5; August 10, 1918, 14:2; Gertz, "Stormy Petrel," ch. 19. At least one of Viereck's employees—his secretary, May Binion—was successfully approached by an investigator, but there is only his word that she was tempted "to bear false witness." Viereck's sons, Peter and George, Jr., were born on August 5, 1916, and April 23, 1918, respectively. Hugo Münsterberg was Peter's godfather.

34. Viereck, *My Flesh*, 203, 300. In 1916, when Viereck learned that Hugo Münsterberg was writing his autobiography, he wrote that he hoped he would appear in it "not merely as a German-American. For after all, I am first of all a poet and a man of letters. At least I was until two years ago." Viereck to Münsterberg, November 6, 1916, MM.

35. Edward J. Wheeler, "A Statement Regarding the Expulsion of George Sylvester Viereck," privately printed, 1918; Viereck, *My Flesh*, 300; Viereck, *Roosevelt*, 43. Among those objecting to Viereck's expulsion were Conrad Aiken, William Ellery Leonard, Edgar Lee Masters, Harriet Monroe, and Padraic Colum. See also Harriet Monroe, "The Viereck Incident," *Poetry* 13 (1919):265–267.

36. Alfred Rau, an intimate friend and best man at Viereck's wedding in 1915, withdrew support from *The Fatherland* because

of Viereck's continued zeal after 1917. Rau to Gertz, undated, Gertz MSS. Other broken friendships included those with Richard LeGallienne, Charles H. Towne, Theodore Roosevelt, Otto Kahn, and Blanche Wagstaff.

37. Quoted in Gertz, "Stormy Petrel," ch. 24, p. 5.

8. *Peace and the Second Coming of War*

1. The *American Monthly* now provided Viereck's chief source of income, which amounted to about $10,000 per year. Viereck to Gertz, undated, Gertz MSS.

2. *American Monthly*, March 1922; *Philadelphia Public Ledger,* September 1, 1919, Viereck SBS.

3. Joseph P. O'Grady, ed., *The Immigrants' Influence on Wilson's Peace Policies* (Lexington: University of Kentucky Press, 1967), 39–53; *American Monthly*, December 1921; March 1922; April 1921. Edmund Robert Otto von Mach, lecturer, editor, and writer on art history, was a close friend of Hugo Münsterberg and an intimate of Viereck. Born in Germany, he came to America in 1891, took a B.A. degree at Harvard in 1896 and a Ph.D. in 1900. He served briefly as an instructor there and from 1911 to 1913 was president of the Boston German Association, following in the footsteps of Münsterberg and Kuno Francke. He became a U.S. citizen in November 1914. He published two books, *What Germany Wants* (Boston: Little, Brown and Co., 1914) and *Germany's Point of View* (Chicago: A. C. McClurg and Co., 1915) that were drawn from his regular newspaper column between 1914 and 1915. His columns and other articles "hovered . . . on the border line between education and propaganda." According to Viereck, he was "one of Germany's most active intellectual propagandists." Viereck, *Germs of Hate*, 81, 87, 95–96. In 1918 von Mach testified before the Senate Committee investigating German propaganda in an attempt to clear himself of charges of disloyalty stemming, in part, from his die-hard defense of German interests. *Brewers Investigation*, II, 2267. Von Mach never admitted to himself his role as a special advocate; as an intellectual devoted exclusively to "higher truths" he did not feel himself bound by any limits on special advocacy. After the war, he argued that Germany had been "betrayed" into surrendering. *American Monthly*, December 1921.

4. Gertz, "Stormy Petrel," ch. 26, pp. 4–5.

5. Viereck, *My Flesh*, 203; *American Monthly*, April 1922.

6. *American Monthly*, March 1922; July 1921; September 1921.

7. Ibid., August 1921; *Milwaukee Journal,* August 20, 1920, Viereck SBS. Viereck apparently turned to the Citizens League after a falling out with the "Steubenites in New York . . . [and] the United German Societies which organized at that time and was an appendix of the *Staats-Zeitung* and was run by small peanut politicians." Viereck to Gertz, undated, Gertz MSS. The chief spokesman of the Citizens League, Dr. Herman Gerhard, was a graduate of Heidelberg and a former editor of the Lincoln, Nebraska, *Freie Presse.* He had been active in Alliance politics and was more ambitious about the league than its president, Ferdinand Walther. Nevertheless, he cautiously told reporters that he "is American in thought and feeling, and that he has always had in mind the interests not of Germany, but of America." *Milwaukee Journal,* 1921. After the 1920 election, Viereck wrote to Harding requesting, as payment for German-American support, the appointment of a German-American to the cabinet and the termination of alien property control. He also petitioned for the release of Debs from prison. Gertz, "Stormy Petrel," ch. 28, pp. 4–6.

8. *American Monthly,* March 1922; April 1921; June 1921.

9. Ibid., April 1921; October 1921; July 1923; June 1921; March 1922. Viereck's investment and security counseling service was organized in 1920 to "protect American investors in Central European securities against the unfair practices of unscrupulous and irresponsible brokers." Ibid., March 1922. He offered to accept Liberty Bonds in payment for German industrial bonds. Ibid., April 1921.

10. Viereck, *Roosevelt,* 12–16, 25, 27. Viereck's allegation of conspiracy, though exaggerated after his fashion, had some basis in reality. In 1919, *Publisher's Weekly* printed an apology for carrying an advertisement of his Roosevelt book. The book, it was said, should be rejected out of hand as malicious and egotistical. *Publisher's Weekly,* June 21, 1919, Viereck SBS. His former publisher, Moffat, Yard, and Co., severed connection with Viereck by returning the plates of all his books published under their imprint. George Sylvester Viereck, *The Haunted House and Other Poems* (Girard, Kan.: Haldemann-Julius Co., 1924), 5. For a time Viereck published under his own imprint, The Jackson Press.

11. Viereck, *Roosevelt,* 55–57. Viereck read Freud avidly in the first decade of the twentieth century. His prewar poetry reveals this influence—which rapidly grew into an obsession. In the 1920s and 1930s Viereck became a popularizer—and vulgarizer—of psychoanalysis. He cultivated Freud's disciples and met Freud himself on several occasions. He consulted Freud about his personal prob-

lems in their correspondence. Freud found Viereck "always interesting" though often a wayward enthusiast of psychoanalysis. In 1933 Freud broke off their correspondence. Sigmund Freud to Viereck, February 2, 1928, among thirty-one letters from Freud to Viereck in *Freud Letters*. See also Gertz, "Stormy Petrel," ch. 37.

12. Viereck, *Roosevelt*, 63–64, 75–83; Viereck, *My Flesh*, 264.

13. Viereck to Roosevelt, February 25, 1915, and March 19, 1915; Roosevelt to Viereck, March 15, 1915. Quoted in Viereck, *Roosevelt*, 118, 128, 125.

14. Viereck to Roosevelt, June 13, 1916; quoted in *Roosevelt*, 135; Viereck, *My Flesh*, 270; *Roosevelt*, 140–141, 143.

15. Viereck, *Roosevelt*, 61. In the first chapter of *Roosevelt*, Viereck singled out Hermann Hagedorn as a particularly odious traitor to the German-American cause. There were many reasons for his hatred of Hagedorn; envy was undoubtedly one of them, for Hagedorn had become Roosevelt's chief German-American lieutenant and protégé.

16. Viereck, *The Haunted House*, 3; George Sylvester Viereck, *The Three Sphinxes and Other Poems* (Girard, Kan.: Haldemann-Julius Co., 1924). In 1935 Viereck observed to Elmer Gertz that these pamphlet collections did not restore "me to respectability; they were not particularly respectable. You might say that they restored my literary status to myself." Viereck to Gertz, undated, Gertz MSS.

17. George Sylvester Viereck, *An Empress in Exile* (New York: J. H. Sears and Co., 1928); *Two Battles of the Marne* (New York: Cosmopolitan Book Co., 1927); George Sylvester Viereck, ed., *As They Saw Us* (Garden City, N.Y.: Doubleday, Doran and Co., 1929); *Glimpses of the Great; Germs of Hate*, xiv. Viereck became a friend of the exiled Kaiser and visited him annually for many years, beginning in 1922.

18. Viereck to Gertz, June 18, 1935, Gertz MSS. Viereck claimed that he had a yearly retainer of $3000 from the *Saturday Evening Post* and that he had earned $500 for news stories and up to $25,000 for his special features. Viereck to Gertz, December 7, 1934, Gertz MSS. His yearly income from the *American Monthly* had been about $10,000. Gertz, "Stormy Petrel," ch. 27, p. 2.

19. George Sylvester Viereck and Paul Eldridge, *My First Two Thousand Years: The Autobiography of the Wandering Jew* (New York: Macaulay Co., 1928).

20. Gertz, "Stormy Petrel," ch. 35, pp. 6, 12. Note the repetition of the primary identification suggested in note 12 of chapter 5,

based on Viereck's taking his father's role in wished-for relations between Louis and himself as a child. Viereck and Eldridge continued their collaboration through succeeding volumes in the Wandering Jew series. *Salome, The Wandering Jewess* (New York: H. Liveright, 1930), tells the story of modern woman's restlessness with bondage to the male principle, and *The Invincible Adam* (London: Duckworth, 1932) relates the misadventures of the exclusively masculine youth Kotikokura, who wanders from conquest to conquest without ever discovering the secret of tender love. Viereck conceived of the series as a trilogy of love.

21. Viereck, *My Flesh*, 104–105, 131, 186, 276, 327; George Sylvester Viereck, *The Seven against Man* (Scotch Plains, N.J.: Flanders Hall, 1941). When Viereck's *My First Two Thousand Years* was confiscated and burned by the Nazis, he said that they had every right to refuse to "harbor so disturbing a guest in their concern to protest against the overemphasis of the purely intellectual point of view [represented by the book's hero] as against the instincts and feelings which may be more infallible than reason." *The Nation* 138 (April 25, 1934):460. In 1935 he observed to Gertz that he had "committed suicide as a poet by learning too much about the mechanisms of the unconscious." Gertz, "Stormy Petrel," ch. 7. Viereck's antiintellectualism may also have been an emulation of his father's self-disgust when he spoke of the "impotence of the Intelligentsia."

22. Viereck, *My Flesh*, 367–373; Viereck to Newton D. Baker, June 23, 1931, House MSS; Viereck, *Strangest Friendship*, xiv, 7. Viereck's interpretation of the Wilson-House relationship centers on the idea that Wilson was ambivalent toward House, that he was dependent on him and yet hated him for his own dependency (p. 279). House reportedly was pleased with the book and much charmed by Viereck, whom he took to be "the foremost German-American" of consequence during World War I. Notes by Gertz on a meeting with House, May 23, 1935, Gertz MSS. *Strangest Friendship* was serialized in *Liberty Magazine* before publication in book form.

23. Viereck to House, March 16, 1933, and Viereck to Dieckhoff, November 21, 1933, House MSS; *New York Times,* June 6, 1934.

24. Carl Wittke, *The German Language Press in America* (Lexington: University of Kentucky Press, 1957), 282; Maldwyn A. Jones, *American Immigration* (Chicago: University of Chicago Press, 1960), 301; Alton Frye, *Nazi Germany and the American*

Hemisphere, 1933–1941 (New Haven: Yale University Press, 1967), 40, 54, 58, 190–191.

25. U.S., 74th Congress, 1st Session, House, Special Committee on Un-American Activities, Report No. 153, *Investigation of Nazi and Other Propaganda* (Washington, 1935), 4–5 (hereinafter cited as *McCormack-Dickstein Report*); Frye, *Nazi Germany*, 63, 80–82, 87, 96. Teutonia was founded in Chicago in 1922. The Friends of New Germany was a front organization for the National Socialist German Labor Party. Spanknoebel and his successor, Fritz Grissibl, were aliens. Later, an American citizen, Walter Reinhold, was placed at the head of the organization to make it look American. In Chicago, the Friends had a membership of 232 in 1934; 146 were German aliens, 2 were native Americans, and 84 were naturalized citizens of German birth. *McCormack-Dickstein Report*, 4–7. The German-American Bund had about 69 local units in 1939; the largest and most powerful was located in metropolitan New York. Almost all of its members were born in Germany, and about half of them remained German citizens through the 1930s. Donald S. Strong, *Organized Anti-Semitism in America* (Washington: American Council on Public Affairs, 1941), 31–34. Pro-Nazi sympathy apparently peaked in 1937 when supporters may have numbered 200,000. In the late 1930s the *New Yorker Staatszeitung*, the German-American League of Culture, and the Steuben Society were openly hostile to the Bund. Richard O'Connor, *The German-Americans* (Boston: Little, Brown Co., 1968), 441; Oscar Handlin, *The American People in the Twentieth Century* (Boston: Beacon Press, 1963), 195–196.

26. *American Monthly*, October 1923; Viereck to Upton Sinclair, September 22, 1934, House MSS; Frederick Hanson to Gertz, June 6, 1935, and Viereck to Gertz, April 23, 1935, Gertz MSS; *McCormack-Dickstein Report*, 6; Frye, *Nazi Germany*, 36, 49, 51. Under the strain of financial reverses, Viereck developed a variety of neurasthenic ailments and was subject to periodic depressions. See "Vorgeschichte" and Viereck to Dr. Harry Benjamin, October 13, 1932, Viereck Papers. Both were written during his "rest cure" hospitalization in Berlin in October 1932.

27. *McCormack-Dickstein Report*, 6; Frye, *Nazi Germany*, 51; Viereck to Editors of *The Nation* (July 19, 1934), VP. Under the terms of Byoir's contract his firm would work to increase travel, promote trade, and build goodwill between the countries, but not to disseminate "political, National Socialist or racial propaganda."

28. Viereck's reports are recorded in "Political and Cultural Propaganda in the United States, 1933–1936," Files of Abteilung

III of the German Foreign Ministry, Foreign Affairs Branch, U.S. Archives (Microfilm Serial K 1053, frames 269616–269686); Frye, *Nazi Germany,* 59; Viereck to Sinclair, September 22, 1934, House MSS.

29. A. A. Brill to Gertz, May 9, 1935, Gertz MSS; George Sylvester Viereck, *The Temptation of Jonathan* (New York: Christopher Publishing House, 1938).

30. Gerhart Falk, "The Immigration of the European Professors and Intellectuals to the United States and Particularly the Niagara Frontier during the Nazi Era, 1933–1941" (Ph.D. diss., University of Buffalo, 1970). Falk's chapter "The German Establishment" is based on a detailed study of the pro-Nazi *Buffalo Volksfreund* from 1933 to 1941. The paper reprinted editorials and news stories from fourteen other German-language papers throughout the country.

31. Viereck to Gertz, November 5, 1938, Gertz MSS; Viereck to Gustav Pabst, March 30, 1933, House MSS; Paul Eldridge to Viereck, February 1934, Viereck SBS; George Sylvester Viereck, "Germany and the Jews," typescript, Viereck Papers; "Speech at Madison Square Garden, May 17, 1934," Viereck SBS. Viereck's comment on the "Jewish-Communist reign of terror" was meant to explain why Gertz was having difficulty finding a publisher for his biography of Viereck.

32. Viereck, *My Flesh,* 145; Viereck to Gertz, March 29, 1939, Gertz MSS.

33. Frye, *Nazi Germany,* 62, 97–98, 161–162; Nathaniel Weyl, *Treason* (Washington: Public Affairs Press, 1950), 331–332; O. J. Rogge, *The Official German Report: Nazi Penetration, 1924–1942* (New York: T. Yoseloff, 1961), 130–172, 184–186; Albert E. Kahn, *High Treason* (New York: Lear Publishers, 1950), 217–219; Michael Sayers and Albert Kahn, *Sabotage! The Secret War against America* (New York: Harper and Bros., 1942), 177–180; "Reply Brief of Appellant in U.S. Court of Appeals, District of Columbia, No. 8205. George S. Viereck, appellant, vs. United States of America, appellee," in Gertz MSS; "U.S. v. Joseph McWilliams, et al., Appendix to Appellant's Brief, District of Columbia, no. 9438, 1946." One of the Flanders Hall books, *Lord Lothian vs. Lord Lothian* (Scotch Plains, N.J.: Flanders Hall, 1940), contained the text of a lengthy speech delivered by Senator Ernest Lundeen (which Viereck probably wrote), and included editorial comment by Viereck under the pseudonym "James Burr Hamilton." Other pseudonyms Viereck used during the 1920s and 1930s were George Four Corners, Don-

ald Furtherman Wicketts, Dr. Claudius Murchison, and Eugen Vroom. In 1935 Viereck observed to Gertz that his father, too, was "compelled . . . to write under noms de plume." Viereck, "Putty," Gertz MSS.

34. Neil M. Johnson, *George Sylvester Viereck* (Urbana: University of Illinois Press, 1972), 194, 201, 215; Viereck to Arnold Gingrich, March 29, 1939, VJ; Frye, *Nazi Germany*, 97.

35. *New York Times*, December 24, 1940, 5:6; *Newsweek* 18 (September 29, 1941): 16–17; 18 (October 20, 1941):21–22; 19 (March 16, 1942):28. In an interview published in the *New Yorker* 16 (June 15, 1940):15–16, Viereck denied any association with German propaganda work: "I am a poet, a journalist, I have even mixed in politics in a small way, but I am not a propagandist." The ostensible purpose of the war debts committees was to secure immediate repayment of war debts through secession of island possessions in the western hemisphere (and cash balances). Both of the committees received funds from the German government. Frye, *Nazi Germany*, 138, 159–161.

36. For a detailed discussion of Viereck's trials and defense see Johnson, *Viereck*, 221 ff.

37. "Statement by Mr. George Sylvester Viereck," October 1941; "Statement before Sentence by George Sylvester Viereck," July 31, 1943. VP.

38. Margaret Viereck to George Viereck, November 24, 1942, and George to Margaret, November 27, 1942, Viereck Papers; Viereck to Gertz, August 26, 1947, Gertz MSS; Viereck to Ferdinand Earle, October 14, 1944, Viereck Papers.

39. *The Nation* 153 (November 29, 1941):551; *New Republic* 108 (January 4, 1943):21; Villard to the Attorney General of the United States, September 24, 1945, VP; Gertz to Viereck, October 24, 1952, Gertz MSS. It was later claimed that Viereck's friend and collaborator, Lawrence Dennis, planted the idea among isolationist leaders that the arrest of Viereck and others represented a move by the FBI to intimidate them. Arthur Derounian, *Undercover* (Philadelphia: Blakiston, 1943), 486, 498. Elmer Gertz was a Jewish lawyer in Chicago, twenty-two years younger than Viereck, who was obviously attracted by flamboyant literary types. He wrote a biography of Frank Harris in 1931. He worked closely with Viereck in gathering material for "Stormy Petrel," and despite differences over Viereck's pro-Nazi, anti-Semitic stance they corresponded occasionally until Viereck's death.

40. George Sylvester Viereck, *Men into Beasts* (New York:

Fawcett Publications, 1952); Stuart Benton (pseud.), *All Things Human* (New York: Duckworth, 1949), 35, 53–54, and passim.

41. Viereck to Gertz, September 16, 1952, Gertz MSS; Viereck to H. Keith Thompson, May 5, 1953, and to Edward Fleckenstein, May 5, 1963, Viereck Papers; George Sylvester Viereck, *The Bankrupt* (Chicago: A Pyramid Publication, 1955); idem, "Laughter in Hell," 16, 31, 37, 40, Gertz MSS.

42. Gertz, "Stormy Petrel," ch. 39.

43. Viereck to Gertz, July 20, 1935, Gertz MSS.

44. Viereck, *My Flesh*, 203.

45. For a discussion of the limited and peripheral role of German-American ethnicity in the American isolationist movement in the 1930s, see Manfred Jonas, *Isolationism in America, 1935–1941* (Ithaca: Cornell University Press, 1969), 20–21, 42. In 1933 there were over a million and a half German-born persons in the United States. Of these, 600,000 were post-World War I immigrants, the main source of Nazi sympathizers. John A. Hawgood, *The Tragedy of German-America* (New York: G. P. Putnam's Sons, 1940), 302; Arthur L. Smith, Jr., *The Deutschtum of Nazi Germany and the United States* (The Hague: Nijhoff, 1965), 85–86, 105.

PART THREE: HERMANN HAGEDORN

9. The Family

1. Hermann Hagedorn, *The Hyphenated Family: An American Saga* (New York The MacMillan Co., 1960), 15. My account of Hagedorn's family background is derived mainly from his autobiography and from "Notes for Family Book," in the Hagedorn Papers. The "Notes" were based, in turn, on family documents and correspondence, also in the Hagedorn Papers.

2. Hagedorn, *Family*, 5, 18.

3. Ibid., 24, 31. Schwedler's entreaty may have provided a model for Hermann Hagedorn's subsequent appeals for "action" on the part of the "Boys and Girls of America," "Americans of German Origin," and especially his call to the "Mothers of New York" on behalf of public school reform in Hagedorn, *Mothers of New York: What of the Children?* (New York: Public Welfare Committee pamphlet, 1927).

4. *Family*, 36.

5. Ibid., 43.

6. Hagedorn, "Notes"; *Family*, 44.

7. *Family*, 43.

8. Ibid., 51.

9. Irma Hagedorn Bensen to Hermann, Jr., April 4, 1952, Hagedorn Papers; *Family*, 57, 58.

10. *Family*, 73–74; Irma to Hermann, Jr., April 4, 1952, Hagedorn Papers.

11. Hermann Hagedorn, Sr., to Charlotte Hagedorn, June 26, 1888, Hagedorn Papers; *Family*, 75.

12. *Family*, 68, 74, 77–78, 88.

13. Ibid., 67, 88–89.

14. Ibid., 90–91.

15. Ibid., 93. Hagedorn's idealization of the American wilderness appears in *The Horse Thieves* (Cambridge: privately printed, 1909), *Roosevelt in the Bad Lands* (Boston: Houghton Mifflin, 1921), and *Leonard Wood* (New York: Harper and Bros., 1931). His romantic attachment to the West provided a common ideal through which he identified with Roosevelt and Wood.

16. *Family*, 20, 77, 99; Irma to Hermann, Jr., April 4, 1952, Hagedorn Papers.

17. *Family*, 102. Irma Hagedorn Bensen reported that even when Father Hagedorn visited his mother in Göttingen before her death, he "generally [managed to be] somewhere else," visiting male friends and relatives or taking "business trips." He "never seemed to miss a chance to go off somewhere . . . leaving us alone with Grandmother and the aunts." Irma to Hermann, Jr., April 4, 1952, Hagedorn Papers.

18. *Family*, 101, 113, 126, 130, 135, 136, 140; Irma to Hermann, Jr., April 4, 1952, Hagedorn Papers.

19. *Family*, 139.

20. Ibid., 64, 140.

21. Ibid., 143, 146; Hagedorn, "Notes." Hagedorn's *The Great Maze and the Heart of Youth* (New York: The MacMillan Co., 1916), is dedicated to The Hill School, which he personifies as a "Mother of boys":

> Not with swords, not with guns,
> Mother of boys, you arm your sons . . .
> With a word you gird their souls
> For storms and starry goals,
> And send them over the lands
> With a torch, a torch in their hands.

22. *Family*, 141–142, 153.

23. Erik Erikson, *Childhood and Society*, 2nd ed. (New York:

W. W. Norton and Co., 1963), 331–332, 335. See also David Rodnick, *Postwar Germans: An Anthropologist's Account* (New Haven: Yale University Press, 1948), and Bertram Schaffner, *Fatherland: A Study of Authoritarianism in the German Family* (New York: Columbia University Press, 1948).

24. Hagedorn, "Notes."

25. Ibid.

26. "Hermann Hagedorn, 1882–1964," privately printed pamphlet, 1964, Hagedorn Papers.

27. On Hagedorn's association with the Society of Friends, Dorothea Hagedorn Parfit, personal communication, May 19, 1970.

28. Geoffrey Gorer, *The American People* (New York: W. W. Norton and Co., 1948), 31. See also "The United States and Germany: A Comparative Study of National Character," in David C. McClelland, *The Roots of Consciousness* (Princeton: D. Van Nostrand Co., 1964), for an analysis that contrasts German and American value systems. The Hill School clearly embodied the code of American values as McClelland describes it.

29. Hermann's correspondence with Marion Meigs, numbering some forty-five letters written between 1900 and 1914, is in the Hagedorn Papers.

10. Finding a Vocation

1. Hermann Hagedorn to Marion Meigs, August 12, 1900; December 10, 1901; January 20, 1902; June 25, 1902, Hagedorn Papers.

2. Ibid., November 14, 1902; Hagedorn, "Diary of Trip to Italy, March, 1903, to June, 1903," Hagedorn Papers.

3. Hermann Hagedorn to Marion Meigs, January 9, 1904; March 31, 1904; September 17, 1914, Hagedorn Papers; *Family,* 162, 169.

4. Hagedorn, "Notes"; idem, "The Artist Must Become a Statesman," National Academy [of Design] *Bulletin,* October 1936, 4–6. The class day poem is reprinted in idem, *A Troop of the Guard* (Boston: Houghton Mifflin, 1909), 14.

5. Hermann Hagedorn to Marion Meigs, June 18, 1907; June 8, 1907, Hagedorn Papers.

6. *Family,* 171–172.

7. Ibid., 176.

8. Ibid., 175; Hagedorn, *The Silver Blade* (Berlin: Verlag von Alfred Unger, 1907), 24.

9. *The Silver Blade,* 53.

10. Ibid., 28, 48, 55, 57–59.

11. Hermann Hagedorn to Annie Hagedorn, October, 1907, and to Marion Meigs, September 26, 1907, Hagedorn Papers. Compare Hagedorn's reflections on the contrast between Europe and America with Viereck's *Confessions of a Barbarian* (1910). To Viereck, America is a "pristine" woman who shares his bed; to Hagedorn, it is a powerful "baby" to whom he defers. The "Micks" in Brooklyn are perhaps discernible behind that "uncultured baby giant."

12. *Family*, 163–164, 167–168, 199–201.

13. Hagedorn, *Faces in the Dawn* (New York: The MacMillan Co., 1914).

14. Ibid., 219.

15. Hagedorn, *The Woman of Corinth* (Boston: Houghton Mifflin, 1908), 30.

16. Hagedorn, *Poems and Ballads* (Boston: Houghton Mifflin, 1912), 26. The image of the closed door is frequently invoked in Hagedorn's writings to indicate that someone feels excluded or separated from a person or thing which is of great value and must be recovered and embraced. *A Troop of the Guard* (1909), written before she died but published afterward, was dedicated to Annie Hagedorn. In a letter dated October 24, 1909, Hermann wrote to his father in a hand trembling with emotion as he mentioned the ceremonial scattering of his mother's ashes. Hagedorn Papers.

17. Hermann Hagedorn to Marion Meigs, July 12, 1911; to Irma Bensen, December 7, 1910; July 9, 1913. Hagedorn Papers. About the visit to New York Hermann wrote, "there was never a chance of getting nearer to him and everyone of us . . . had moments when we wanted to jump out of our skins." Hagedorn to Irma Bensen, December 7, 1910, Hagedorn Papers.

18. Interview in the Boston *Evening Transcript*, December 19, 1931; *Family*, 182–183, 202–203.

19. Hagedorn, *The Great Maze*, 41–42; *Family*, 204–205.

20. *The Great Maze*, 9–11, 24, and passim.

21. Ibid., 62, 74, 75, 81.

22. Ibid., 59.

23. *Outlook* 93 (December 18, 1909):878; *Independent* 74 (January 2, 1913):53; *New York Times* March 12, 1916, 7:87; *Outlook* 112 (April 26, 1916):999. Hagedorn received particular praise for being "free of the pose of cynicism, skepticism, and worldly fatigue which often disfigures the early work of prominent poets."

Outlook 93 (December 18, 1909):878. In all likelihood, the allusion was to George Sylvester Viereck.

24. *Family*, 174.

25. Ibid., 209.

11. The Battlefield: Public and Private

1. Alma Hagedorn to Adolph Hagedorn, September 12, 1914; Hermann, Sr., to Adolph and Hermann, Jr., September 13, 1914, and September 24, 1914; Irma to Hermann, Jr., October 13, 1914; Hermann, Sr., to Hermann, Jr., November 5, 1914. Hagedorn Papers. *Family*, 217; Hagedorn, "Notes."

2. *Family*, 222; Hagedorn, *Makers of Madness* (New York: The MacMillan Co., 1914); idem, *Hymn of Free Peoples Triumphant* (New York: The MacMillan Co., 1918). See also idem, "Germany Interpreted by a German-American," in William H. Skaggs, ed., *America and the War in Europe* (pamphlet, 1914), 20–24. This short essay takes a sympathetic view of the Kaiser and asserts that the German people are partially justified in believing that everyone is against them.

3. Hermann, Jr., to Irma, July 7, 1915, Hagedorn Papers; Hagedorn to Kuno Francke, February 1915, Francke MSS; Hagedorn, *Leonard Wood*, II, 158.

4. Hermann, Jr., to Irma, July 7, 1915, Hagedorn Papers; *Family*, 98, 223.

5. *Family*, 224, 136; Hagedorn, "Notes."

6. *New York Times*, August 17, 1917, 8:8; *Family*, 229.

7. See Charles A. Fenton, "A Literary Fracture of World War I," *American Quarterly* 12 (Summer 1960):119–132.

8. Draft proposal of the Vigilantes, and Hagedorn to Woodrow Wilson, undated, Hagedorn File; Hagedorn, *You Are the Hope of the World: An Appeal to the Boys and Girls of America* (New York: The MacMillan Co., 1917). Among the founders of the Vigilantes were Porter Emerson Browne, Charles Hanson Towne, and Julian Street.

9. *Family*, 233; Porter Emerson Browne, "The Vigilantes," *Outlook* 119 (May 8, 1918):67–69; Amy Lowell to Hermann Hagedorn, April 21, 1917, Hagedorn Letters. Among the four hundred contributing writers of the Vigilantes were Booth Tarkington, Charles Dana Gibson, George Ade, Mary R. Rhinehart, Irwin S. Cobb, Rex Beach, Hamlin Garland, Bruce Barton, Don Marquis, William A. White, Albert Bushnell Hart, Ralph Barton Perry, Emer-

son Hough, Gustavus Ohlinger, Hendrik van Loon, Ida Tarbell, William English Walling. Its financial backers included Cleveland H. Dodge, Samuel Lewisohn, Jacob Schiff, George F. Baker, Vincent Astor, Paul D. Cravath, and Willard Straight. Browne, "The Vigilantes"; *New York Times,* March 18, 1917, II, 3:7.

10. John Higham, *Strangers in the Land* (New Brunswick: Rutgers University Press, 1955), 198.

11. Theodore Roosevelt to Ralph M. Easley, July 5, 1917, in Elting Morison, ed., *The Letters of Theodore Roosevelt* (Cambridge: Harvard University Press, 1954), VIII, 1, 207; *New York Times,* July 5, 1917, 3:3; July 15, 1917, 4:1; August 12, 1917, 3:6.

12. *New York Evening Sun,* November 22, 1917; Viereck, *Roosevelt,* 37–38; Hagedorn, "Notes"; *Family,* 234.

13. *Family,* 223–227, 234.

14. Hermann, Sr., to Irma, February 1, 1915, and April 2, 1917, Hagedorn Papers; *Family,* 235; Hagedorn, *The Roosevelt Family of Sagamore Hill* (New York: The MacMillan Co., 1954); typescript of unaddressed letter supporting Hughes, undated, Hagedorn Papers.

15. *New York Times,* August 5, 1917, II, 2:7; Hagedorn, "The Menace of the German Language Press," *Outlook* 116 (August 15, 1917):579–581; Rudolph Heinrichs (pseud.), "A Family Letter from a German American to His Brother," *Atlantic Monthly* 120 (December 1917):739–745. During the summer of 1917, Hagedorn wrote numerous letters to editors and short articles calling for the suppression of the German-language and other pro-German press. He repeatedly called for vigilance against the "fanatical" pro-German element. At the same time, he placed an ad for a cook in his local Connecticut newspaper that bore the admonition that "only honest to goodness patriots need apply." Clipping in Hagedorn Correspondence.

16. Hagedorn, "Notes." Hermann, Sr., to Hermann, Jr., August 28, 1914, and November 4, 1915; to Adolph Hagedorn, January 13, 1917; Adolph to Hermann, Jr., December 22, 1917. Hagedorn Papers. Hagedorn to Harold T. Pulsifer, September 12, 1941, Pulsifer Letters; Hagedorn, "My Forty-five Year Miracle," Hagedorn Papers.

17. Heinrichs, "Family Letter," 740–741, 744.

18. Ibid., 744; Hagedorn, "Notes for Sequel to The Hyphenated Family," Hagedorn Papers.

19. Hagedorn, *Where Do You Stand? An Appeal to Americans of German Origin* (New York: The MacMillan Co., 1918), 108–109 and passim. See also Julius A. Coller, *The Loyalty of German-*

Americans to the United States Government (Washington, 1918), for a similar attack on "nonloyalty."

20. Hagedorn, *Where Do You Stand*, 3, 38–39, 44–49, 52, 54, 78, 111; idem, *Wood*, II, 183.

21. *Family*, 244. Kuno Francke wrote a public letter of support for *Where Do You Stand?*, but in private chastised Hagedorn for "serious" factual errors in his description of the German system of government. Francke to Hagedorn, April 6 and 7, 1918, Hagedorn Correspondence.

22. *Family*, 245; *New York Tribune*, May 15, 1918, and June 11, 1918.

23. *Family*, 235, 244–248; *New York Times*, April 20, 1918, 14:1,7; Hagedorn, *Wood*, II, 217.

24. Hagedorn, "Miracle."

25. *Family*, 240, 241; Hagedorn to Mark Sullivan, August 16, 1922, Hagedorn Letters; Hagedorn, *The Roosevelt Family*, lv; Hagedorn, "Theodore Roosevelt, The Father," *Red Cross Magazine*, October 1919, 16–19.

26. Hagedorn, *The Roosevelt Family*, 18, 190, 193; idem, *Roosevelt in the Bad Lands*, ix–x.

27. *Family*, 229; Hagedorn, *The Roosevelt Family*, 356, 387, 405.

28. Hermann, Sr., to Irma Bensen, July 12, 1919; Hermann, Jr., to Marianne and Gidel von Poschinger, 1960. Hagedorn Papers. *Family*, 257, 260.

29. *Family*, 254–255.

12. The Dénouement

1. Hagedorn to Mark Sullivan, August 16, 1922, Hagedorn Papers; Hagedorn, *Where Do You Stand?*, 95; *Family*, 244–246; Hermann, Jr., to Irma Bensen, December 15, 1920, Hagedorn Papers.

2. Typescript of article for *Outlook*, Hagedorn Papers; Hagedorn to The Editor of *Outlook*, August 30, 1922, Hagedorn Papers; Hagedorn, *The Roosevelt Family*, 420; idem, *Wood*, II, 321–322.

3. Hagedorn, "Notes for Sequel to The Hyphenated Family"; Hermann, Jr., to Irma Bensen, May 29, 1924, and January 10, 1920; to Willy Bensen, February 23, 1922. Hagedorn Papers. Hagedorn, *Ladders through the Blue* (Garden City, N.Y.: Doubleday, Page Co., 1925), 39, 51.

4. Hagedorn, *That Human Being, Leonard Wood* (New York: Harcourt, Brace and Howe, 1920); idem, *Wood*, I, 371–372.

5. Hagedorn, *Wood,* II, 125, 154, 197, 217, 317, 337, 375, 469. Interestingly, Fred Hagedorn later shared the same response to his ouster from the German civil service in 1933: it occurred, he wrote, "because a fear engulfed the leading people that they would perhaps be put into the shadow." Fred Hagedorn to Hermann, Jr., May 6, 1938, Hagedorn Papers. Fred was indicted on charges of tax evasion and of mishandling his office in the Ministry of Agriculture. He won his case in 1936. Jurgen Hagedorn, personal communication, September 10, 1970.

6. Copy of application to the Pelman Institute in Hagedorn Papers; Hagedorn, leaves from notebook, in Hagedorn Correspondence; idem, "Notes for Sequel to The Hyphenated Family." Although he had moved often, among rented houses, in the course of his childhood, Hagedorn differentiated his own family's peregrinations by purchasing at least five houses at various times. *Family,* 67, and Dorothea Hagedorn Parfit, personal communication, May 19, 1970.

7. Hadley Cantril, *The Psychology of Social Movements* (New York: J. Wiley and Sons, 1941), 144–168; Tom Driberg, *The Mystery of Moral Re-Armament: A Study of Frank Buchman and His Movement* (New York: Knopf, 1965); Allan W. Eister, *Drawing-Room Conversion: A Sociological Account of the Oxford Movement* (Durham: Duke University Press, 1950). Hagedorn had already proclaimed his "spiritual solution" to the economic crisis before he took up with the Oxford Group. In 1932 he published the poem, *The Three Pharaohs* (New York: The John Day Co., 1932), which he delivered as a Phi Beta Kappa address at Harvard; in it he denounced the "Black Pharaoh" of industrialism and the "Red Pharaoh" of Communism, commending to his listeners the way of the "Third Pharaoh"—the voice of God in the human heart.

8. Hagedorn, "Notes for Sequel to The Hyphenated Family"; Hagedorn, "Faith in Our Time," typescript of a radio broadcast delivered August 9, 1953. As one in a series of speakers, Hagedorn responded to the question of what religion meant to him. In 1937 and 1938 he was active in organizing a movement for National Rededication in America.

9. Hagedorn, "Notes for Sequel to The Hyphenated Family." Hagedorn's belief in miracles is frequently reiterated in his writings. Typically, when he exhausted his resources or found himself in a quandary, he would resign himself to waiting for God to take care of him. See Hagedorn to Harold T. Pulsifer, September 12, 1941, Pulsifer Letters.

10. Hagedorn, *Combat at Midnight* (New York: The John Day Co., 1940), 102. The poem takes off from a phrase of Whitman's.

11. Hagedorn to Harold T. Pulsifer, December 27, 1939; to Sam Shoemaker, June 11, 1945. Pulsifer Letters.

12. Hagedorn, *Wood*; idem, *The Magnate: William Boyce Thompson, 1869–1930* (New York: Reynal and Hitchcock, 1935); idem, *Brookings: A Biography* (New York: The MacMillan Co., 1936). Hagedorn to Richard Nixon, November 12, 1962; to Herr Lindemann, December 10, 1947; copy of report on manuscript entitled "History Takes a Holiday." Hagedorn Papers. William Boyce Thompson was a mining operator and financial giant who had been chairman of the American Red Cross Commission to Russia in 1917–1918. He urged the American government to aid Kerensky and, later, to recognize the Soviet regime. Hagedorn saw him, as he saw the businessman and philanthropist Robert S. Brookings, as a strong-minded go-getter who was also a sensitive dreamer, an idealist, and a responsible citizen.

13. Hagedorn, *Combat at Midnight*, 95–96.

14. Hagedorn to Harold T. Pulsifer, March 21, 1942, Pulsifer Letters.

15. Hagedorn, *The Bomb That Fell on America* (Santa Barbara: Pacific Coast Publishing Co., 1946).

16. George S. Viereck to Elmer Gertz, November 20, 1956; Hermann Hagedorn to Elmer Gertz, July 6, 1935. Gertz MSS.

17. *Family*, 263–264. Hagedorn's son, David, attended Harvard College and became an engineer and businessman. He died after heart surgery on July 27, 1946. A third child, Mary, was also devoted to MRA, but Dorothea, who married a like-thinking English parson named Eric Parfit, was most active in the movement.

18. Clipping in Hagedorn Papers; Hagedorn, "Notes." Hagedorn lived in Santa Barbara at several times during his life: in 1911, from 1926 to 1928, from 1940 to1946, and from 1960 until his death in 1964.

19. Edith Hagedorn to Hermann, Jr., October 31, 1960; Marie Hagedorn to Hermann, Jr., September 9, 1960; Walter Hagedorn to Hermann, Jr., December 18, 1960. Hagedorn Papers.

EPILOGUE

1. Nathan Glazer and Daniel P. Moynihan, *Beyond the Melting Pot* (Cambridge: M.I.T. Press, 1963), 311.

2. For a set of stimulating essays on the experiences, concerns, and leadership patterns within American ethnic groups, see John Higham, ed., *Ethnic Leadership in America* (Baltimore: Johns Hopkins University Press, 1978).

INDEX

(father of Hermann Hagedorn),
191–192, 201, 202, 210, 242;
dominance of his mother over,
192–196 passim; marriage to Annie
Schwedler, 193; ambivalence of his
personality, 195–196, 202–203; response to his mother's suicide, 198–
199; son Hermann's ambivalence
toward, 203–205, 215, 241, 254–
255; fortune amassed by, 208;
financial support for son Hermann,
209, 217; mansion built by, in
Germany, 211, 213; marriage of his
son to Dorothy Oakley, 213; stay in
sanitarium, 217–218; influence on
son's writings, 220; unhappiness
living in Germany, 220–221; and
WWI, 222, 223, 225, 230, 239–240;
estrangement from his son, 231–
232, 237; death and legacy of, 240–
241; political views of, 249–250;
The Hyphenated Family on, 253,
255
Hagedorn, Irma, 195–196, 198, 243,
244; and WWI, 222, 224
Hart, Albert Bushnell, 95
Harvard Advocate, 209
Harvey, Alexander, 137
Haywood, William (Big Bill), 44
Henry, Prince, of Prussia, 79, 231
Hermine, Empress, of Germany, 170
Herzl, Theodor, 6
Hexamer, Charles J., 2, 82
Hill, David Jayne, 62–63, 87
Hiroshima, atomic explosion at, 251,
252
Hitchcock, Gilbert M., 157
Hitler, Adolf, 175, 177; Viereck's at-
titude toward, 176, 178; Hagedorn's
view of, 250
Hocking, William E., 107–108, 109
Hodges, George, 113
Hoe, Richard March, 213
Holleben, Ambassador, 79
Holt, Edwin B., 28, 31, 287; *The
Freudian Wish*, 45, 103; quarrels
with Münsterberg, 45, 103–104
Hoover, Herbert, 165, 166, 206
House, Edward M., 174

Hughes, Charles Evans, 152–153
Hymn of Free Peoples Triumphant
(Hagedorn), 223
*Hyphenated Family, The: An Ameri-
can Saga* (Hagedorn), 219–220,
253, 255

"Impeachment of the German-Ameri-
cans, The" (Münsterberg), 94–96
"Innocent Rebellion" (1912), 135
International, The, 139–140, 143, 144
Islands for War Debts Committee, 181

Jagemann, Hans C. G. van, 78
James, Henry, 41
James, William, 38, 45, 56, 104; on
Willenshandlung (Activity of the
Will), 23–25; and Hugo Münster-
berg, 25–26, 27, 29, 39; philosophi-
cal perspective compared with
Münsterberg's, 33–34; estrangement
from Münsterberg, 40–42; and
psychic phenomena, 42, 43
Janet, Pierre, 24, 47
Jastrow, Joseph, 43
Jones, Ernest, 48
Jordan, David Starr, 88

Kahn, Otto, 139
"Keeper of the Light, A" (Hagedorn),
225
Kellor, Frances, 235
Kiep, Otto, 176
Kinderlaube, 10
Kuhn, Fritz, 176

LaFollette, Robert, 171, 243
Lange, Carl George, 24
Langfeld, Herbert, 112
Lassalle, Ferdinand, 7
Lawrence, Cyrus J., 213
League of Nations, 162, 165
League to Enforce Peace, 88
Leonard, William Ellery, 130–131,
154
"Letter from the Journey, A"
(Münsterberg), 35
Levinson, Salmon O., 87–88
Lewisohn, Ludwig, 131, 132, 179